Palgrave Shakespeare Studies

General Editors: Michael Dobson and Gail Kern Paster

Editorial Advisory Board: Michael Neill, University of Auckland; David Schalkwyk, University of Cape Town; Lois D. Potter, University of Delaware; Margreta de Grazia, Queen Mary University of London; Peter Holland, University of Notre Dame.

Palgrave Shakespeare Studies takes Shakespeare as its focus but strives to understand the significance of his oeuvre in relation to his contemporaries, subsequent writers and historical and political contexts. By extending the scope of Shakespeare and English Renaissance Studies, the series will open up the field to examinations of previously neglected aspects or sources in the period's art and thought. Titles in the *Palgrave Shakespeare Studies* series seek to understand anew both where the literary achievements of the English Renaissance came from and where they have brought us.

Titles include:

Pascale Aebischer, Edward J. Esche and Nigel Wheale (*editors*)
REMAKING SHAKESPEARE
Performance across Media, Genres and Cultures

Mark Thornton Burnett
FILMING SHAKESPEARE IN THE GLOBAL MARKETPLACE

David Hillman
SHAKESPEARE'S ENTRAILS
Belief, Scepticism and the Interior of the Body

Jane Kingsley-Smith
SHAKESPEARE'S DRAMA OF EXILE

Paul Yachnin and Jessica Slights
SHAKESPEARE AND CHARACTER
Theory, History, Performance, and Theatrical Persons

Forthcoming titles:

Timothy Billings
GLOSSING SHAKESPEARE

Erica Sheen
SHAKESPEARE AND THE INSTITUTION OF THE THEATRE

Palgrave Shakespeare Studies
Series Standing Order ISBN 978-1403-911643 (hardback) 978-1403-911650 (paperback)
(*outside North America only*)

You can receive future titles in this series as they are published by placing a standing order. Please contact your bookseller or, in case of difficulty, write to us at the address below with your name and address, the title of the series and the ISBN quoted above.

Customer Services Department, Macmillan Distribution Ltd, Houndmills, Basingstoke, Hampshire RG21 6XS, England

Also by Paul Yachnin

STAGE-WRIGHTS: Shakespeare, Jonson, Middleton, and the Making of Theatrical Value

THE CULTURE OF PLAYGOING IN SHAKESPEARE'S ENGLAND: A Collaborative Debate *(with Anthony Dawson)*

SHAKESPEARE AND THE CULTURES OF PERFORMANCE *(co-edited with Patricia Badir)*

Shakespeare and Character

Theory, History, Performance,
and Theatrical Persons

Edited by

Paul Yachnin and Jessica Slights

**Property of
Department of Theatre
LIBRARY**

palgrave
macmillan

Introduction, selection and editorial matter © Paul Yachnin & Jessica Slights 2009
Individual chapters © contributors 2009

All rights reserved. No reproduction, copy or transmission of this publication may be made without written permission.

No portion of this publication may be reproduced, copied or transmitted save with written permission or in accordance with the provisions of the Copyright, Designs and Patents Act 1988, or under the terms of any licence permitting limited copying issued by the Copyright Licensing Agency, Saffron House, 6-10 Kirby Street, London EC1N 8TS.

Any person who does any unauthorized act in relation to this publication may be liable to criminal prosecution and civil claims for damages.

The authors have asserted their rights to be identified as the authors of this work in accordance with the Copyright, Designs and Patents Act 1988.

First published 2009 by
PALGRAVE MACMILLAN

Palgrave Macmillan in the UK is an imprint of Macmillan Publishers Limited, registered in England, company number 785998, of Houndmills, Basingstoke, Hampshire RG21 6XS.

Palgrave Macmillan in the US is a division of St Martin's Press LLC, 175 Fifth Avenue, New York, NY 10010.

Palgrave Macmillan is the global academic imprint of the above companies and has companies and representatives throughout the world.

Palgrave® and Macmillan® are registered trademarks in the United States, the United Kingdom, Europe and other countries.

ISBN-13: 978-0-230-57262-1   hardback
ISBN-10: 0-230-57262-6   hardback

This book is printed on paper suitable for recycling and made from fully managed and sustained forest sources. Logging, pulping and manufacturing processes are expected to conform to the environmental regulations of the country of origin.

A catalogue record for this book is available from the British Library.

Library of Congress Cataloging-in-Publication Data

Shakespeare and character : theory, history, performance, and
  theatrical persons / Paul Yachnin and Jessica Slights.
      p. cm.
   Includes bibliographical references and index.
   ISBN 978-0-230-57262-1 (alk. paper)
  1. Shakespeare, William, 1564–1616—Characters. 2. Shakespeare,
  William, 1564–1616—Knowledge—Psychology. 3. Characters and
  characteristics in literature. 4. Identity (Psychology) in
  literature. 5. Personality in literature. I. Yachnin, Paul
  Edward, 1953– II. Slights, Jessica, 1968–

PR2989.S525 2009
822.3'3—dc22   2008030680

10 9 8 7 6 5 4 3 2 1
18 17 16 15 14 13 12 11 10 09

Transferred to digital printing in 2009.

*To the founders of the Shakespeare and Performance
Research Team*

*Michael Bristol
Leanore Lieblein
Patrick Neilson
Edward Pechter
John Ripley
Denis Salter
Catherine Shaw*

Contents

Acknowledgments ix

Notes on the Contributors and Editors x

Introduction 1
Paul Yachnin and Jessica Slights

I Theory

1 Confusing Shakespeare's Characters with Real People: Reflections on Reading in Four Questions 21
 Michael Bristol

2 The Reality of Fictive Cinematic Characters 41
 Trevor Ponech

3 Character as Dynamic Identity: From Fictional Interaction Script to Performance 62
 William Dodd

II History

4 *Personnage*: History, Philology, Performance 83
 André G. Bourassa

5 The Properties of Character in *King Lear* 98
 James Berg

6 Embodied Intersubjectivity and the Creation of Early Modern Character 117
 Leanore Lieblein

III Performance

7 Metatheater and the Performance of Character in *The Winter's Tale* 139
 Paul Yachnin and Myrna Wyatt Selkirk

8 Character, Agency and the Familiar Actor 158
 Andrew James Hartley

9 The Actor-Character in "Secretly Open" Action: Doubly Encoded Personation on Shakespeare's Stage 177
 Robert Weimann

IV Theatrical Persons

10 Is Timon a Character? 197
   Anthony Dawson

11 When Is a Bastard Not a Bastard? Character and 214
   Conscience in *King John*
   Camille Slights

12 Arming Cordelia: Character and Performance 232
   Sarah Werner

   Index 250

Acknowledgments

Five contributors to this volume are members of the Shakespeare and Performance Research Team, which is headquartered at McGill University and includes team members from Concordia University, the Université de Montréal, and the Université du Québec à Montréal. The robust literary-critical and theatrical life of the Shakespeare Team is, we think, well reflected in this volume. For one thing, the vitality of the team's collaborative, interdisciplinary work over the past fifteen years (coupled of course with the timeliness and importance of the topic) has helped to recruit a number of other scholars who have added immeasurably to this book's ability to rethink the category of character in Shakespeare studies.

Our gratitude is threefold. We thank Tiffany Hoffman PhD student and research assistant for her excellent editorial work. We gratefully acknowledge the splendid support of the Fonds québécois de la recherche sur la société et la culture (FQRSC). Mostly, however, we wish to acknowledge the vision, energy, and intellectual generosity of the founders of the Shakespeare Team, to whom this book is admiringly and affectionately dedicated.

Notes on the Contributors and Editors

James E. Berg is Visiting Assistant Professor of English at Middlebury College in Vermont. Since receiving his PhD at Columbia University, he has taught Shakespeare and Renaissance Literature at Iowa State University and in the Harvard Expository Writing Program. He is currently working on a book, *The Character of Shakespeare's Plays*. His other publications include an article on John Donne's *Holy Sonnets*, in vol. 1 of the Scribner's British Classics series, ed. Jay Parini, and articles in *English Literary Renaissance* ("This Dear Dear Land: Dearth and the Fantasy of the Land-Grab" in *Richard II* and *Henry IV*), and *Studies in English Literature* ("*Gorboduc* and the Tragic Remembrance of Feudalism").

André G. Bourassa is Professor Emeritus at the École supérieure de théâtre at the Université du Québec à Montréal (UQÀM). He has published many articles on surrealism, literature, and theater. From 1979 to 1997, he directed an editorial project on the works of Paul-Émile Borduas. He is a founding member of the journal, *Lettres québécoises*, of the Union des écrivaines et écrivains du Québec, and of the Société québécoise d'études théâtrales, where he was for a number of years the president and editor of the journal, *L'Annuaire théâtral*. As a member of Commission des études de l'UQAM, he collaborated in the founding of the doctoral program in Études pratiques des arts.

Michael Bristol's (Department of English, McGill) work is primarily concerned with situating Shakespeare's work in the social contexts of their production and reception. He has written three book-length studies of Shakespeare's theater: *Carnival and Theatre*, *Shakespeare's America/America's Shakespeare*, and *Big Time Shakespeare*.

Anthony Dawson is Professor Emeritus at the University of British Columbia. His research interests include literary-historical scholarship on Renaissance drama, performance theory and history, and textual editing and theory of the text. He is presently writing a book on the Jesuit Relations. Among his publications are the books, *Indirections* (1978), *Watching Shakespeare: A Playgoer's Guide* (1988), *Hamlet* (Shakespeare in Performance) (1995), and *Shakespeare and the Cultures of Performance* (with Paul Yachnin; Cambridge, 2001). He has also published editions of *Tamburlaine* for the New Mermaids series (1996), *Troilus and Cressida* (Cambridge, 2003), and *Timon of Athens* (with Gretchen Minton; Arden 3, 2008).

William Dodd retired recently after teaching English Literature at the Universities of Bologna and Siena since 1967. His writings include studies of the poetry of Donne, Shakespeare, Keats, Lawrence, Muir, a book on *Measure for Measure*, and a wide range of essays on Shakespeare's plays. He has written on the issue of characterization in "Metalanguage and Character in Drama"; *Lingua e Stile* (1979) 14, 1; "Destined Livery? Character and Person in Shakespeare"; *Shakespeare Survey* 51 (1998); "Impossible Worlds. What happens in *King Lear* Act 1 Scene 1?"; *Shakespeare Quarterly*, 50 (1999) 4. He is at present working on the impact of the Chamberlain's/King's Men actors on Shakespeare's construction of characters and on what performance-related quartos may be able to tell us about how his actors voiced and embodied their characters.

Andrew James Hartley is the distinguished Chair of Shakespeare Studies at the University of North Carolina, Charlotte. He is the author of *The Shakespearean Dramaturg: A Theoretical and Practical Guide* (Palgrave Macmillan, 2006) and of articles on performance-related issues in journals such as *ELH* and *Medieval and Renaissance Drama in England*. Dr. Hartley is resident dramaturg for the Georgia Shakespeare Festival and the editor of the performance journal *Shakespeare Bulletin*, published by Johns Hopkins University Press. His current work includes a forthcoming chapter in *Shakespeare Re-Dressed: Cross-gender Casting in Contemporary Performance* (ed. Bulman) and a book on *Julius Caesar* for Manchester University Press's plays in performance series. He is currently directing *Dr. Faustus* on the main stage at UNCC.

Leanore Lieblein's (English Department, McGill) research is situated at the intersection of the page and the stage. She has published widely on both Elizabethan and contemporary plays in performance, and has edited a special issue of *L'Annuaire théâtral* on Shakespeare in Québec. Her recent research has focused on the performing body.

Trevor Ponech is Associate Professor of English at McGill University, and he specializes in analytic-philosophical approaches to cinema and literature. He's the author of *What Is Non-Fiction Cinema?* (Westview Press, 1999) and *Kitchen Stories*, a monograph forthcoming in the University of Washington Press' Nordic Film Classics Series. His current research, focusing on the ontology of cinema, includes the recent "The Substance of Cinema" (*Journal of Aesthetics and Art Criticism* 64, winter 2006) and "External Realism About Cinematic Motion" (*British Journal of Aesthetics* 46, October 2006).

Myrna Wyatt Selkirk (Drama and Theatre Program, English Department, McGill) has been an assistant director at the Neptune Theatre (Halifax) and the Shaw Festival (Ontario). At McGill she has directed numerous full-scale productions, including Michel Tremblay's *Bonjour, là, Bonjour*, Shakespeare's *Twelfth Night* and *The Merchant of Venice*, *The Castle* by Howard Barker, and Brian Friel's *Dancing at Lughnasa*.

Camille Wells Slights (PhD Cornell University) is Professor Emerita at the University of Saskatchewan. She has published *The Casuistical Tradition in Shakespeare, Donne, Herbert, and Milton* (Princeton, 1981), *Shakespeare's Comic Commonwealths* (Toronto, 1993), and articles in such journals as *PQ, ELR, PMLA,* and *SQ*. She is working on an essay on John Donne's epithalamia and a study of conscience in seventeenth-century English literature.

Jessica Slights is Associate Professor of English at Acadia University. She has written about and lectured on various aspects of early modern literature and culture, and her work has appeared in *English Studies in Canada, Studies in Philology,* and *Studies in English Literature*. Her most recent project is a book-length manuscript entitled *Everyday Shakespeare: The Ethical Architecture of Shakespearean Comedy*.

Robert Weimann is Professor of Emeritus in the Department of Drama, University of California, Irvine. He is an honorary member of MLA, a past President of the German Shakespeare Society, and a member of the Berlin-Brandenburg Academy of Fine Arts. His recent books are *Author's Pen and Actor's Voice: Playing and Writing in Shakespeare's Theatre* (Cambridge University Press, 2000) and *Prologues to Shakespeare's Theatre*, co-authored with Douglas Bruster (Routledge, 2004).

Sarah Werner is author of *Shakespeare and Feminist Performance: Ideology on Stage* (Routledge 2001) and performance editor for *Shakespeare Quarterly*. She is currently working on a production history of *As You Like It* for Manchester University Press's series, Shakespeare in Performance, and editing a collection of essays on the methodology of performance criticism. She is the director of the Folger-GW Undergraduate Research Seminar at the Folger Shakespeare Library.

Paul Yachnin is Tomlinson Professor of Shakespeare Studies and Chair of the English Department at McGill University. He is co-director of the Shakespeare and Performance Research Team and director of the Making Publics project. His books include *Stage-Wrights: Shakespeare, Jonson, Middleton, and the Making of Theatrical Value* (1997); *The Culture of Playgoing in Shakespeare's England* (with Anthony Dawson, 2001); and *Shakespeare and the Cultures of Performance* (with Patricia Badir, 2008). He is an editor of *The Works of Thomas Middleton* and is editing Shakespeare's *Richard II* (Oxford). Work-in-progress includes an edition of *The Tempest* for Broadview Press and a book, *Making Theatrical Publics: A Social History of Drama in Shakespeare's England*.

Introduction

Paul Yachnin and Jessica Slights

I

Character has made a comeback. Having all but disappeared from Shakespeare criticism as an analytic category in the second half of the twentieth century, the idea of character has now begun to reemerge as an important—perhaps even an essential—way of thinking about the political, ethical, historical, literary, and performative aspects of early modern theater. The present volume recognizes the development in Shakespeare studies of what might best be termed a "new character criticism," by bringing together of a group of scholars whose work touches in one way or another on the fundamental question: what is character? That these scholars approach the question from a wide variety of perspectives and with disparate methodological tools suggests how valuable their answers might be to an increasingly interdisciplinary study of Shakespeare's plays.

The study of Shakespearean drama has had a long and rich, if often vexed, relationship to the idea of character. When, in 1664, Margaret Cavendish published a collection of mostly fictional letters on a variety of topics and included among them an epistolary essay in defense of Shakespeare, she anticipated what would later become the focus of much eighteenth- and nineteenth-century criticism by arguing that Shakespeare's "persons" are what make his plays praiseworthy. According to Cavendish: "*Shakespear* did not want Wit, to Express to the Life all Sorts of Persons, of what Quality, Profession, Degree, Breeding, or Birth soever; nor did he want Wit to Express the Divers, and Different Humours, or Natures, or Several Passions in Mankind."[1] The assumption that it is both possible and desirable for theatrical texts to "express [persons] to the Life" continued to dominate responses to Shakespeare in England and continental Europe for the next 250 years. In 1753,

Samuel Johnson argued that Shakespeare's "chief Skill was in Human Actions, Passions, and Habits," and that "his Works may be considered as a Map of Life, a faithful Miniature of human Transactions."[2] The focus and the specific terms of reference have shifted here in interesting ways—away from Cavendish's naturalizing of Shakespeare's accomplishment and her distinctively seventeenth-century humoral discourse and toward an emphasis on Shakespeare's "skill" and the economic model of human interaction implied by Johnson's use of "transactions," but the fundamental assumption remains the same: that Shakespearean characters are best understood as mimetic representations of imagined persons.

The claim that Shakespeare's characters are most usefully considered as though they were real people perhaps found its most eager proponent in Maurice Morgann, whose *Essay on the Dramatic Character of Falstaff* (1777) mounts a vigorous defense of the knight against accusations of cowardice. As Morgann's own description of his essay emphasizes, he saw his project as altogether larger than a simple defense of a single character. He had written, he explained, "An Essay professing to treat of the Courage of Falstaff, but extending itself to his Whole character; to the arts and genius of his Poetic-Maker, SHAKESPEARE; and thro' him sometimes, with ambitious aim, even to the principles of human nature itself."[3] This wider goal, of exploring human nature through an analysis of Shakespearean character, marks Morgann's essay not only as a precursor of such Romantic and post-Romantic critics as S. T. Coleridge, August Wilhelm Schlegel, William Hazlitt, and Anna Jameson, for whom Shakespeare becomes an embodiment of genius whose characters "are complete individuals, whose hearts and souls are laid open before us,"[4] but also a critical antecedent of A. C. Bradley,[5] whose work is often considered the grand finale of nineteenth-century Shakespeare criticism, and whose monumental *Shakespearean Tragedy* (1904) is often seen as the definitive synthesis of this long tradition of celebrating Shakespeare's ability to portray psychological depth.

The first major statement rejecting this psychological approach was L. C. Knights's famous essay "How Many Children Had Lady Macbeth?"(1933), which directs the reader away from what Knights constructs as irresponsible speculation about the psychological mechanics of fictional characters, and toward an emphasis on a play's theme, form, and literary language. Knights's vehement attack on Bradley's characterological approach ushered in the era of New Criticism in Shakespeare studies, and until the latter half of the twentieth century studies of stagecraft, imagery, theme, and intellectual history dominated the critical field. As the interpretive priorities of Knights and the New Critics began to give way to critical approaches influenced by poststructuralism, however, references to Bradleian character criticism began to spring up again, this time as a convenient critical shorthand for a particular set of naïve assumptions about universality and transhistoricity. For critics eager to differentiate their New Historicist, cultural materialist, materialist feminist, and postcolonialist projects from what they saw as the pernicious influence of a hegemonic New Criticism, distinctions between Bradley's psychological approach to plot and character and Cleanth Brooks's focus on figurative language and imagery were of less concern than their shared tendency to assume the existence of a timeless, universal, unified self by whom, for whom, and about whom literary texts might be written. The poststructuralist case against character has two major strains. The first *theoretical* challenge argues for the impossibility of inward, agential personhood altogether on the grounds that subjects are merely the effects of the social, linguistic, and ideological determinations of individual identity. The second *historical* challenge argues that inwardness as we understand and experience it did not exist in the early modern period. On both of these accounts, readings of Shakespeare that presuppose an inward, agential personhood are certainly anachronistic and probably also politically retrograde.

Although recognizing "character" as a valid analytic category became anathema for many scholars, Shakespeare's characters have continued to have a lively existence for theater practitioners, playgoers, students, and general readers. This does not mean, of course, that the theater has not struggled with the issues surrounding character; some of the most powerful critiques, whether in discursive or dramatic form, of the idea of inward characterization have come from theater professionals such as Bertolt Brecht, Antonin Artaud, Samuel Beckett, and Charles Marowitz. Indeed, one of the central arguments of this volume is that much greater attention needs to be paid to the contributions made by the theater and the performance environment as we attempt to re-articulate a notion of character in the twenty-first century. If an emphasis on character has remained prominent in the theatrical setting, it has also continued to dominate responses to Shakespeare in many high school and undergraduate classrooms, as well as among the general public. Both the vernacular intuition that characterization is central to Shakespeare's art and his politics, and the instinct to connect observations about dramatic characters and communities to their own life experience, are common among both readers and audience members. While we have an obligation as scholars to apply the twin pressures of history and theory to the claims of non-specialists, as Michael Bristol points out in the powerful essay that opens this collection, ignoring their contributions risks impoverishing our understanding of the ethical dimensions of early modern drama.

II

Over the past thirty years, a number of influential critics have called into question the prominence traditionally accorded Shakespeare's characters in literary studies.[6] Jonathan Goldberg—with Catherine Belsey, Jonathan Dollimore and others—enjoined critics to put aside "notions of character as self-same, owned, capable of autonomy and change."[7] In a learned, imaginative essay, Peter Stallybrass analyzed Desdemona as a discontinuous effect of the ideological functions and formal features of the text:

> Desdemona, I suggest, fulfils two different functions. The Desdemona of the first half of the play is an active agent, however much she may be conceived of as the "spiritualization" of Othello's legitimation. She is accordingly given the freedom we tend to associate with the comic heroine. In fact, in the first two acts it is Othello who is the primary object of scrutiny . . . it is only when Desdemona becomes the object of surveillance that she is reformed within the problematic of the enclosed body. Hence, in the second half of the play, the worse Iago's insinuations, the more she is "purified." In other words, the play constructs two different Desdemonas: the first, a woman capable of "downright violence" (1.3.249); the second, "A maiden never bold" (1.3.94). Desdemona's subservience, enforced by her death, has already been enforced by the play's structure.[8]

This reduction of character to the effects of what are claimed to be larger and more stable entities—such as dramatic genres, texts, or social structures—has come to seem dated over the past twenty years. Certainly, the materialist understanding of *persons* as effects of ideology has lost ground in the face of work on the historical embeddedness of early modern personhood by scholars such as Katharine Maus, Theodore Leinwand, Wes Folkerth, and others.[9] But Shakespearean characters, who have been de-realized and whose influence has been severely diminished by materialist critique, have not fully recovered their prominence or vitality within Shakespeare studies. Shakespeare criticism, we suggest, has been rendered tongue-tied by the absence of a coherent account of what Trevor Ponech in this volume calls "real fictive characters."

What would an account of the nature of Shakespearean characters look like? First of all, even if it could be demonstrated that Shakespeare himself, the actors, playgoers, and readers of early modern drama experienced theatrical character and themselves as discontinuous (and that they paid attention to the social and political dimensions of the plays rather than the characters), or if it emerged that early modern ideas about character were so at odds with modern views as to constitute an essentially different understanding of the term—none of that would change the historical fact that character, defined more or less as self-same, capable of autonomy and change, and possessed of some measure of inwardness and inscrutability, has stood at the center of the literary and theatrical engagement with Shakespeare for at least the past 350 years. That engagement has come to form an integral part of what Shakespeare means, and of how his plays connect with and influence the world. Even if the modern emphasis on character turns out to have been a massive mistake, it could not now be prised away from Shakespeare.

Of course, we do not think that it is a mistake. At the start of his essay in this book, Michael Bristol cites Dr Johnson in support of a widespread intuition about the reality of fictional characters, but we can reach back earlier than the eighteenth century for valuable insights. Consider, for example, this seventeenth-century recollection of Shakespeare's dramatic art, with its emphasis on the wonder aroused by his characters, an effect that is highlighted by comparison with what the author represents as the pallid characterization and text-boundedness of Jonson's drama:

> So I have seene, when Cesar would appeare,
> And on the stage at halfe-sword parley were,
> *Brutus* and *Cassius*: oh how the Audience,
> Were ravish'd, with what wonder they went thence,
> When some new day they would not brooke a line,
> Of tedious (though well laboured) *Catilines*;
> *Sejanus* too were irkesome, they priz'de more
> Honest *Iago*, or the jealous Moore.[10]

According to this account, engagement with character in the playhouse is more moving than are lines of poetry, however well-crafted. By the way, it should not be surprising that Shakespeare's characters are as effective and affecting for readers as they are for playgoers. The characters were conceived with performance and with the actors in mind: Shakespeare builds a gestural, kinesthetic, and vocal dimension into how he writes his characters; he also engineers something like a contest of perspectives on the dramatic action among major characters that unfolds first before the eyes of the audience and that carries over into the experience of reading the plays. Think about the scene where Richard II and Henry Bolingbrook both grasp the crown of England: "Here, cousin, seize the crown," Richard says, 'On this side my hand, and on that side thine" (4.1.181–83). Both on stage and in the study, the scene is filled with physical and political tension borne from the kinesthetic, emotional, and ideological differences between the two characters, here captured and stretched taut by both their hold on the crown and the hold the crown has on them. We can almost feel them feeling the hard edges of the embellished metal, not to mention feeling each other's desire for the crown between them. An eyewitness report by one Henry Jackson of a performance of *Othello* at Oxford in 1610 makes clearer the centrality of character as an organizing and effective feature of the play, and it also shows how actor and character interpenetrate along the "double-voiced" lines explained by Robert Weimann in this volume (note that while the character Desdemona is dead at the end of the play, the boy actor does not cease acting and interacting with the spectators)[11]:

> They also had tragedies, which they acted with propriety and fitness. In which (tragedies), not only through speaking but also through acting certain things, they moved (the audience) to tears. But truly the celebrated Desdemona, slain in our presence by her husband, although she pleaded her case [*causam egit*] very effectively throughout, yet moved (us) [*movebat*] more after she was dead, when, lying on her bed, she entreated [*imploraret*] the pity of the spectators by her very countenance.[12]

Desdemona's character, which here includes the words of the text and also the vocal, gestural, and facial expressiveness of the boy actor, provides the through-line of the action for this playgoer, serves as the center of emotional and cognitive response for the spectators, and perhaps stands as the focus of their collective deliberation and judging. Even when she is dead, Desdemona keeps on "speaking," as it were, to the audience. She is, from the 1610 reporter's point of view, evidently the principle of continuity in *Othello*.

In what follows, we suggest that character is the organizing principle of Shakespeare's plays—it organizes both the formal and ideological dimensions of the drama and is not organized by them—and we also argue that character is the principal bridge over which the emotional, cognitive, and political transactions of theater and literature pass between actors and playgoers or between written texts and readers.

How is character the organizing *formal* principle of the plays? The answer, we think, is straightforward. Aristotle places plot ahead of character:

> But most important of all is the structure of the incidents. For Tragedy is an imitation, not of men, but of an action and of life, and life consists in action, and its end is a mode of action, not a quality. Now character determines men's qualities, but it is by their actions that they are happy or the reverse. Dramatic action, therefore, is not with a view to the representation of character: character comes in as subsidiary to the actions. Hence the incidents and the plot are the end of a tragedy; and the end is the chief thing of all. Again, without action there cannot be a tragedy; there may be without character.[13]

Shakespeare tends to overturn the Aristotelian ranking of plot and character by reworking traditional narrative types such as revenge tragedy, romantic courtship, struggle for mastery between husband and wife, or the story of growth-into-adulthood so that character displaces plot as the center of interest in ways that determine the kinds of elements we find in the plays and how those elements are organized. Each major character is fashioned by what William Dodd in this volume calls a "discourse biography." As a consequence of both the inversion of plot and character and the prominent unfolding of discourse biographies, we are far more interested, say, in how the action of revenge seems to Hamlet than we are in the working out of the revenge plot. The centrality of the character Hamlet is also enforced by (and underlies) the number and the nature of soliloquies, which do little to provide exposition or advance the plot, but which contribute to the development of Hamlet's thinking about action in relation to an increasingly complex world. Indeed, actions are not actions in a meaningful way in this play unless they are so conceived by the major character. This re-ordering of character and plot is not a uniform feature of the plays, but it is certainly an important one. The central plot-points of plays such as *Hamlet, Henry IV, The Taming of the Shrew, Measure for Measure*, and others depend for their meaning on how they are performed and grasped by the central characters. The knotted thread of the action of *All's Well that Ends Well* untangles into a romantic courtship narrative or knots further into something far darker depending on what we are able to determine about the protagonist Helena's motives and perhaps also how we view Bertram's capacity for remorse and moral amendment. And those questions cannot be addressed by an analysis of the plot, of course; they must emerge from an examination of the characters' discourse biographies.

Important also is how the characters gather into themselves the competing ideological positions that circulate in the play worlds. It is worth bearing in mind André Bourassa's observation (in Chapter 4) that "the word personage [i.e., character] . . . refers first of all to masked acting, but it means more than 'mask' since its complete source is *personam agere*, that is, to lead, to manage the mask, which refers to *agens*, the agent or actor. The personnage is thus seen as the principal 'carrier of meaning'" (85–6). That this is true is clear enough in *Hamlet*, where the competing ideals of violence and piety, laid out by the Ghost's instruction to Hamlet to kill Claudius but to leave Gertrude to heaven (1.5.24–86), work their way through Hamlet's conflicting acts of death-dealing and sermon-giving and also his strenuous thinking about the moral value of violent action. Witness the exquisite balance between his appreciation of Fortinbras' *virtus* and his recognition of the utter futility of the young warrior's military campaign (4.4.32–56). Or, to take Desdemona as an exemplary figure of how ideology is mediated by character and how, more generally, character is the quantum of meaning-making in Shakespeare's plays, let us compare what Stallybrass and Henry Jackson have to say about the arc of her role in *Othello*.[14]

While both agree, in general terms, that Desdemona's value is seen to increase the closer she comes to death, the differences are certainly more important than the similarities, and the differences are also telling about the two men's opposite views of the place, nature, and purpose of character. Here the modern response is characterized by a preponderance of passive constructions ("She is . . . given the freedom we tend to associate with the comic heroine . . . she is reformed within the problematic of the enclosed body . . . she is 'purified'"); the earlier description gives us an active, acting Desdemona ("she pleaded her case [*causam egit*] very effectively . . . [she] moved (us) [*movebat*] . . . she entreated [*imploraret*] the pity of the spectators by her very countenance"). The passive, artifactual, discontinuous Desdemona of materialist criticism could not be more unlike the agential character whose tragic movement from life to death seems unable to still her active pursuit of recognition and respect.

Jackson's report of the Oxford audience's response to Desdemona is not innocent of the gender bias so well described by Stallybrass. She moves them more after she is dead than when she argues her case; and, once she is dead, he says, she entreats their pity. "Misericordia" is a more complex word than the English "pity" since it includes an idea of fellow feeling, but it nevertheless contrasts tellingly with the even-handed judgment demanded explicitly by Othello: "When you shall these unlucky deeds relate, / Speak of me as I am; nothing extenuate, / Nor set down aught in malice" (5.2.341–43). Beyond the particular differences of tone of the performance and reception of the deaths of the female and male protagonists is the plain fact that Desdemona dies silently (though Emilia provides a powerful chorus of enlightenment and grief) while Othello is given a lengthy speech by which he may exculpate his uxoricide and express his remorse, and he is able to arrange and stage his own death. The point, then, is not that boy actor playing Desdemona in 1610 somehow transcends the gender system that is one of the conditions of possibility for the writing and performance of the play, but that the character Desdemona that the boy plays speaks both from within and about the system of gender. The character is in part product of the patriarchal idea of woman, and she is able also to contest and complicate that idea.

The characters' ability to put in question the ideological conditions of possibility of their own creation is one of the most significant artistic and political achievements of Shakespeare's drama. Another example comes from the category of race rather than gender. Shakespeare seems to have conceived the character Shylock in large measure in terms of caninity. He is, Salerio says, "A creature that did bear the shape of man" (3.2.275). Shylock's canine Jewishness is in the language thrown at him ("the dog Jew" [2.8.14], "impenetrable cur" [3.3.18], "inexecrable dog" [4.1.128], "this currish Jew" [4.1.292]), but it is also in his language. His first exchange with Bassanio, with its uncomfortably threatening repetition of his interlocutor's words (1.3.1–10), suggests his dogged style of conversation, but his speech and vocabulary become increasingly aggressive and iterative. Since his words enact a refusal to enter into a human, verbal exchange, they are more of the nature of a barking than a speaking:

[A]ntonio
Hear me yet, good Shylock.

[S]hylock
I'll have my bond, speak not against my bond,
I have sworn an oath that I will have my bond.
Thou call'dst me dog before thou hadst a cause,

> But since I am a dog, beware my fangs.
> The Duke shall grant me justice. I do wonder,
> Thou naughty jailor, that thou art so fond
> To come abroad with him at his request.
>
> *Antonio*
> I pray thee hear me speak.
>
> *Shylock*
> I'll have my bond; I will not hear thee speak.
> I'll have my bond, and therefore speak no more.
> I'll not be made a soft and dull-ey'd fool,
> To shake the head, relent, and sigh, and yield
> To Christian intercessors. Follow not.
> I'll have no speaking, I will have my bond.
>
> (3.3.3–17)

Shylock's dog-words are of a piece here with the unaccountable and irresistible desire for human flesh that rises within him toward the end of his part in the story. It begins as the vaguely threatening "merry bond" that Shylock proposes in 1.3 and from the faintly cannibalistic remark to Antonio in the same scene: "Rest you fair, good signior, / Your worship was the last man in our mouths" (1.3.59–60). These seem at first merely curious violations of contractual and conversational decorum, but they are in fact indicators of a deeper division between the Jew and his Christian interlocutors. Shylock's insistence on what he calls justice in the trial scene, but which is in the play's terms the Jewish hunger for Christian flesh, sets Shylock definitively against what is experienced in the play as the human community and reveals Shylock's essential nature as a "currish Jew" (4.1.288)

Shakespeare's caninization of Shylock is of a piece with the anti-Semitism of early modern Christian culture. The association between dogs and Jews was widespread, which makes Shylock's caninity seem more or less natural and to be expected, but Graziano helpfully provides a genealogy for Shylock, a metamorphosis from currish wolf to inexecrable dog that suggests why Shakespeare seized on and developed Christopher Marlowe's caninization of the figure of the wolfish usurer (in the character Barabus in *The Jew of Malta*):

> O, be thou damned, inexecrable dog,
> And for thy life let justice be accused!
> Thou almost mak'st me waver in my faith

> To hold opinion with Pythagoras,
> That souls of animals infuse themselves
> Into the trunks of men. Thy currish spirit
> Governed a wolf who, hanged for human slaughter,
> Even from the gallows did his fell soul fleet,
> And whilst thou layest in thy unhallowed dam,
> Infused itself in thee; for thy desires
> Are wolvish, bloody, starved and ravenous.
>
> (4.1.127–37)

The wolf is—in nature and in human imagination—alien to humanity; a creature whose predation is an upsurge of unchecked appetite into human society, and a figure of bottomless hunger as an aspect of human society itself; but the wolf whose hanging yielded the currish spirit that transmigrated into Shylock's dam was already somehow inside human society, since it suffered the legal penalty of hanging. Even in his ancestry, Shylock is therefore inside the human community, yet not of it. Dogs have a place with us; they are bred, valued, and trained for service; but curs are low-bred, uncontrolled, unwanted denizens in our communities. Shylock is a cur, according to this idea, because Jews are similarly animal strangers in our midst. According to Bruce Boehrer, it was traditional to represent Jews as "feral, interloping scavengers," a characterization that contributed to the "practice of hanging Jews between two dogs in an inverted parody of the crucifixion."[15]

There is thus no transcendence of anti-Semitism in *The Merchant of Venice*; but the fact that Shylock is in large measure a product of Christian prejudices against Jews is not a weakness of the play or in the characterization of the Jewish antagonist; rather, it is a great strength of the character Shylock in both artistic and political terms. Without being able to escape his less-than-fully-human caninity, Shylock challenges the distinction between Christians and Jews as well as the graduated scale from animality to humanity that was another, related condition of imaginative possibility in early modernity. He does so by explicit rebuttal in the "Hath not a Jew eyes" speech ([3.1.53–73]; importantly, the speech can be performed as a rationalization of revenge), by being injured by the loss of his daughter and the eradication of his blood-line, and by being mocked, humiliated, and forced to convert in the presence of a crowd that can be played as more animalistic than the "currish Jew" who is the object of their Christian "mercy" (4.1.378). Again, though, there is no transcendence of ideology in the play. Even when he gets his day in court, just when he has the chance to make a public case for his injured fatherhood and manhood, Shylock is still a dog that lifts its leg, as it were, against the Venetian state ("Some men there are love not a gaping pig . . . And others, when the bagpipe sings i' th' nose, / Cannot contain their urine" [4.1.47–50]). As the audience at Oxford in 1610 attended to Desdemona's eloquent argumentative speeches without leaving behind certain rooted ideas about women and silence, so early moderns, and playgoers and readers since, have been confronted by Shylock and have been thereby invited to think through entrenched ideas about race, animality, and religion from inside the world that produced these ways of ordering social reality. On this account, finally, character is important as the organizing formal feature of Shakespeare's drama and also the heart of audience engagement with his plays. In view of our present, pressing concern with the political dimension of works of art, character particularly merits our attention and study because it is by coming face to face with characters such as Hamlet, Desdemona, and Shylock that playgoers and readers can think feelingly about social life and the ideological shaping of the human.

III

Shakespeare and Character is divided into four sections. The first three of these group essays according to the primary critical approaches of their authors, while the fourth and final section offers three essays that demonstrate what a theoretically sophisticated and historically informed new character criticism can accomplish when it is alert to the nuances of theatrical performance and intellectual history. The progress from section to section moves according to a linear logic; over the course of the book, that linear movement is enhanced by an equally important recursive and dialogical principle of organization. Section 1 considers certain foundational questions. In what ways are characters like real people? In what ways are characters real *tout court*? What is the relationship between characters and language? Section 2 explores the emergence of Shakespearean character in early modernity, starting with a historical taxonomy of terms, moving to an analysis of the relationship between character and early modern commodity, and concluding with a discussion of character and early modern corporeality. Section 3 focuses on character and performance: metatheater, audience engagement, and character; character and particular actors; and doubleness in sixteenth-century practices of personation. Finally, Section 4 turns to particular characters—Timon of Athens, the "Bastard" Faulconbridge, and Cordelia. Overall, this development allows for the logical elaboration of an account of character that is then tested on particular cases.

The first section of the volume raises a series of foundational questions about characters and how they ought to be studied. Michael Bristol's essay "Confusing Shakespeare's Characters with Real People," which opens the section, takes as its starting point the contentious claim that talking about Shakespeare's characters as though they were real people can be productive for scholars. First, Bristol suggests that by drawing on the tools we use to know our friends and family as we seek to understand a character like Shylock, we can allow ourselves to recognize broad areas of convergence as well as difference among people across times, places, and cultures. On Bristol's account, then, resisting an unselfconscious essentialism need not entail dismissing all attempts to recognize elements of a sense of shared humanity. Second, and by contrast, Bristol uses a discussion of Rosalind to demonstrate that reading characters as though they were real people also allows us to recognize the importance of the notion of coherence to our conception of the self and so to recognize the fundamental singularity of every person. Third, Bristol discusses the pathos of Viola's solitude in *Twelfth Night* in order to argue that the process of reading character requires that we engage in the practice of ethical reflection; a practice that allows us to understand the roles of moral agency and moral problem-solving in constructions of the self and community. Finally, Bristol reminds us that when it is used as a verb, the word "character" means to write, and that writing—that is, the text—is our source for representations of people. Reading characters is about reading people, and reading people is a crucial part of being human. In "The Reality of Fictive Cinematic Characters," Trevor Ponech approaches the issue of character as an analytic philosopher, advancing a strong form of realism about fictional characters. Arguing against the ontological austerity of a literary criticism that is suspicious of characters because the meanings they contain lack independent causal powers, Ponech demonstrates the philosophical viability of a realist account of characters. Traditionally, philosophers have supposed that there is a problem with asserting facts about imaginary beings. Surely it is impossible, or at least epistemologically suspect, to assert a belief about something that one knows has never existed? Ponech demonstrates by way of response that it is both possible and necessary to challenge such reductive ontological strictness.

Section 1 concludes with William Dodd's "Character as Dynamic Identity." Like Bristol, Dodd begins from the premise that dramatic characters often give the impression of behaving much like real persons. These "person-effects," Dodd argues, are not manifestations of some mystical human essence or absolute individuality, but products of dynamic interactional phenomena, of dialogical events not classified by traditional rhetoric. Such phenomena may be said to personalize characters rather than individualize them, but the sequence of discourse events that constructs the characters as persons is unique: each character acquires a discourse biography of its own as a result of the pragmatics of its interactions with other characters. Grounding his thinking about character in an analysis of *Othello*, Dodd explores how such dynamic discourse biographies can interact with historically and ideologically specific discourses and with the semantic dimension of characters.

Section 2 continues the task of developing a substantial, interdisciplinary re-articulation of character by tracing its emergence in early modern literature and culture. In "Personnages: History, Philology, Performance," André Bourassa asks us to consider the etymological history of the French term "personnage" for what this can teach us about the relationship between people and dramatis personae now. His new philological, diachronic interpretation of "personnage" provides the foundation for a critical reassessment of the modern idea of theatrical character, a synchronic study that examines the formal and functional dimensions of the theatrical performance of character and then concludes by considering the multivalence of theatrical character, especially as a function of its transmutation from one production to another. His discussion adds a valuable historical taxonomy, as well as a discussion of the relationship between the textuality and performance of "personnage," to the volume's overall understanding of character.

In "The Properties of Character in *King Lear*," James Berg develops a historical theory of Shakespearean character, suggesting that the aesthetic pleasures and materialist insights afforded by the play are not at odds, as so many critics have assumed, but rather enhance each other. Drawing on the early sense of character as interpretable sign, Berg identifies early modern character as everything about a person that can be read, a definition which includes a character's material possessions. Berg argues that the play nostalgically remembers a mythic age when what a person was, what a person owned, and what a person meant could not be distinguished. The commodification of things owned (as represented, for instance, by Lear's alienation from his land) disrupts these identifications. For Berg, then, as commodity, character is continually altered, overwritten, deleted, but as what indelibly belongs to persons, giving them meaning and being, it leaves traces of itself in the form of ownership history—history concealed by commodification, yet rediscovered and remembered throughout the play. It is such history, Berg argues, that gives character in *King Lear* a "depth" beyond individual interiority.

Leanore Lieblein's "Embodied Intersubjectivity and the Creation of Early Modern Character" draws upon both Thomas Heywood's *Apology for Actors* (1612) and early modern rhetoric manuals to argue in phenomenological terms that the actor participates in the authoring of what can be understood as a dramatic character. Pointing out that for Renaissance rhetoricians the communication of emotion was a physical as well as an imaginative process, Lieblein considers the early modern sense of the word "character" as a form of writing and develops a case for the rhetorical concept of *actio* as a writing on the actor's body. Finally, she argues from early modern sources that spectators, like actors, are "body-subjects," with corporeal histories, and that the "person personated," whom we think of today as a dramatic character, can be viewed as the corporeal product of an intersubjective communication between the actor and the spectator.

From Lieblein's focus on accounts of character in early modern stage practice, we move to the discussions of character and contemporary stage practice that constitute Section 3 of the volume. Paul Yachnin and Myrna Wyatt Selkirk's essay opens this section with an exploration of the theoretical and practical implications for the idea of character of a classroom experiment in which the students in a Theater Lab course performed a series of scenes from *The Winter's Tale*. In "Metatheater and the Performance of Character in *The Winter's Tale*," Yachnin and Selkirk reflect on what the actors achieved in performance and what they wrote afterwards about the experiment in order to suggest that Shakespeare's drama has a more ubiquitous and fluid metatheatrical dimension than is usually thought. Metatheater, they conclude, deepens rather than undermines the reality-effect of characterization, and so promotes ethical spectatorship in ways that answer age-old antitheatrical arguments, from St Augustine to Emmanuel Levinas.

Andrew Hartley's "Character, Agency, and the Familiar Actor" also anchors its analysis of character in the specificities of performance. Arguing that character is crucially tied less to actorly motivation than it is to the actor's performative habitus, Hartley suggests that the staged character's pursuit of agency is generated not simply by barriers of plot or social structure, which have to be overcome within the fiction, but also by the actor's attempt to "own" the linguistically alien role even as his or her own voice, body and gestural vocabulary foregrounds the performer through the performed. As he demonstrates by means of a discussion of a Georgia Shakespeare production of *The Comedy of Errors*, in which a locally well-known actor played both Antipholi, this sense of the character as hybrid striving for agency is particularly conspicuous in Shakespeare. This is doubly so in regional Shakespeare festivals where actors can develop a special visibility over long careers, playing numerous Shakespearean parts.

Robert Weimann's essay on "Doubly Encoded Personation on Shakespeare's Stage" extends his ground-breaking earlier work on the social politics of the drama and theatrical spaces ("locus" and "platea") toward a new understanding of early modern performance practice. Weimann rechristens character as "actor-character," a hybrid figure that brings into dynamic interrelationship the popular traditions of playing and the neoclassical traditions of literary drama. This argument for the "double-voiced" nature of performance yields some startling new insights into particular moments in the plays. Troilus' angry, bewildered remark, "This is, and is not, Cressid" includes a metatheatrical observation on the presence of the boy actor in the part that deepens rather than alleviates the question of Cressida's character. Beyond these new readings of particular passages, the essay looks closely at two scenes from two different plays (featuring Falstaff and Autolycus) in order to demonstrate that the performance practice of Shakespeare's playhouse, with the consistently dialogic work of the actor-characters, was itself an important form of social and cultural critique.

The final section of the volume grounds its project of providing a theoretically, historically, theatrically, and critically substantial account of Shakespearean character in explorations of three "theatrical persons": Timon of Athens, *King John*'s Faulconbridge, and *King Lear*'s Cordelia. In "Is Timon a Character?" Anthony Dawson notes that if we understand Shakespearean character as distinct from either allegorical personage or satirical caricature, because it entails a certain roundness and psychological complexity, Timon cannot fully count as a character. On Dawson's account, Timon's intense experience of envy gives him the kind of interiority that enlivens figures like Macbeth or Antony, but his lack of introspection denies him the complexity of full characterization. Nevertheless, Dawson argues, it is useful to understand Timon as a figure on the extremity of the category of character. Camille Slights also investigates the limits of character, arguing in "When is a bastard not a bastard?", that conscience, a concept including both self-reflection and knowledge of moral principles, was basic to early modern self-understanding and that it provides historical grounding for the analysis of characters on the early modern stage. She points out that a taxonomy of characters in Shakespeare's *King John* from the perspective of conscience includes most characters in such traditional categories as those who deliberately act contrary to the judgment of their consciences, those who ignore their consciences, and those who struggle with difficult cases of conscience. The most interesting character, however, does not fit easily into any of these categories. Instead of judging himself and others on the basis of moral standards articulated in religious and political traditions, Philip Faulconbridge, known as the Bastard, develops a personal sense of right and wrong through a process of inward reflection—what Hannah Arendt has called "a dialogue carried on by the mind with itself" by which "the moral precept rises out of the thinking activity itself." Slights argues that through the Bastard, who develops an individual conscience when traditional values and principles fail, *King John* explores the transition from a universalized conscience, the voice of God speaking within each person, to an individualized conscience, which is characteristic of modern Western culture.

In the essay that closes the volume, "Arming Cordelia: Character and Performance," Sarah Werner works from a single stage direction in the Folio text of *King Lear* as a means of interrogating the interpretive tools that scholars use in studying Shakespearean character. In the Folio text, Cordelia's re-emergence onto the stage—and into the action of the play—is marked by the stage direction, "Enter with drum and colours, Cordelia, Gentleman, and Soldiers" (4.3.0) Werner points out that, while it has rarely been commented on, this stage direction is crucial for understanding Cordelia. Along with her subsequent exchange with the Messenger, it suggests not only that Cordelia is at the head of the French army but that she is dressed in armor. To imagine an armed Cordelia here, Werner argues, is both to reshape the usual interpretation of her character as docile and to recover a more complicated gender ideology for the play. Further, she argues, the possibility of an armed Cordelia raises questions about the relationship between performance and textual interpretation since it requires not only an ability and a willingness to imagine women soldiers, but also a recognition that dramatic character is created not only by words on the page, but also by actions on stage. Thus, for Werner, reading early modern dramatic character requires reading stage directions—explicit and implicit—as carefully as we read dialogue.

Notes

1. Margaret Cavendish. *CCXI. Sociable Letters* (1664), 245.
2. Samuel Johnson, from the Dedication to Charlotte Lennox. *Shakespeare Illustrated* (1753), 9–10.
3. Maurice Morgann, *Essay on the Dramatic Character of Falstaff* (1777), 189.
4. Anna Murphy Jameson, *Shakespeare's Heroines* (1832), ed. Cheri L. Larsen Hoeckley. (Broadview, 2005), 55.
5. Indeed, Bradley reportedly said of Morgann's rereading of Falstaff: "[T]here is no better piece of Shakespearian criticism in the world." Quoted in Hardy, J. P. Review of *Maurice Morgann: Shakespearian Criticism*, edited by Daniel A. Fineman. *The Review of English Studies* 24.96 (November 1973): 496–99.
6. The practice of "character assassination" was particularly popular several decades ago. Among the most influential works were Francis Barker, *The Tremulous Private Body* (New York: Methuen 1984); Jonathan Dollimore, *Radical Tragedy: Religion, Ideology, and Power in the Drama of Shakespeare and his Contemporaries* (Chicago: University of Chicago Press, 1984); and Catherine Belsey, *The Subject of Tragedy: Identity and Difference in Renaissance Drama* (London: Routledge, 1985). More recent work has prosecuted the case against character with greater theoretical sophistication, interpretive nuance, and historical depth. See especially Margreta de Grazia, *Hamlet without Hamlet* (Cambridge: Cambridge University Press, 2007).
7. Jonathan Goldberg, "Shakespearean Inscriptions: The Voicing of Power," in *Shakespeare and the Question of Theory*, eds Patricia Parker and Geoffrey Hartman (New York: Methuen, 1985), 118–19.
8. Peter Stallybrass, "Patriarchal Territories: The Body Enclosed," in *Rewriting the Renaissance: The Discourses of Sexual Difference in Early Modern Europe*, eds Margaret Ferguson et al. (Chicago: University of Chicago Press, 1986), 123–42, at 141.
9. Katharine Maus, *Inwardness and Theater in the English Renaissance* (Chicago: University of Chicago Press, 1995); Theodore B. Leinwand, *Theatre, Finance and Society in Early Modern England* (Cambridge: Cambridge University Press, 1999); and Wes Folkerth, *The Sound of Shakespeare* (London and New York: Routledge, 2002).
10. Leonard Digges, "Poets are borne not made," in *Riverside Shakespeare*, ed. G. Blakemore Evans (2nd ed. Boston: Houghton Mifflin, 1997), 1972.
11. The phrase "double-voiced" is from M. M. Bakhtin, *The Dialogic Imagination: Four Essays*, ed. M. Holquist (Austin: University of Texas Press, 1981), 324.
12. Henry Jackson, [*Othello* at Oxford, 1610], quoted and translated in *Riverside Shakespeare*, 1978.
13. *Aristotle's Poetics*, trans. S. H. Butcher, intro. Francis Fergusson (New York: Hill and Wang, 1961), 62–3.
14. For a discussion of the person as the measure of meaning-making in Shakespeare, see Paul Yachnin, "Personations: *The Taming of the Shrew* and the Limits of Theoretical Criticism," *Early Modern Literary Studies* 2.1 (1996): 2.1–31 <URL: http://purl.oclc.org/emls/02-1/yachshak.html>.
15. Bruce Boehrer, *Shakespeare Among the Animals: Nature and Society in the Drama of Early Modern* England (New York: Palgrave Macmillan, 2002), 26.

Part I Theory

1
Confusing Shakespeare's Characters with Real People: Reflections on Reading in Four Questions

Michael Bristol

Whenever I teach a Shakespeare play, or discuss one with a friend, or attend a performance, I find myself relating to the characters just as I do with real people. I don't think I'm really confused. Dr Johnson didn't think so either: "[S]pectators are always in their senses, and know, from the first act to the last, that the stage is only a stage, and that the players are only players."[1] Fair enough, but why do I puzzle over Macbeth's real motives or speculate about Lady Macbeth's children? And why do I think that the basic intuitions I use to understand my friends and relatives are appropriate tools for getting at a fictional character? This essay is about some of my assumptions about notions like human nature, the self, individuality, and how these categories have been articulated by Shakespeare in his characters. It is not really a theory about fictional characters. For that, it's best to consult Trevor Ponech's essay in this volume.[2] Rather, this essay is more concerned with articulating what I think I've learned about the way Shakespeare characterizes his make-believe people.

Why is it possible to ride a bicycle?

On the face of it, it's not really obvious that it can be done at all. Picture a silent movie with Buster Keaton. He sets up a bike on its wheels, hitches up his pants, and in that tiny interval the bike falls over. No matter how carefully he tries to position the bike, it will fall over every time. But after a while he gives it a push. It stays up for a while, then falls over, but something has been learned: stationary wheels fall over; spinning ones stay balanced. This is the physical principle of the gyroscope, used for guidance systems in spacecraft, but the basic idea is known to any child who has ever spun a top.

Back in our silent movie, Buster Keaton has managed to make the bike stay up in a shaky sort of way, but he's not really riding yet. Once he has confidence that there's a way to keep the bike from just falling over, he tries out the idea of getting on and then giving it a good push-off to keep it moving. Soon he can even ride with no hands! How did he learn so fast? This is possible because the organs of balance can regulate the bike's momentum as the rider pedals along his chosen path. The principle of the gyroscope, average balance, and reasonably well functioning arms and legs constitute the conditions of possibility for bike riding. And anyone can do it. The *possibility* of riding a bicycle is independent of its historical context; it's part of human nature, like speaking a language or solving problems by trial and error.

The ability to ride a bicycle is, we might say, a latent potentiality of all human beings. The actual riding of bicycles is another matter. For someone living in Ancient Egypt, bicycle riding would not just have been impossible, it would have been inconceivable. For actual bicycle riding to be possible, there have to be bicycles and places to ride them; or, in other words, historically specific social conditions and technical discoveries that actualize any potentiality of human nature. Understanding these conditions is the task of historical inquiry, which is concerned with "bringing out, as vividly as possible, the peculiar and transient idiosyncrasy of the individual or social group under study."[3] People living in Ancient Egypt or in Early Modern England must undoubtedly be shaped by all kinds of contingent states of affairs. Still, the underlying point of historical inquiry must be that there are underlying regularities that make historically specific differences intelligible within our own similarly peculiar and transient conditions of life.

Human nature has become a problematic idea for most of the people now writing criticism of Shakespeare. This is partly due to the extraordinary success of historical inquiry in bringing out specific complexities in Shakespeare's works. Feelings, attitudes, ways of relating to other people, the very idea of "self," all look very different in Shakespeare's culture from what we are used to in our everyday lives.[4] Even something as "natural" as bodily experience is culturally constructed to a surprising degree, as Gail Kern Paster has shown.[5] In addition, specific claims about human nature often exhibit a degree of ideological blindness that confuses our "peculiar and transient idiosyncrasy" with universal characteristics of all human beings.[6] Jonathan Dollimore's sustained critique of "essentialist humanism" is perhaps the most thorough and persuasive account of this view for early modern literary studies. Dollimore is certainly right to take on the intellectual complacency often on display in claims people have made about human nature. But it does not follow from his critique that there can be no "essential" features of human experience that register across different cultural and historical settings. "Claims regarding cultural constructs cannot simply be assumed as a priori truths blocking interpretive inquiries that may give us cause to reject them."[7]

I think it's desirable to think about a general human nature if only in the sense of exploring areas of convergence as well as areas of difference, and indeed to distinguish between the two. Noam Chomsky has argued for a latent potentiality for learning language as both innate and central to a shared human nature.[8] An acquaintance of mine who teaches Mathematics is convinced that human beings in all cultures are in some way attuned to the Pythagorean harmonic proportions expressed in musical intervals.[9] We can certainly say that there is a "history of sex" but let's not forget that there is also "a biology of sex."[10] The relationship between "history" and "biology" is what Sandra Harding has called an "organic social variable."[11] Her idea is that a number of features of our common evolutionary development, notably human reproductive physiology, demand a specific articulation in every cultural setting. This is very different from the approach taken in socio-biology, which usually gets into trouble by trying to do too much.[12] Harding's identification of the sex-gender system as an organic social variable combines a sensible acknowledgement that some things are invariant in every social context with an awareness of cultural diversity. Martha Nussbaum tries to take this idea much farther, suggesting that all human cultures recognize such things as friendship and affiliation, skills for problem solving, humor, sexuality, infant and child development, among other things.[13]

For Shakespeare, the idea of human nature appears tragically in the image of unaccomodated man, the "poor bare forked animal" (3.4.99–100)[14] that remains when false and dissembling garments are stripped away. The notion of "unaccomodated man" (99) clearly speaks to a general "human condition" of radical physical vulnerability. It means, literally, a man without any commodities, without the barest minimum of social amenities or even basic needs. Lear wonders if a man is "no more than this,"(95–96), but what he has evidently seen is that a person is certainly no less than this. *King Lear* is a play that gives us a lot to think about, but one thing seems consistent and unambiguous. No social position or moral attitude confers immunity to loss and suffering. Human fragility, "the thousand natural shocks that flesh is heir to," rather than any latent potentiality like bicycle riding, is the common and natural condition of human personhood.

For Shakespeare, this sense of human nature as vulnerability to harm makes a powerful claim on our attention as moral imperative rather than as sociobiological explanation. This claim finds its most startling, difficult, and disturbing articulation in the words of a character fundamentally alien and inimical to the ethos of the community in which he resides. Shylock hopes to be permitted to live his life as a Jew in Venetian society, a desire protected by the laws of the Republic of Venice, but not, apparently, by many of its citizens.[15] Antonio never denies spitting upon him, and his friends Salario and Salarino continue to taunt him when his daughter absconds with his money. Just in case we in the audience are tempted to join in the fun, however, Shylock confronts his tormentors with a question: does the fact of being Jewish provide any reason or give permission to insult, harm, and humiliate someone?

> *Shylock:* Hath not a Jew eyes? Hath not a Jew hands, organs, dimensions, senses, affections, passions; fed with the same food, hurt with the same weapons, heal'd by the same means, warm'd and cool'd by the same winter and summer, as a Christian is? If you prick us, do we not bleed? If you tickle us, do we not laugh? If you poison us, do we not die? And if you wrong us, shall we not revenge? If we are like you in the rest, we will resemble you in that. If a Jew wrong a Christian, what is his humility? Revenge. If a Christian wrong a Jew, what should his sufferance be by Christian example? Why, revenge. The villainy you teach me, I will execute, and it shall go hard but I will better the instruction.
> (*The Merchant of Venice* 3.1.49–61)

Shylock's resistance to the jeering disrespect of his Christian neighbors is based on an appeal to human nature. This idea includes, but is not limited to, the shared physiological condition of organic function and vulnerability. There is also a psychological element here—"if you wrong us, shall we not revenge?"

For Shylock, the Christian privilege conferred by the doctrine of "turning the other cheek" will always express itself in accordance with a human nature that seeks retribution for every injury. This speaks very specifically to the historical antagonism between Christian and Jew; it also speaks to the question of Shylock's Jewish identity as sufficient warrant for the hatred displayed towards him.[16] What are we to make of this remarkable intervention in what is otherwise a comic tale about overcoming obstacles to a series of happy marriages? Salario and Salarino basically have nothing to say; they're interrupted—they have to go and see Antonio. Charles Spinosa has shown that the dispute between Shylock and Antonio recapitulates certain fundamental changes in the understanding of the law of contract in Early Modern England.[17] For Henry Turner, the play is concerned with changing ideas about friendship, affiliation, and citizenship.[18] Edward Andrew sees in this speech a powerful articulation of a theory of human rights, based on a robust picture of a common physical and psychological nature.[19]

I very much admire the intelligence in these examples of historical inquiry, but they all tend to diminish what Harry Berger calls the "fatness of the character."[20] Berger's intuition is that the language of a Shakespeare character—like the Duke in *Measure for Measure*; or like Shylock—is not well elucidated as the expression of a generic or historical type. For Berger, an utterance always presupposes an actual person. Following Berger, I wonder if there is something even more basic and also more personal in Shylock's speech. "Hath not a Jew eyes?" What does this Jew see with his own eyes? He sees other people who hate him *because he is a Jew*. And so Shylock hates: "Hatred, it seems, cannot be bought . . . no amount of money will buy Shylock."[21] This is specifically Shylock's nature, but it is not his human nature. In the world of *The Merchant of Venice*, hatred is what we necessarily are to expect. Human nature as it is articulated by Shylock is not so much about having human organs, or desires, or attitudes. It is basically a kind of moral entitlement, a "right" to be recognized and respected as a human being.[22] It's an odd thing for Shylock to be saying, but then who else would there be to say it?

How does a small child build a tower of wooden blocks?

The answer to this question has something in common with the possibility of riding a bicycle. The task involved has to be possible. So things don't fall through the floor; towers can be made of blocks, but not sour cream. The task involves learning, discovery, and problem solving. And it is a potential that exists in all children, independent of their historical context. But this is not a question about why something is possible, it is rather about how something is done. Unlike the case of bicycle riding, the answer seems obvious: put one block on top of another; what's the problem? Marvin Minsky points out that "An idea will seem self-evident—once you've forgotten learning it."[23] This is what he calls "the amnesia of infancy: . . . though all grown-up persons know how to do such things, *no one understands how we learn to do them.*"[24]

It turns out that building a tower of blocks is a complex achievement. Minsky describes the child's mind as a kind of "society" consisting of "mental agents," each one capable of accomplishing a specialized function.[25] "Builder" is one of these agents, whose specialization is constructing towers. To do this, however, builder acts only as a general contractor, drawing on the skills of other agents known as "begin", "add", and "end." Begin decides where to put the tower and End decides when it is high enough. Add has the job of placing blocks, but to do this she has to recruit agents called "find", "get", and "put" who in turn depend on "see", "grasp", "move", "release", and so on. It's no wonder that small children find playing with blocks so fascinating. Some of them eventually grow up to be stone-masons, contractors, or architects. Most of us do other things when we grow up, but the agents that enable us to build towers are still there, even if we can't remember where they came from.

The amnesia of infancy refers not only to things we had to learn, but also to things that weren't learned at all. "Prior to the greater part of specific cultural shaping, though perhaps not free from all shaping, are certain areas of human experience and development that are broadly shared . . . all humans begin as hungry babies, perceiving their own helplessness . . . "[26] Clearly, many of the "mental agents" we need for the basic activity of everyday life look like standard equipment—impersonal logical routines for picking up a cup of coffee that aren't distinguishing traits of anyone in particular but form part of a more general human nature. Such logical routines might include mental agents like builder, wrecker, bicycle rider, and so on, according to an inventory of stock human functions. Not everyone gets exactly the same standard package of skills. It is said that there are men who cannot boil an egg. But if people are inhabited by whole societies of distinct agents, what does it mean to speak of a self?

Descartes famously thought there was some kind of co-ordinating agency that thought and therefore was. He called this magisterial agent "reason" and considered it as sovereign.[27] This picture of the self, often characterized as the "ghost in the machine," conforms to our common sense intuition about ourselves, but it doesn't withstand much close scrutiny.[28] The idea of a centralized self somehow regulating all our diverse and conflicted mental agents has been rejected as an illusion by many different modes of inquiry, including historical research about early modern drama.[29] The most brilliant critique of the Cartesian "ego" that I have encountered was in a skit performed many years ago by Sid Caesar as "the brain." Seated in front of a bank of phones, he received messages from "the knee", "the eyes" and "the ears", and tried to issue instructions to the various organs. The inputs were so fast and furious that all efforts at co-ordination very quickly broke down.

But if there is no one in charge, how do our minds function? For Nietzsche "reason" is neither unified nor the dominant cause of action:

> The assumption of one single subject is perhaps unnecessary; perhaps it is just as permissible to assume a multiplicity of subjects, whose interaction and struggle is the basis of our thought and our consciousness in general? A kind of aristocracy of "cells" in which dominion resides? To be sure, an aristocracy of equals, used to ruling jointly and understanding how to command?[30]

The important point here is the idea of equals used to ruling jointly, as in the well ordered *polis* described by Aristotle. Nietzsche's idea is more traditional than it sounds, since the "mental aristocrats" presumably have common interests and mutual respect for each other. But Nietzsche's idea of a society of aristocrats "used to ruling jointly" itself now seems a bit idealistic. The society of mind looks more like a bunch of disorganized street people dressed in "borrowed robes," a kind of shabby vaudeville with unreliable and inept management. Minsky's reference to "the amnesia of infancy" is interesting in this respect, since it reminds us that the "mental agents" we rely on so much are not even indigenous, but come from outside ourselves as part of a diaspora of hand-me-down selves in the form of an anonymous repertoire of gestures, attitudes, and personality traits.

Is there really a "core of interiority" where a unified and coherent self can be found? Sid Caesar as "the brain" just had way too much to do, and his performance would suggest that the idea of a central self just can't be made to work. But if the "single self" view is unworkable, what about the "plural self" picture of things? Minsky thinks we're never fully satisfied with either of these alternatives; that we need to recognize both interpretations to represent our own *rapport a soi*. Self, on his account, corresponds to a conservative function, some process that maintains a relatively stable continuity in our lives. A well functioning self, even if we don't know where it is or how it works, makes it possible to have plans and purposes, instead of trying to do everything at once.[31] Keeping track of self and its purposes is not about unity so much as it is about coherence. Maintaining coherence is a more complex task than putting one block on top of another. Stuff happens. The world presents us with distractions, crises, and complicated problems to solve.

Rosalind is a beautiful young princess whose father has been banished by her not-very-nice uncle. She falls in love with a beautiful young man called Orlando. Her uncle sends her into exile. She gets disguised as a boy because she is "uncommon tall" and goes to the forest of Arden. She pretends to be Ganymede. She meets the beautiful boy. She pretends to be Rosalind and helps Orlando woo her. Her goal is to marry Orlando. But Rosalind's over-riding purpose is to survive, to keep on being Rosalind, which isn't easy because she also has to keep on being Ganymede. And, of course, Ganymede has troubles of his own, one of which is called Phoebe.

Pretending to be myself at the same time as I'm pretending to be somebody else is a conventional device in literature, but it's probably most familiar to most of us as something we do every day.[32] Shakespeare is quite interested in situations like this one, and not just in his comedies. Viola's disguise as Cesario is one kind of analogue, Hamlet's "antic disposition" is another. The survival involved in these situations is really a kind of ethical self-preservation, maintaining integrity by a strategic practice of disintegrity. Versatility, change, dissimulation are all placed at the service of the conservative self. Rosalind wants to be sure that Orlando really loves her, and so she asks him how long he would "have her." He tells her "forever and a day." But this is the wrong answer. She doesn't want a conventional response; she wants a reality check.

> *Rosalind:* Say "a day" without the "ever." No, no Orlando, men are April when they woo, December when they wed; maids are May when they are maids, but the sky changes when they are wives. I will be more jealous of thee than a Barbary cock-pigeon over his hen, more clamorous than a parrot against rain, more new-fangled than an ape, more giddy in my desires than a monkey. I will weep for nothing, like Diana in the fountain, and I will do that when you are dispos'd to be merry. I will laugh like a hyen, and that when thou art inclin'd to sleep.
> (*As You Like It* 4.1.124–33)

What Rosalind wants Orlando to understand is that when you marry someone you don't get a fairy tale; what you get is a person with a mind. In Rosalind's case, her mind is not just a diverse society of mental agents; it's a veritable zoo of emotions, impulses, and perversities.

Rosalind doesn't want to be loved forever and a day. She wants Orlando to love her even when she's acting like a hyena, whether he is sleepy or depressed or in a good mood. This is what "marriage" means in *As You Like It*; it's a way to augment the faculty of self-conservation by means of another's recognition of a real person within an entire menagerie of conflicting dispositions. "Forever and a day" expresses the conventional view of marriage as an institution for maintaining an established order. Rosalind wants to take things one day at a time, hoping she won't have to impersonate herself all the time.[33]

We don't remember learning how to build a tower of blocks and we don't remember learning language either. These are things that Mikhail Bakhtin refers to as "exotopy"—things that come from outside the self that are necessary for its completion.[34] There may be no core of interiority in the early modern subject, or in anyone else for that matter, but "self" is probably better understood as "authority" rather than as "inwardness." For Rosalind, language is a performance, a way to avoid danger and to get what she wants. She wants Orlando to quit writing bad sonnets and say something simple, from the heart. Her authority is not so much about performing as it is about her capacity to utter the performative.[35] "I do take thee, Orlando, for my husband. There's a girl goes before the priest, and certainly a woman's thought runs before her actions" (4.1.117–19). Rosalind understands how to use language to execute her own thoughts and turn them into actions. That's why the character is so much fun to perform.

If I am not for myself, then who will be for me?

Hillel's aphorism is not just about sticking up for oneself, though that is certainly part of what he intends.[36] "Hath not a Jew eyes?"—draws some of its force from this aspect of Hillel's teaching. "I" here has the sense of a core self, though "inwardness" is probably not the best way to think about the meaning of Hillel's first-person singular. What's intended here is better represented in the wanderings of Abraham: "Now the LORD had said unto Abram, Get thee out of thy country, and from thy kindred, and from thy father's house, unto a land that I will shew thee" (Genesis 12:1) This verse implies a self that exists independently of one's situatedness in a nation or family. Its physical location is not what matters. Abraham, I was always told, wouldn't accept conventional wisdom; he thought things through for himself. This led to his *demarche* and his encounter with "I am". Hillel's aphorism speaks to a "responsible self," something other than the social roles, conventions, and habits acquired from others. This is a self that exists without any alibis.

"If I am not for myself, then who will be for me?" is sticking up for oneself but also taking responsibility for oneself. Hillel's second question—"But if I am only for myself, who am I?"[37] suggests an expanded sense of what responsibility means.[38] There is a story that one day a pagan came to see Hillel and said that he would convert to Judaism if the Rabbi could recite the whole of the Torah while standing on one foot.[39] "Do not do unto others as you would not have done unto you. That is the whole of the Torah: now go and learn it." Jesus' golden rule enjoins you to do unto others as you would have others do unto you. This makes no sense unless the second-person singular addressee (you) is a first-person singular (I) that "you" are an "I" with a strong sense of self-worth and personal dignity. If my own *rapport a soi* is based on respect, consideration, and recognition for myself, I am empowered to adopt such dispositions towards others. If I live as a slave, always at the call of another's well-being, "I" have nothing to offer.

Hillel's question bears on Aristotle's discussion of the virtue of friendship. Aristotle wonders if *philautia* (self-love) is justifiable for the virtuous man. He distinguishes between a bad kind of self-love that translates as something like self-indulgence and something altogether different that looks more like a responsible self-care. " . . . It is right for the good man to be self-loving, because then he will both be benefitting himself by performing fine actions, and also help others . . . For intelligence always chooses what is best for itself, and the good man obeys the guidance of intelligence."[40] This has something in common with Nietzsche's master morality, his idea that " . . . the noble man lives for himself in trust and openness . . . ".[41] For Nietzsche, this is the only possible way to treat others—even enemies—with genuine respect.

"If I am not for myself" is not only about the possibility of an ethics, however. There is a tragic sense to Hillel's aphorism. It means that no one else can be expected to act on my behalf. Personhood, the responsible self, is singularity and aloneness. What is there to say about this solitude other than taking note of suffering and death, the common fate of "unaccomodated man." Emmanuel Levinas wants to say something more about solitude than simply describing it as unhappiness. "Solitude is not tragic because it is the privation of the other, but because it is shut up within the captivity of its identity, because it is matter."[42] The singular self, the individual, is hard to find not because it is hidden away "deep inside" but because its existence presupposes diaspora, banishment, or possibly shipwreck.

Viola has left her country, her kindred, and her father's house. She didn't actually decide to do this; the shipwreck leaves her a stranger in a strange land. Viola has next to nothing in the sense that the network of social relationships in which she has, up to now, been supported, has been radically effaced, wiped out, literally drowned in the ocean. The ship's captain thinks her brother might still be alive, but there is not really much hope. But Viola, though she is alone, is not completely bereft of resources. She has some money. She is sturdy, resilient, probably a good swimmer, and she demonstrates alacrity in coping with very difficult situations. She is able to act on her own behalf when she has no alternative. When you've just survived a shipwreck, "if I am not for myself, then who will be for me?" is not an academic question.

In addition to her gold, Viola has an improvisatory competence, a basic package of verbal skills that enable her to speak in "many sorts of music" (1.2.54). To cash this in she decides it would be best to apply to Duke Orsino, disguising herself as a "eunuch" whose skills in the various arts of giving pleasure may be "very worth his service" (55). Viola has to take a chance here and she decides that the Captain is someone she can trust. In fact, he is her only chance. Basically, she is going to give him her clothes for safe-keeping; or, in other words, she is going to trust him with the secret of her sex. She asks him if he will "Shape thou thy silence to my wit" (57). The captain agrees: "Be you his eunuch, and your mute I'll be; When my tongue blabs, then let mine eyes not see" (58–59). Your secret, he says, is safe with me. Both eunuchs and mutes are physically incomplete or compromised men whose task is to guard female chastity. And this language speaks both to Viola's empowerment and her disempowerment. She is going to be the guardian of her own chastity by becoming a eunuch. She bets on her own assets as the guarantee of her survival and her personal integrity. She loses the bet not because her chastity is compromised, but because she becomes trapped by her own versatility. "Disguise I see thou art a wickedness wherein the pregnant enemy does much" (2.2.25–26).

Viola has the very bad luck to fall in love with her master, Duke Orsino. She has even worse luck when the Duchess Olivia, to whom she has been sent to woo on behalf of Orsino, falls in love with her, thinking Viola is really a young man.[43] Her disguise as a young man is so good, in fact, that she gets embroiled in a duel over the affections of the Duchess. The whole thing looks like an implausible farce, but in *Twelfth Night*, as in many of Shakespeare's other comedies, something more is at stake than the elaboration of a conventional dramatic formula. Viola's predicament represents a problem of moral orientation.[44] She would like to express her feelings directly to Orsino, but he thinks she is really a boy whose feelings are not to be taken seriously. Viola resorts to something a bit like Rosalind's self-impersonation, saying what she feels by not saying it, by telling the history of a sister she doesn't really have.

> *Viola:* . . . She never told her love,
> But let concealment, like a worm i' the bud,
> Feed on her damask cheek: she pined in thought,
> And with a green and yellow melancholy
> She sat like patience on a monument,
> Smiling at grief. Was not this love indeed?
>
> (2.5.109–14)

Mourning for her lost brother, she becomes her brother, and seems condemned either to lead a completely false and absurd life of unrequited love or to be exposed as an imposter. When the Duke asks if the sister died of her love she tells him the truth:

> I am all the daughters of my father's house,
> And all the brothers too: and yet I know not.
>
> (2.5.119–21)

She doesn't know if "her sister" died of love, because she doesn't know how her own story will end.

"If not now, when?" Viola's predicament here, and throughout *Twelfth Night*, represents the pathos of solitude as a deferral of recognition. To guard her chastity, to maintain her integrity as Viola, she has to make herself vanish. Feste has promised Orsino that "Journey's end in lovers meeting" but that doesn't quite happen. Viola and Sebastian recognize each other, but it's not clear if they embrace.

> Do not embrace me till each circumstance
> Of place, time, fortune, do cohere and jump
> That I am Viola.
>
> (5.1.244–46)

Yu Jin Ko describes a performance where they do not and she relates this to the moment in John 20:17 when Jesus says to Mary Magdalene, "Touch me not, for I am not yet ascended to the Father." The joy of reconciliation is deferred here until Viola's absent self can be brought back into view. The pain of deferral suggests that there is "no promise of transcendent fulfillment."[45]

All that has to happen now is for the Captain to re-appear and confirm Viola's identity by producing discarded clothing. But this is what really happens in the story:

> The captain that did bring me first on shore
> Hath my maid's garments. He upon some action
> Is now in durance, at Malvolio's suit,
> A gentleman and follower of my lady's.
>
> (5.1.267–70)

Somewhere, we don't know the exact location, the "real Viola" or at least her maid's garments, are held in trust by the Captain. The relationship between Viola and the Captain is a bargain between wit and silence, between being the "versatile" object of desire Viola has to become in order to survive and the lost self indefinitely held "in durance." Viola's own garments are going to be produced tomorrow—but not now. Then she will become "Orsino's mistress and his fancy's Queen." Is this going to be the "when" of self-reconciliation or just a different kind of durance? When is the self present? Hillel has an answer for this: "Appear neither naked nor clothed, neither sitting nor standing, neither laughing nor weeping."

What's in the brain that ink may character
Which hath not figured to thee my true spirit.

Used as a verb, character means to engrave or to write. This really is a *literal* usage of the word, since it refers to the idea of written marks or letters of the alphabet.[46] Sonnet 108 asks how ink can be used to display what's in the brain, which otherwise cannot be seen. The answer is not only that ink can represent the mind; it can even represent the "true spirit," the breath of life or essence of a person. The sonnets are deeply preoccupied with writing, and with ink as an expressive medium; a black substance that, paradoxically, can illuminate what's dark. Ink is black, like the black bile associated with melancholia; and indeed the whole enterprise of the sonnets represents the pathology of writing.[47] This sonnet suggests that "mind" can be exhaustively represented in writing, not because the poet has anything new to say, but because the love that motivates the verse can somehow bring dead metaphors back to life: " . . . eternal love in love's fresh case / Weighs not the dust and injury of age."

Shakespeare uses character as a verb several times in his plays, usually in reference to things that can be written into the mind. When Polonius wants Laertes to follow his fatherly advice, even when he's away in Paris, he tells him "these few precepts in thy memory see thou character" (*Hamlet*, 1.3.58–59). The precepts have to be written down, charactered, so that Laertes won't forget them. In *Two Gentlemen of Verona* Julia wants "advice" about how she can undertake a journey to see "my loving Proteus":

> *Julia:* Counsel, Lucetta; gentle girl, assist me;
> And even in kind love I do conjure thee,
> Who art the table wherein all my thoughts
> Are visibly character'd and engraved.
> (*Two Gentlemen of Verona*: 2.7.1–4)

The basis for this odd request is that Lucetta knows all Julia's thoughts, which she has confided or "visibly character'd," as if to say "you are the person who knows me best." The idea of trust here is figured as an act of writing thoughts in another person's mind. Lucetta's counsel is sensible and prudent: "don't do it." Julia's response is "hinder not my course" (33). She doesn't want advice. She wants a strategy which will take the form of "weeds as may beseem some well-reputed page" (42–43).

These examples suggest that writing down thoughts and precepts from another person in your mind should promote rational behavior. But Hamlet, after seeing the Ghost, wants to *erase* everything he's learned so that "thy commandment all alone shall live / Within the book and volume of my brain" (1.5.102–3). The idea of the mind as a commonplace book, full of trivial records and maxims collected from books, doesn't correspond to a genuine self capable of acting authentically. Hamlet wants only one thing to be written in his mind:—his father's commandment. But it's not really clear that this will lead to a sensible course of action.

Polonius wants to give his son maxims designed to help him live a good life and so he tells him to "character" his father's precepts so that they will be part of the son's identity. Hamlet wants to erase everything he knows so that he can follow his father's writ. But there are things that can be written in the mind that don't help with living a good life and that can't be erased either. Lady Macbeth is "troubled with thick coming fancies, / That keep her from her rest" (5.3.40–41) Macbeth thinks her doctor should be able to do something about it:

> *Macbeth:* Cure her of that.
> Canst thou not minister to a mind diseased,

> Pluck from the memory a rooted sorrow,
> Raze out the written troubles of the brain
> And with some sweet oblivious antidote
> Cleanse the stuff'd bosom of that perilous stuff
> Which weighs upon the heart?
>
> (5.3.42–47)

This is an extraordinary insight into the way the mind works. Lady Macbeth's sleeplessness, her obsessive fantasies, her delusions, are not caused by an excess of black bile or by any "chemical imbalance."[48] Macbeth knows that his wife's suffering is caused by something in her memory and that she lacks the capacity or the will to "an active forgetfulness . . . preserving mental order, calm, and decorum."[49]

If psychoanalysis is what Macbeth has in mind as the remedy for Lady Macbeth's illness, he is bound to be disappointed. The Doctor tells him, "Therein the patient must minister to himself" (5.3.47–48). Why does he say "himself" when the person they're talking about is Lady Macbeth? The Doctor understands what's really going on and he knows that the Queen is not the only one who exhibits symptoms of serious mental illness. He also knows the signs of a bad conscience, but as a physician he also understands that there are times when it's best to be discrete. He does, however, manage to give Macbeth some therapeutic advice, if only obliquely. The patient must "minister to himself" through confession and contrition of heart. It won't "raze out the written troubles" (5.3.44), but it might make you feel better about them. Macbeth isn't much interested in heeding the Doctor's advice, any more than Julia is in heeding Lucetta's. He does what men often do when they're depressed and anxious: he decides that action is the best remedy.

The "written troubles" in Lady Macbeth's brain clearly have something to do with her remorse over killing Duncan. But there might have been other things written there that made her want to do such a deed in the first place. And what about Macbeth? Did he kill Duncan because he wanted to be king? Or was wanting to be king simply an excuse for killing? There is reason to think that Macbeth didn't really want to kill Duncan at all and that he acted against his own best judgment in carrying out the murder. What's in the brain can be "charactered"—expressly written out as the record of someone's "true spirit." Even so, other people are hard to understand; everyone has "written troubles" of their own.

Like Macbeth, Angelo in *Measure for Measure* is a man much admired for his virtues. Also like Macbeth, his exemplary behavior is rewarded with trust, authority, and status. When the Duke appoints him Deputy, with full power to govern the city of Vienna, this is how he explains his decision:

Duke: There is a kind of character in thy life,
That to th'observer doth thy history
Fully unfold. Thyself and thy belongings
Are not thine own so proper as to waste
Thyself upon thy virtues, they on thee.
(Measure for Measure 1.1.28–31)

What does the Duke mean by telling Angelo "there is . . . a character in thy life"? At face value, the phrase means that what's written down—"a character"— in Angelo's life makes his history explicit—"unfolds it fully"—to the observer. Angelo's "character" then, is somehow transparent, and that is why he has earned the Duke's confidence. But then why does the Duke go to such lengths to caution Angelo that his virtues are not his exclusive possession? In the OED, this passage is cited for the usage of "character" to mean "a cipher for secret correspondence." Maybe the Duke is saying there is a secret code in your life that makes your history explicit, if we can find a way to decipher you. But what are the "written troubles" in Angelo's brain that would account for his creepy assault on Isabella? Does a virtuous man suddenly decide to act on his fantasies of domination and rape just because he can? It's possible that Angelo really believes in his virtue, but acts against his own all-things-considered best judgment. His actions in this sense are incontinent. Like Ovid's Medea, Angelo thinks, "Against my own wishes, some strange influence weighs heavily upon me, and desire sways me one way, reason another. I see which is the better course, and I approve it: but still I follow the worse" (*Metamorphoses*: 7.13–23). Or should we consider Angelo's caddish behavior towards Marianna, along with his extortion and subsequent betrayal of Isabella, as compelling evidence that he is just vicious to the core? One doesn't care to think of what was done in that darkened bedroom.

"Who will believe my verse in times to come?" In Sonnet 17 Shakespeare wonders about the skepticism of future readers, who may not believe in what he has written, in the way he has characterized the beauty of his beloved young man. "The age to come will say 'this poet lies.'" Well, maybe not lying, just exaggerating. People often do when they think about their loved ones. The French Princess Constance in *King John*, for example, thinks Prince Arthur, her son, the most "gracious creature born" since Abel. And when he is captured by the English, her sorrow is extravagant. Constance's mind is not so much a written document as it is a theatrical mise-en-scene in which grief plays the principal role:

> *Constance:* Grief fills the room up of my absent child,
> Lies in his bed, walks up and down with me,
> Puts on his pretty looks, repeats his words,
> Remembers me of all his gracious parts,
> Stuffs out his vacant garments with his form;
> Then, have I reason to be fond of grief?
>
> (*King John* 3.4.93–98)

In a way, this can be made to appear disingenuous. Constance has a political interest in her son's dynastic entitlement that she expressed earlier as grievance and complaint. It doesn't require much historical inquiry to realize that she is politically ambitious and calculating. Even so, notwithstanding the histrionics, I think this verse expresses how grief acts in the mind and why a person would be fond of it. I don't need historical evidence or a biographical correlative to be affected by this. The loss of a child is part of the story. For me to understand what's happened to a character in a fiction I really need to face up to what can happen to a real person.

Constance is not the central figure in *King John*. She appears in only a few scenes and she plays no significant role in the great military conflict between England and France. When King Philip tells her she is "fond of grief" his admonition may not be meant unkindly. To be "fond" of grief is, in a sense, to be infatuated, foolish, and even a bit crazy. Cardinal Pandulph's charge is less tender: "you hold too heinous a respect of grief" (3.4.90). A conscientious historical inquiry could help explain the tradition of Christian Stoicism behind the Cardinal's statement and the sense that Constance's love for her child is excessive, or even sinful. Another line of historical inquiry could explain that a noblewoman like Constance is expected to maintain her dignity even in these dire circumstances. But what is any of this to Constance—or to me—at this moment? "He talks to me that never had a son" (3.4.91). Constance recognizes and rejects the shabby explanations of the men in power who can always find ways to make brutality appear reasonable. As for me, I think I'm supposed to bear witness to Constance's suffering, not to try and explain it away.

Constance's refusal to be silenced or intimidated is *intended* to explode complacency. It is a direct challenge both to the make-believe Cardinal

Pandulph in *King John* and to the real Cardinal Pandulph in every one of us. It happens again when Shylock asks Antonio's friends "hath not a Jew eyes" and again when Lady Macduff confronts the lame excuses offered by Ross to "justify" her husband's abandonment of his wife and children: "All is the fear and nothing is the love" (4.2.12). What's charactered by Shakespeare in this way shows up again and again. His characters are like us, but sometimes they are more courageous than most of us manage to be. They are people who live in a world we can understand. We don't need any specialized historical knowledge to understand Constance or Shylock or Lady Macduff if we are really alive to our own feelings and capable of empathy with other people—the real ones, I mean. Our response to these dramatic moments is underwritten by the shared complexity of our human nature. Engagement with a character has a moral dimension; it corresponds to the imperative of respect for our human vulnerability to loss and grief. We learn about our own complex human nature by thinking about and coming to respect Shakespeare's characters.

Notes

1. Samuel Johnson, *Preface to Shakespeare*, in *The Yale Edition of the Works of Samuel Johnson*, 16 vols, ed. Arthur Sherbo (New Haven: Yale University Press, 1968), 7: 20–22.
2. Trevor Ponech, "Realism About Fictional Characters," in *Shakespeare and Character*, ed. Jessica Slights and Paul Yachnin (London: Palgrave Macmillan, 2009).
3. Stuart Hampshire, *Morality and Conflict* (Cambridge, MA: Harvard University Press, 1983), 69.
4. Katherine Eisamann Maus, *Inwardness and Theater in the English Renaissance* (Chicago: University of Chicago Press, 1995).
5. Gail Kern Paster, *The Body Embarrassed: Drama and the Disciplines of Shame in Early Modern England* (Ithaca, New York: Cornell University Press, 1993).
6. Catherine Belsey, *The Subject of Tragedy* (London: Methuen, 1985).
7. Tzachi Zamir, *Double Vision: Moral Philosophy & Shakespearean Drama* (Princeton: Princeton University Press, 2007), 199.
8. Noam Chomsky, *Syntactic Structures* (The Hague: Mouton, 1957).
9. Such a view was well understood in Early Modern European culture. See e.g. Gary Tomlinson, *Music in Renaissance Magic: Toward a Historiography of Others* (Chicago: University of Chicago Press, 1993); David Lindley, *Shakespeare and Music* (London: Arden Shakespeare, 2006).
10. Michel Foucault, *The History of Sexuality*, Trans. Robert Hurley (New York: Vintage Books, 1980); Thomas Laqueur, *Making Sex: Body and Gender from the Greeks to Freud* (Cambridge, MA: Harvard University Press, 1990).
11. Sandra Harding, "Why Has the Sex / Gender System Become Visible Only Now?" in *Discovering Reality: Feminist Perspectives on Epistemology, Metaphysics,*

Methodology, and Philosophy of Science, ed. Sandra Harding and Merrill B. Hintikka (Dordrecht: Kluwer Academic Publishers, 2003), 311–24.
12. Donald E. Brown, "Human Nature and History," in Theme Issue 38: The Return of Science: Evolutionary Ideas and History, *History and Theory*, vol. 38, no. 4 (December, 1999): 138–57.
13. Martha Nussbaum, "Non-Relative Virtues: An Aristotelian Approach," in *The Quality of Life*, ed. Martha C. Nussbaum and Amartya Sen (Oxford: Oxford University Press, 1993), 264.
14. Quotes from each play are taken from *The Norton Shakespeare*, ed. Stephen Greenblatt et al. (New York: Norton, 1997).
15. Julia Reinhard Lupton, "Arendt and Shakespeare: Emancipation and Its Equivocalities," *Revista Dramateatro Digital* (2004), http://dramateatro.fundacite.arg.gov.ve/teoria_teatral/arendt_shakespeare.html.
16. James Shapiro, *Shakespeare and the Jews* (New York: Columbia University Press, 1996); John Gross, *Shylock: A Legend and its Legacy* (New York: Simon and Schuster ,1992); Kenneth Gross, *Shylock is Shakespeare* (Chicago: University of Chicago Press, 2006).
17. Charles Spinosa, "The Transformation of Intentionality: Debt and Contract in *The Merchant of Venice*," ELR 24 (1994): 370–409.
18. Turner, Henry S. "The Problem of the More-than One: Friendship, Calculation, and Political Association in *The Merchant of Venice*," *Shakespeare Quarterly*, vol. 57, no. 4 (Winter, 2006): 413–42.
19. Andrew, Edward, *Shylock's Rights: A Grammar of Lockian Claims* (Toronto: University of Toronto Press, 1988).
20. Harry Berger Jr, *Making Trifles of Terrors: Redistributing Complicities in Shakespeare* (Stanford: Stanford University Press, 1997), 337–39 .
21. Tzachi Zamir, *Double Vision*, x1.
22. Avishai Margalit, *The Ethics of Memory* (Cambridge, MA: Harvard University Press, 2002).
23. Marvin Minsky, "How Towers Work," in *The Society of Mind* (New York: Touchstone Books, 1986), 128.
24. Minsky, "The World of Blocks," in *The Society of Mind*, 21.
25. Minsky, "The World of Blocks," 21.
26. Nussbaum, "Non Relative Virtues," 264.
27. René Descartes, *Discourse on Method and Meditation*, Trans. Laurence J. Lafleur (Indianapolis: Liberal Arts, 1960).
28. Gilbert Ryle, *The Concept of Mind* (New York: Barnes & Noble, 1949).
29. Charles Taylor, *Sources of the Self* (Cambridge: Harvard University Press, 1989); Daniel Dennett, *Consciousness Explained* (Boston: Little, Brown and Co., 1991); Stephen Greenblatt, *Renaissance Self-fashioning: From More to Shakespeare* (Chicago: University of Chicago Press, 1980); Katherine Eisamann Maus, *Inwardness and Theater in the English Renaissance* (Chicago: University of Chicago Press, 1995).
30. Friedrich Nietzsche, *The Will to Power*, Trans. Walter Kaufmann and R. J. Hollingdale , with facsimiles of the original manuscript (1885; York: Vintage Books, 1968), 490.
31. Minsky, *Society of Mind*, 40–42.
32. Wendy Doniger, "Self-Impersonation in World Literature," *Kenyon Review* 26, no. 2 (2004): 101–25.

33. Desmond Manderson and Paul Yachnin, "Love on Trial: Nature, Law, and Same-Sex Love in the Court of Shakespeare," *McGill Law Journal*, 49 (2004): 475–511.
34. Tzetvan Todorov, *Mikhail Bakhtin: The Dialogical Principle*, trans. Wlad Godzich (Manchester: University of Manchester Press, 1984), 109ff.
35. Susanne L. Wofford, "To You I Give Myself, For I am Yours": Erotic Performance and Theatrical Performatives in *As You Like It*, in *Shakespeare Reread*, ed. Russ McDonald (Ithaca: Cornell University Press, 1994), 147–70; William O. Scott, "'A woman's thought runs before her actions': Vows as Speech Acts in As You Like It," *Philosophy and Literature* 30 (2006): 528–39. On the definition of "performative" see J. L. Austin, *How to Do Things With Words*, 2nd. ed. (Cambridge: Harvard University Press, 1962), 22. On speech act theory more generally, Mary Louise Pratt, *Toward a Speech Act Theory of Literary Discourse* (Bloomington: Indiana University Press, 1977); Joseph A. Porter, *The Drama of Speech Acts: Shakespeare's Lancastrian Tetralogy* (Berkeley: University of California Press, 1979).
36. Hillel's saying is from *Pirkei Avot*, (Ethics of the Fathers): 1:14. The sense of the aphorism is expounded in various ways in rabbinical tradition. My interpretation reflects the way it was taught to me at various times in my early education. On Hillel see also Judah Goldin, "Hillel the Elder," *The Journal of Religions* 26 (1946): 263–77.
37. Judah Goldin, *Hillel the Elder*, 275
38. Moshe Gold, "Ethical Practice in Critical Discourse: Conversions and Disruptions in Legal, Religious Narratives," *Representations* 64 (1998): 21–40.
39. Raphael Jospe, "Hillel's Rule," *Jewish Quarterly Review*. N.S. 81 (1990): 45–57.
40. Aristotle, *Ethics*, trans. J. A. K. Thomson (Harmondsworth: Penguin, 1953), 276.
41. Friedrich Nietzsche, *The Genealogy of Morals*, trans. Douglas Smith (Oxford: Oxford University Press, World's Classics), 24.
42. Emmanuel Levinas, *Time and The Other*, trans. Richard A. Cohen (Pittsburgh: Duquesne University Press, 1987), 57.
43. David Schalkwyk, "Love and Service in *Twelfth Night* and the Sonnets," *Shakespeare Quarterly*, 56 (2005): 76–100.
44. Mustapha Fahmi, "Shakespeare: The Orientation of the Human" in Harold Bloom's *Shakespeare* (Basingstoke: Palgrave Macmillan, 2001), 97–108.
45. Yu Jin Ko, "The Comic Close of *Twelfth Night* and Viola's *Noli me Tangere*," *Shakespeare Quarterly*, 48 (1997): 391–405.
46. Jonathan Goldberg, *Shakespeare's Hand* (Minneapolis: University of Minnesota Press, 2003).
47. W. G. Sebald, "Constructs of Mourning," in *Campo Santo*, ed. Sven Meyer, trans. Anthea Bell (London: Hamish Hamilton, 2005), 102–29.
48. Michael Bristol, "How Many Children Did She Have?" in *Philosophical Shakespeare*, ed. John Joughin (London: Routledge, 2000), 18–34.
49. Friedrich Nietzsche, *On the Genealogy of Morals*, trans. Douglas Smith (Oxford: Oxford University Press World's Classics, 1996), 39.

2
The Reality of Fictive Cinematic Characters

Trevor Ponech

This paper is about the metaphysics of fiction. It outlines a case for the existence of "fictional characters," more precisely, fictive characters encountered in narrative fictions. In doing so, it tries to secure a niche for such entities within the familiar world of material objects, artefacts, and properties. Thus I advocate realism about fictive characters. "Realism" here denotes an ontological thesis. To be a realist about something is to believe it exists and is what it is independently of how one takes it to be. Realism, then, is associated with mind-independence. Macbeth and company may strike us as poor candidates for realism. But let's not be hasty.

Much of what I shall say holds for imaginary beings wheresoever and howsoever they arise and are encountered. My overall goal is to ground a deflationary argument for the existence of fictive characters *simpliciter*; an argument according to which they are ordinary psychohistorical facts—where "fact" refers to some state of affairs that obtains in reality. Literary critics and other humanities scholars who are interested in the ultimate defensibility of resuscitating character-based critical appreciation—or who suspect that character-talk is an ineluctable if intellectually problematic, even retrograde, part of their interpretive and pedagogical practices—can expect encouragement to treat such discourse as an opportunity for successful, serious investigation of actual features of narrative art works. My special interest, however, is in the ontology of cinematic works. Cinematic characters shall therefore take center stage. Their objective reality seems precluded by the very nature of the medium in which they are instantiated. I hope that by thinking about what would be required for cinematic characters to exist, I shall be able to survey the grounds for the reality of characters in general.

My conjectures about fictive (cinematic) characterhood adopt a naturalistic ontology somewhat disconnected from how aesthetic philosophers, cinema scholars, and literary critics usually think about fictional characters. I flag a few of its underlying, formative premises at the outset. I then proceed to sketch what a cinematic image might be: namely, a *stroboluminescent display* (SLD). A cinematic fictive character is not, strictly speaking, an intrinsic part or property of a cinematic image any more than, say, a literary character is actually "in" a text. Rather, a character is a *public agent-concept*: a certain kind of psychological item standing in a reciprocal, historical relation to a certain vehicle of expression. In the case of cinema, this vehicle is a property, or family of properties, borne by an SLD. After examining the substance of this public agent-concept, I attend to some problems of individuating and identifying fictive characters. Finally, I offer some general comments on my concept ontology's implications for critical appreciation.

Some ontological premises

On my desk sits a green apple. What is there to its existence? A unique story could be told about any one green apple, a story about precisely where, when, and how it comes to be, about the situations and events it enters into until its destruction. A select few are subjects of scholarly ruminations. Its vicissitudes aside, green applehood essentially involves being a macroscopic object. Here, "object" denotes an individual property-bearing entity. On the compositional model, any familiar object with which we have mundane interactions is best regarded as a complex configuration of substantial parts and particles. It is an object, of the familiar macroscopic sort, by virtue of being a particular arrangement of substantial parts and particles having a particular history and standing in particular relations to other arrangements of particles. It is complex, being composed of other things that are objects in their own right. Under a gross description, my apple is composed of its outer skin, flesh, core, seeds, and stem; a slightly finer-grained description identifies its cellular, chemical, and molecular constituents.

The apple counts as an object insofar as it is *one* spatially-temporally extended thing. An object's being a single item—an individual or particular—depends on there being unifying interrelations and interactivities between its constituent elements. This organization can persist across some limited range of instabilities and alterations. Material parts and particles can be subtracted, added, reconfigured, or qualitatively changed without necessarily destroying the object or changing its identity.

A stone statue can, for a time, survive continuous erosion of its surface molecules; a growing lion, thanks to its metabolic processes and molecular bonds, is the same particular lion despite the added matter and the increasing distance between its nose and tail; the apple on my desk is the same one from three days ago, though softer now.

Speaking of the apple's features, philosophers often distinguish between two kinds of properties. Sphericity and weighing 144 grams seem to be so-called qualitative or structural properties—qualities narrowly possessed by objects themselves owing to the particles they're made of and the manner in which these are arranged. Greenness, on the other hand, is often thought a purely dispositional property. Like a square peg's fitting a square hole, such a property is supposedly not "in" the object. It is contingent, dependent on the right ambient conditions obtaining or the object's standing in the appropriate relation to something else. Hence a dispositional is a broad, relational or, as some philosophers like to say, higher level supervenient property.

The compositional view of objecthood does not distinguish between qualitative and dispositional properties.[1] There are simply properties. Here, properties are understood as *particular ways objects intrinsically are*, as modes of objects, in ontologists' patois. Property possession is a matter of simultaneously and indissolubly having intrinsic, particular qualities and intrinsic, particular dispositions. Spherical is one structural way the apple is. Its being this way is inseparable from the apple's disposition, its power, to roll or leave a concave impression in sand. Green is another way the apple is. Its particular greenness is a matter of its skin's microstructural condition. This condition is inseparable from the skin's built-in powers, manifested or not, to structure reflected light in a particular way, thereby triggering certain experiences in percipients with visual systems of a given type. Understanding properties and their individuation will be crucial to grasping the ontology of cinematic fictive characters.

An individuation problem

Motion pictures pose a classic individuation problem directly bearing upon the ontology of cinematic fictive characters. Screening Akira Kurosawa's *Throne of Blood* (1957) to its finale, we watch the collective murder of improvident Washizu, a character based on Macbeth. The Great Lord Washizu, portrayed by Toshiro Mifune, is trapped on a gallery overlooking his besieged castle's inner courtyard, where his now restive soldiers congregate. A single arrow issues from the crowd, narrowly missing his feudal lordship. For several more seconds, the camera tracks Mifune, framed within an uninterrupted medium shot, as he pulls the missile from the post, throws it back down at the men, and is soon sent reeling backwards when the mob launches a second arrow, this one striking his upper body. Throughout this shot, we have an experience as of one unitary, continuously existing entity: an image-of-a-man.

According to conventional wisdom, what is really on the screen is a rapid succession of discrete, discontinuous frozen images, 24 of them a second. Standard explanations of this apparent discrepancy are constructivist, insofar as they hold that my experience of a single, unitary onscreen item is the law-like reaction of my perceptual system to a barrage of fragmentary, transient, but visible stimuli. The constructivist thesis comes in two flavors. Illusionism, the orthodoxy, maintains that human vision botches the job of detecting what really is there to be seen.[2] Response-dependence realism, the heterodoxy, finds something mundane about cinematic individuals. It is inspired by putative relational ontologies, of which color is thought paradigmatic. Greenness, construed as a specifically dispositional property, is nowhere to be found on the apple's surface. But that fact does not make greenness illusory. Rather, green supervenes on the apple's skin. Its being green *just is* its triggering of a certain response in observers, a response which depends on its standing in the normal causal relation to percipients with the normal human visual system. So maybe cinematic images have response-dependent existence.[3] The image-of-a-man consists of transitory patterns of colored light reflected against a surface—color taken to include black, white, and gray shades. Analogous to how the apple's greenness is nonetheless real, despite being extrinsically sustained, maybe this single, continuous image-of-a-man supervenes on the screen by virtue of the transitory patterns of colored light being reidentified by normal viewers' perceptual systems, under normal circumstances, as the same individual.

Our visual experience of the image vividly, indefeasibly seems to be of and about an individual external to ourselves. In the face of constructivist intuitions, one wonders what, if anything, could make it true that the referent of "image-of-a-man" is a single, mind-independent item residing throughout its brief career within the display itself. This problem concerns individuation in the metaphysical sense. Its focus is not what spectators do, what cognitive powers underpin or constitute their capacity to individuate cinematic imagery. It is the logically prior question of whether there are some individuals nested within the visual display—entities already individuated by their own mode of being and just waiting for us to spot them. To tackle this individuation problem, it helps first to think a bit about cinema's ontology.[4]

The stroboluminescent display (SLD)

Suppose you're watching a single, uninterrupted shot of MM—which, without prejudice to the example, could designate a photographic image of Marilyn Monroe or a cartoon image of Mickey Mouse. Whatever else this movie image might mean or be — however else theorists might understand the term "movie image," that which you gaze at is invariably an area of illumination on a reflectant, approximately flat, surface. This area is produced by mechanically coupling a template with a projection device. A template is a storage or delivery format the form or content of which has the power to change a display's visible condition. A 35mm film print is an example of a template. So is a broadcast television signal, as is a videotape, DVD, or MPEG data file.

The illuminated area and screen are collocated but not identical. To establish their separateness, simply turn off the film projector (television, computer monitor): the light-diffusing screen is there, in front of you; but your perceptual target, the luminescent display, has disappeared. The display itself consists of a great many points of light, varying individually with respect to their spectral distribution and brightness. These pixels are the display's own resolution elements.

Different kinds of templates and light propagation devices produce correspondingly different displays. A black and white film print consists of layers of silver grains dispersed in a transparent gelatin through which light is beamed. These particles, measuring from 0.002 millimeters to one-tenth that size, are opaque. Hence the projected display is a latticework of unilluminated points and pixels reflected off the grains' edges. A color print, too, consists of a plastic strip coated in gelatin. Suspended therein are clouds of colored dye left behind where specially treated silver halide grains dissolved during developing. Some clouds are so dense they occlude the projector's light; and like any photographically produced film print, there are opaque unexposed/ undeveloped areas on the print associated with areas that received no light during photography. A film print's silver particles and dye pools are randomly distributed; where pixels and points of negative illumination occur in the display is thus correspondingly random. Contrastingly, television and computer monitors, including liquid crystal and plasma displays, contain lines of rigidly fixed resolving elements. A monitor only illumes where tiny trichromatic dots are situated. Between these sites are unilluminated spaces.

Pixels are also separated temporally. Whenever and however a movie is displayed, it involves rapid alternations between illuminated onset phases and unilluminated or less brightly illuminated offset phases. Projecting one second of a film print, for instance, typically involves 72 flashes. During that second, each of 24 separate Mickey Mouse or Marilyn Monroe patterns printed on the translucent acetate strip is advanced into a gate, where it's briefly immobilized between the projector's light beam and focusing lens. While stalled in the gate, an episcotister—a rotating disk with open segments—interrupts the beam three times. Consequently, the projector's beam penetrates each of mm^1 through mm^{24} three times.

Like the film projector, the video optical system is stroboscopic. It illuminates the display periodically. In a standard television monitor, an electron beam scans every horizontal line of pixels 60 or more times per second. In a plasma screen monitor, also having a "refresh rate" of at least 60 hertz, pixels are generated from gas bubbles glowing intermittently when excited by electrical current flowing through a matrix of wires. Each of these systems, and others fundamentally similar, produces a *stroboluminescent display* (SLD). The SLD, described synchronically, is an illuminated field composed of pixels, plus any unilluminated areas and periods situated spatially-temporally between those points. If we switch emphasis to a diachronic description, the SLD comprises a rapid, continuous cycle of phase changes during which the pixels are refreshed and their spectral distributions vary. This high-frequency redistribution of illumination, a continuous play of light across a reflective or light emitting surface, is what I intend by "stroboscopic" luminescence.

Cinematic individuals

Recall the shot of beleaguered Washizu. Ignore for now that it photographically depicts Mifune and is meant to represent the fictive Washizu. Consider only the visible singleton W, that is, a certain physical pattern of illumination in the SLD about which we usually predicate various Mifune and Washizu statements. This item is not, of course, literally identical either to Washizu or to Mifune. W nevertheless is just what it looks to be: *one* mind-independent entity, one among many such items, persisting throughout its brief career within the display. The current problem is how to conceive of W as an external target rather than as a product of our perceptual experiences. The solution, I suspect, is that W is a complex property of the SLD. It is a particular way a particular SLD is, for a time.

An SLD might seem an insubstantial, gappy thing, but it satisfies the constraints on objecthood no less than do apples and desks. It is, for instance, spatially and temporally extended. A *Throne of Blood* display occupies so much space in your den or at the front of the theater from time t, when the screen first illumes, until t^n, when the projection device is extinguished. Its bounds are established by an assembly of simple physical elements, the pixels, existing in various unifying interrelations and interactivities. Again, displays appear ephemeral, less solid or "thingy" than apples and desks. But their constitutive parts are no less real than the fundamental constituents of any ordinary object. The SLD's resolving elements comprise packets of photon particles themselves possessing wave, momentum, energy, and spin properties.[5] Evidence of the display's substantial reality comes from its participation in the world's causal order, as a source of ambient energy triggering cascading responses in percipients' visual systems.

Another mark of objecthood is property-possession. If W is a mode of some radiant light source, it is a complex one composed of collections of properties. These include the shape, size, brightness, intensity, and color of each individual pixel; the spatial relations between these pixels, including any unilluminated areas between them; and the temporal frequency with which pixels stroboscopically succeed each other. The intuition, then, is that W exists by virtue of the juxtaposition or mix of properties borne by the individual pixels occupying some spatial-temporal region of the display. W stands out visibly from the rest of the display because the brightness, intensity, and color of a certain cluster of pixels delineate its edges, contours, lines, shapes, and volumes. Notice that W is not here thought to be itself an object. It is hard to conceive of a particular, unified entity, W, which *has* the visible properties with reference to which we identify W. Once we abstract the pixels' brightness and so on—imagine, say, that every pixel in the SLD has the same spectral and luminance values—no W remains to bear properties.

W is not an object. It is another sort of garden-variety individual; namely, a particular property of some object. This claim invites the objection that W's persistence over time is merely apparent. Pointing to five seconds of the aforementioned shot, an opponent could argue that all there really is on screen is a series of about 360 numerically distinct, immobile images. It is approximately true that the display, considered synchronically, contains successive still images w^1, w^2, w^3, *et seq.*, separated from one another by unilluminated fields. Yet it seems ontologically negligent to equate a display with a series of frozen, primordial moments. Such a description discloses little about cinema's constitutive parts and their properties. It leaves open what w^1 and so forth are, what they're made of (pixels), and what kind of existence they have (complex properties of pixels). It also ignores a display property essential to cinema's nature. Rather than being simply a location in which a series of still images appears, an SLD comprises a process. Something is always happening to its resolving components; they and their properties are continuously changing. Change is not here reducible to an item having one property at a certain time and not having it at another. It is an event taking place over and through time. This event—stroboscopy—is integral to the cinematic display's existence.

It is also essential to W's persistence. Thanks to stroboscopy, the property W is continuously distributed and redistributed within the SLD. In other words, stroboscopy permits W to undergo and survive various changes. During t^1–t^5, individual pixels come and go, but properties by virtue of which W's edges and so forth are delineated are continuously being borne to the display. Indeed, W just is a stroboscopically maintained way the display is, stroboscopy being itself one of the properties out of which this relatively more complex property is made. W's existence is thus roughly akin to that of an oval *café-au-lait*-colored skin blemish. This blemish is a region of epidermis constantly shedding old and moving up new skin cell layers bearing to the surface the pigmentation by virtue of which the region maintains its shape and color. Of course, W is volatile. It, and the patterns inside its edges, change size, shape, color, resolution, attitude, pitch, and rotation. W also changes location. Between t^1 and t^5, it is continuously redistributed within the display space such that it moves therein from center left to bottom right, when Washizu throws the arrow back at his soldiers.

Realism about cinematic imagery says that W and the like exist out in the world, no cognitive assembly required. They are neither illusions nor response-dependent entities having disjunctive, externally sustained existences. If an SLD's being W involves its having certain color properties—where color includes black, white, and gray shades—then realism about W leans for support on color objectivism. Color objectivism posits that "x is green" is made true by x's intrinsic disposition to produce various visual experiences in us. There is not necessarily any one physical basis for this power. If x is a solid object, its disposition is a matter of its having just the microphysical surface properties it has; if a light source, a matter of x's radiant light being structured as it is. X's disposition does not depend upon or alter in relation to *our* disposition under various circumstances to experience green or judge that the object is green. Only its manifestation depends on a partnership with us. A disposition is not a relation. It is an intrinsic way an object unconditionally is—one that, in C. B. Martin's words, is "ready to go" in the sense of always being present and ready to manifest itself.[6] Water is disposed to dissolve salt; salt is disposed toward solubility in water. The exercise of either disposition needs the other. The water and salt mutually exercise their powers in partnership with one another. On the present thesis, our experience of the color green, versus x's being green, is a reciprocal manifestation of x's inherent disposition and our visual system's inherent disposition.[7] Our experience of W, its looking to us as it does, is likewise a reciprocal manifestation. One partner is our perceptual system, with its complex dispositionalities. The other is a particular ongoing stroboscopic pattern of illumination, with its own accompanying dispositionalities.

The paradox of fictive existence

W and other display properties resembling it are vehicles for the fictive character Washizu. Yet Washizu is not W. Saying what Washizu is, establishing what reality, if any, it has, and explaining the link between items like W and entities like Washizu, means delving into the ontology of fictive characters.

We often think and talk about fictive characters as if they were real people. Washizu, I believe, is afflicted by weakness of the will, his considered better judgment against murderously usurping the Great Lord being overthrown by irrational fears and selfish desires. The trouble is, Washizu does not, and never did, exist. How can I have a true and justified belief about something that not only doesn't exist, but that I know not to exist? And since the name "Washizu" has failed, empty reference, how can it have reference at all? The muddle deepens when we consider the puzzling sentence "Washizu does not exist." Surely this proposition assertively uttered is true. After all, we know that no such person as Washizu ever lived. Yet the truth of the above sentence implies that Washizu in some sense *is*—that Washizu has being *of some sort*. How else could we refer to this entity and say truly of it that it does not exist? Apparently, Washizu and the like nevertheless are creatures that simply *are*, or else we could not coherently and truly deny they exist. They must have being, if only so they can have nonbeing.

I cannot canvas all viable solutions to the paradox of fictive existence, so I will settle here on mentioning only two kinds. The first is antirealist. It denies Washizu is an actual object or property residing in the ordinary world. Positively, it holds that the welter of apparent epistemic and logical problems are avoided when we understand the distinctive practices and conventions associated with fiction's production and appreciation. A fictional work, in any medium, is one which invites audiences to make-believe or imagine various situations, events, and individuals.[8] Readers are supposed to imagine, to think and speak as if, there is a general named Macbeth celebrated by his kinsmen for unseaming a traitor from nave to chaps; viewers are supposed to imagine a warlord named Washizu who rides on horseback through the forest, searching for the evil spirit who knows his destiny. These imaginings are not about anyone or anything. We do not make-believe of some particular object that it can be destroyed by no man of woman born. "Macbeth," then, is not a proper name but a sort of label or abbreviation for myriad definite descriptions (is a man, is married, unseams a traitor) some text or movie furnishes—descriptions audiences use to stoke their imaginations. Correspondingly, assertions about fictive characters' traits and doings do not report what some being or item is really like. They are assertions regarding what some fictional work authorizes its audience to imagine. "Washizu is a 16th-century warlord" thus paraphrases as "In Kurasawa's *Throne of Blood*, it is true in the fiction that Washizu is a 16th-century warlord."

An alternative analysis proposes that antirealism toward fictive characters is controvertible insofar as it conflicts with a commonsense, plausible assumption: authors, filmmakers, and other artists can form or make something, bring into existence a novel entity, while composing fictional works. Shakespeare's Macbeth is a now familiar item—one occurring time and again in myriad representations—inexistent prior to 1605, around which time Shakespeare, maybe helped by artistic collaborators, created this character, thereby beginning its career. Like tables, champagne, and computers, Macbeth and Washizu are artifacts. They are products of the imaginative, purposive activity of some person(s), working with words, images, sounds, etc. Unlike concrete artifacts, though, characters are abstract objects, as they lack a spatiotemporal location. Macbeth is not identical to or part of any particular text of *The Tragedy of Macbeth*. Aside from possessing properties, like courage in battle, that these physical items lack, Macbeth's existence continues when any given copy of the text is destroyed. Similarly, Washizu's existence is not associated with that of any one *Throne of Blood* template or visual display. Nor is Washizu identical to Mifune, who is but an actor playing at being a warlord; indeed, Washizu, like Macbeth, can be played by other actors without fatal loss of identity to the character.

The statement, "Macbeth is Thane of Glamis" describes no concrete person or thing, but an abstract object the properties of which were stipulated by Shakespeare in writing his play. "Macbeth does not exist" is a paraphrase of "No such person as Macbeth exists."

With Amie Thomasson, whose artifactual theory I cite, I believe characters are real items issuing from artists' creative-imaginative actions.[9] Thomasson construes characters as "higher-level dependent entities."[10] A character's existence depends historically on the creative activities of its author; it is maintained in existence by the existence of at least one copy of a text, and by at least one conscious agent able to understand that text. Yet, ontologically speaking, its existence as an abstract artifact is irreducible to, and partially independent of, these underlying entities. Authors die without their characters being destroyed; individual copies and readers cease to exist without thus annihilating the character. A character is one of those things that, as philosophers often say, supervenes on lower-level, underlying entities.

In contrast, my analysis is deflationary. It holds fictive characters to be residents of the familiar physical world, not the realm of abstracta. It also denies that they are novel, semiautonomous phenomena existing over and above texts, authors, and audiences. I incline towards denying characters any sort of objecthood, artefacthood, or autonomy. Nonetheless, I treat them as real, categorically distinct, and, I suppose, entirely ordinary items. "Washizu," on the present account, refers to an occurrent or dispositional condition of some actual mind (or minds), this mental item having a certain kind of content and history. Its ontogenesis includes its standing in formative reciprocal relations to other real items—like W and the display in which W appears. In turn, W is a vehicle for the open expression of the aforementioned mental item. Partly by perceptually engaging with such vehicles of expression, competent observers recover the psychohistorical facts pertaining to someone's effectively expressed idea of Washizu. I propose to identify the character "Washizu" with this WASHIZU concept.

Fictive characters and public agent-concepts

A fictive character might be equated with an ordinary if hitherto untheorized psychological item:

> *Fictive character*=a vacuous agent-concept, as prescribed by some author(s) or maker(s) of a literary, cinematic, or other expressive work.

Although fictive characters seem profoundly linked to narrative fiction, I leave open the question of whether this association is essential to their being.[11] "Agent" applies to any conscious being capable of feats of self-direction triggered by beliefs, desires, intentions, practical reasoning, and so forth—fiction being full of the bric-a-brac and ascribed powers of agency exhibited by human persons. A "vacuous agent-concept" describes a nonexistent agent. No causal encounter with a substantial individual grounds this concept, and its content is not made true by virtue of what an actual, particular agent is like.

The nature of concepts is subject to intricate philosophical debates.[12] Without delving into these, I avail myself of a few general assumptions so as to eke out a basis for linking characters with concepts. One supposition is that concepts are concrete representational states of concrete minds. Concept possession consists of a mind *being* in a certain way or of its *being disposed to being* in a certain way when activated under the right circumstances. Another supposition is that concepts are basic constituents of thought. To possess a concept is to have a vehicle for thought, belief, and action. Having a MONEY concept is that which permits you to think about money, to recognize instances of it, to go looking for money, to investigate, disambiguate, and hypothesize money's nature, and to introspect and revise the content of your MONEY concept. This internal representation also serves as repository and unifier for your disparate money-thoughts and as a disposition to assimilate some though not other experiences and ideas into this repository.

Suppose *Throne of Blood* counts as fiction because Kurosawa intends audiences not to believe but merely entertain the thought, or imagine, that certain situations and events transpire as described by his movie's imagery and sounds. WASHIZU is a vacuous agent-concept Kurosawa creates in making this narrative cinematic fiction. We viewers do not imagine that WASHIZU is a warlord. We imagine there is a man, Washizu, who is a warlord. In the process, we replicate somebody's concept of an inexistent agent, WASHIZU, along with beliefs and other attitudes about that concept.

Kurosawa's WASHIZU concept is a decisive input to the sprawling, causally networked course of events comprising *Throne of Blood*'s production. WASHIZU itself is a vehicle for Kurosawa's private cogitations about a certain imaginary agent and his story. It also informs and constrains his involvement in—and contributions to—scripting, casting, make-up and wardrobe, set design, mise-en-scène, direction of acting, cinematography, and so forth. I do not claim that WASHIZU or its content independently exert control over directorial actions. An agent-concept's effectiveness is somewhat mediated, its power to shape the cinematic work depending on its content being nested within the artist's relevant intentions. Here I follow Paisley Livingston in regarding intentions as distinctive mental states composed of a content or plan component conjoined to an identifying functional attitude.[13] The plan, which might be quite schematic and adjustable, represents some prospective situation or goal, plus some means to that end. It is part of an intention just in case one takes an executive attitude towards it. To have an intention is to settle on (trying to realize) a certain plan, this commitment serving to initiate and sustain actions appropriate to its realization. My proposal, then, is that fictioneers' agent-concepts contribute content to their intention-embedded narrative plans.

WASHIZU emerges as Kurosawa decides what story-related imaginings to prescribe and how to prescribe them. Doing this evidently involves his turning to Shakespeare as well as Noh theater for inspiration.[14] Presumably it also involves exercising his own imagination, settling on stylistic and thematic preferences, and meshing these with the imaginative, as well as practical, inputs of the artistic collaborators under his direction. Kurosawa's WASHIZU concept thus evolves over a course of spontaneous, intentional creative activities. Said activities commence with the filmmaker's preliminary *Throne-of-Blood*-related thoughts and plans, and continue over his practical engagements with the cinematic medium until he deems this movie completed. Throughout, WASHIZU is reciprocally related to the visual display's imagery and accompanying aural tracks. These serve as a vehicle of expression. They also function heuristically, as a resource for solving creative problems. By grappling with how the display should look and the audio should sound, Kurosawa clarifies, critically evaluates, reformulates, and finally executes some of his preferences regarding what his character looks and sounds like, how he acts, and what differentiates him from other characters. He thereby fills in to his own satisfaction WASHIZU's content.

The WASHIZU concept Kurosawa creates is a public concept. By "public," I mean neither that it is a social, intersubjective construct, nor that it is possessed by more than one member of a population. What I mean is this: Kurosawa uses cinematic means to invite some target audience to imagine a sixteenth-century warrior named Washizu. In doing so, he establishes and attempts to share with his audience part of WASHIZU's content. An agent-concept therefore counts as public by virtue of the history of its conception. This history comprises its being conceived and openly expressed by appropriate means, like making some intersubjectively accessible artifact, textual or cinematic, adapted to the job of conceiving and expressing agent-concepts.

Perhaps Kurosawa also imagined his character to have halitosis. If so, he took no effective steps toward indicating this content to viewers and couldn't rationally believe he had built this esoteric idea into the intersubjectively accessible WASHIZU. WASHIZU-making, then, is not a covert psychological act culminating in a private mental representation. To confect an agent-concept is to clarify it by expressing it, where its expression consists of trying overtly to steer people toward it.

Individuation and identification

Recall that cinematic individual W, a physical property of a certain artifact, *Throne of Blood*'s stroboluminescent display. W and WASHIZU, a mental property of some actual agent, are fundamentally related even if they are not identical. W is something Kurosawa relies on to establish and indicate his WASHIZU concept. The way it looks helps us to figure out what to imagine; for example, that Washizu is bearded. At the same time, W's appearance, plus other display and aural properties, including linguistic items, help us to discover how the director conceives of his protagonist. W thereby subserves WASHIZU's creation and dissemination.

The claim that W is an SLD property should not be taken to imply that it is one selfsame thing intermittently appearing in the display throughout a screening of *Throne of Blood*. "W" actually refers generically to a multitude of individual, numerically distinct display properties. W is one way my display is during the shot of Washizu flinging the arrow down at his troops. At other moments, my display lacks this property. But during previous and subsequent shots from different scenes, my display is W again. The term "W" applies to many particular display properties—to many particular, numerically distinct ways my SLD sometimes is; and to many particular ways other SLDs at other locations sometimes are. These are very—perhaps precisely—similar display modes. However visibly similar, I count them as disparate brute properties, not as the selfsame *in rebus* universal occurring in many instances, nor as individual tokens of the same abstract type.

There is normally another similarity between these particulars: their shared function to clarify and convey Kurosawa's WASHIZU concept. Possessing this similarity depends less on pixels and stroboluminescence than on a contingent psychohistorical relation. To wit, a display is apt to be a vehicle for WASHIZU if generated from (a copy of) some template Kurosawa intended for that purpose.

"Washizu exists" is made true not by W's existence but by that of a public agent-concept WASHIZU. "WASHIZU exists" is made true by complex psychohistorical facts about Kurosawa. These pertain to his possessing, clarifying, and effectively expressing a certain vacuous agent-concept. Washizu's existence is nothing over and above this public concept, WASHIZU. Any informative account of how WASHIZU comes to be will tacitly presuppose, if not explicitly stress, Kurosawa's relevant creative-imaginative thoughts and actions, and their reciprocal relations with the cinematic medium. Indeed, a monstrously complicated arrangement of objects, properties, and events is implicated in WASHIZU's existence, not the least of these involving Shakespeare's brain, medieval Japanese feudal society, cinema's invention, and Toshiro Mifune. All this and more help realize WASHIZU. Acknowledgement of WASHIZU's dependence on other entities and their relations is not acceptance of Thomasson's ontology of fictive characters as higher-level abstract-artifactual objects supervening on some combination of lower-level items. To be realists about fictive characters, we need not posit a novel, distinct kind of object existing in addition to mental states, texts, SLDs, audiences, and so on. Creating a public agent-concept does depend on myriad entities and their relations. But a public agent-concept is what a fictive character is.

The foregoing denies that fictive characters are artifacts. The ontology of artifacts is itself obscure.[15] In standard, relatively uncontroversial cases, an artifact is an extramental, spatiotemporally located object. Construed as either abstract objects or concepts, characters are poor candidates to be paradigmatic artifacts. Depriving fictive characters of extramental status might seem to play them into antirealist hands. There's no loss of realism here. Minds are what they are independent of how we take them to be. An artist's having a certain mental property, an agent-concept, no more depends on my believing him to have it than does my belief require his believing me to have this belief. Short of revising a work, not even an author can modify the psychohistorical fact of his or her public agent-concept. Were Kurosawa, his movie completed, to reconceive Washizu as rationally and autonomously desiring to commit regicide, this change of mind would happen too late to make a difference to his public concept.

The SLD, unlike WASHIZU, is an artifact. I have called this item a vehicle for the character concept. It makes psychohistorical facts about how the filmmaker conceived of his character available to competent audiences long after the artist has left the scene. It also falls within the display's ambit to serve as a proxy for WASHIZU. W is, for both Kurosawa and his audience, a vivid, externalized model or simulation of some of the perceptible ways Kurosawa conceives his fictive agent to be. Experiencing this model is one route by which we discover both what to imagine about Washizu and what to believe about WASHIZU. It is a proximal source of our own concepts of this character.

Kurosawa exploits this proxy to fill in WASHIZU's content and thereby help fix this character's identity. Something's identity is that by virtue of which it differs from other things. If we equate fictive characters with concepts, then their identities devolve to the identities of concepts. And a concept's identity evidently comes from its content and ontogenesis. Grossly simplifying, WASHIZU's content is its referent: an agent having such and such traits, and engaging in certain actions. Being vacuous, WASHIZU lacks extramental extension, picks out no nonconceptual entity. This representation could nonetheless be confected from various empirical experiences; for example, of men, social hierarchy, leadership, violent rivalry, loss of self-control, and so forth. WASHIZU's confection is part of its ontogenesis. One concept diverges from others with respect to how it comes to be acquired or formed by some agent(s) at a given time and place. Here ontogenesis pertains to the routes, be they mental acts or causal-perceptual relations with extramental items, by which someone comes to have a concept. It also evokes the intramental and practical functions a concept facilitates for some particular conceiver or conceivers. To possess a concept is to possess a vehicle for thought, belief, and action. WASHIZU's identity, then, is partly associated with its roles in *Throne of Blood*'s making. It would, for example, be an inner representation serving as repository and unifier for Kurosawa's accumulating Washizu-thoughts and as a disposition to assimilate some though not other ideas into this repository.

Being public, fictive character concepts exist to be shared. Consider Kurosawa and Roman Polanski, director of *Macbeth* (1971), both of whom employ MACBETH concepts. As competent members of a literature-appreciating public, both are historically linked via some non-deviant causal chain—one excluding acquisition by head injury or by reading a Borgesian Pierre-Menard-authored *Macbeth*—to Shakespeare's public character concept as disseminated via assorted texts and performances. Thanks to these links, the two directors' concepts stand in similar historical relationships to Shakespeare's MACBETH and have similar, though surely not identical, content. These concepts correspond insofar as their representations of the imaginary agent, Macbeth, overlap.

Kurosawa's and Polanski's respective MACBETH concepts likewise enable them to think about a Scottish traitor-unseaming, dagger-hallucinating usurper named Macbeth, to track occurrences of Macbeth across texts and performances, and to investigate and form beliefs about the nature of Macbeth. Acquiring a concept copying at least some of the content of Shakespeare's MACBETH concept is necessary if interpreters are to have any specifically MACBETH thoughts of their own. Otherwise, they could not think about *Shakespeare's* Macbeth.

Kurosawa's MACBETH and Polanski's MACBETH are imperfect copies, their content and ontogenesis departing in countless ways from one another and from Shakespeare's public concept. Their *conceptions* of MACBETH are surely different, too. A conception is what one knows, believes, or thinks about some concept, its referent, and its content.[16] There are many ways in which our various potentially incompatible conceptions of the world's parts and properties can not only differ but also be faulty or confused. Fictive characters present no exception. One might possess MACBETH unaware it is vacuous, or the product of a certain artist's imaginative activities.[17] Possessing a MACBETH concept, one can accumulate knowledge about this concept's identity. Sophisticated, penetrating conceptions would comprise beliefs to the effect that Macbeth is indeed fictive; that is, a vacuous concept lacking nonmental, nonconceptual reference; that it is some fictioneer's imaginative creation; that it has certain artistic values and applications.

The realist premise that there are at least some facts about MACBETH's identity—about its content and connection to Shakespeare's relevant creative activities—does not imply that all such facts are either accessible or interesting to every sensitive interpreter. Nor does it imply that learning facts exhausts the possibilities for engaging with and interpreting fictive characters. Interpreters appropriately give free play to their imaginative explorations of what a fictive character could be like, filling in for themselves an agent-concept's content without necessarily being concerned with whether their conceptions coincide or cohere with the author's public concept.

Kurosawa and Polanski do different things with their respective MACBETH concepts. Kurosawa's is an input to a novel creation. *Throne of Blood* is not a performance of *Macbeth*. And Washizu is not Macbeth. He is ethnically and culturally Japanese; he does not believe himself indestructible by one of woman born; he is settled on his murderous course less by vaulting ambition than by maddening fear that he will fall victim to the cycle of distrust and betrayal that brought the previous sovereign to power. Polanski, on the other hand, treats *Macbeth* as what it is: explicit instructions for and constraints on the realization of a right performance of a theatrical work. Subsequently, the public MACBETH concept he prescribes by cinematic proxy is similar to the one Shakespeare prescribes by textual proxy. Naturally, Polanski prescribes his own idea of Macbeth, a more resolute Macbeth less weakened by the milk of human kindness. But while watching his movie, we encounter Macbeth again rather than a different if not entirely new character with an old name.

The theory I have outlined precludes saying that Polanski's modern cinematic MACBETH is Shakespeare's early seventeenth-century literary MACBETH. Strictly speaking, these two public concepts cannot be identical. Perhaps our intuition of identity in such cases detects a privileged psychohistorical relationship between certain concepts. Arguably, Polanski's MACBETH effectively though imperfectly copies Shakespeare's MACBETH. This claim's truth requires the former stand in a nondeviant causally-historically dependent relation to the latter. Its truth is also a matter of the degree to which their prescribed contents overlap. Given this sort of identity relation, Macbeth can persist indefinitely as a familiar item in ordinary reality, Shakespeare's public agent-concept being made available to audiences time after time, across media.

Realism and appreciation

Realists about fictive characters may wholeheartedly embrace them as legitimate, worthy targets of critical appreciation. I have suggested that critical appreciation comprises acquisition of public agent-concepts, along with conceptions of—attitudes toward, beliefs about—those concepts. Evidently, character appreciation also involves a further, quasi-interpersonal dimension. For we often think of engagements with characters as being like interpreting and responding to real persons.[18] For example, we might wonder about the strength of Macbeth's will to be king and suspect that he murders Duncan against his own—all things considered—better judgment.

According to a concept ontology, to think about characters at all is to think about agency. Characterization, the production of a character, is the achievement of some actual agent(s). To discover that character is to gain access to a highly structured mental representation embedded within the fictioneer's narrative intentions. Moreover, public agent-concepts, even vacuous ones, are to a degree functionally equivalent to agent-concepts acquired more directly via encounters with real people. A vacuous public agent-concept encompasses neither the existential commitments nor the dispositions to trigger practical, what-should-I-do-now reasoning and action that agent-concepts comprise. No interpreter in their right mind tries to do something to prevent Macbeth's killing Duncan. However, possessing an agent-concept, or copy of one, involves having a vehicle for thinking about an entity's beliefs, desires, and other action-orienting states and how they are meaningfully interrelated. To acquire and mobilize a public agent-concept is to have a capacity central to story-making and comprehension. Without it, there is not the faintest chance of reasoning competently about fictional truth; that is, the states of affairs, situations, and events that narrative works like *Macbeth* prescribe or license audiences to imagine. I think understandingly of Macbeth and his doings by holding my MACBETH concept occurrently in mind, just as I think of someone named Paul Yachnin by holding my YACHNIN concept in mind. Facts about Yachnin are the truth-makers for my YACHNIN concept. Lacking a real agent as its extension, my MACBETH concept is made true by facts about the content of Shakespeare's public agent-concept.

Any accurate conception of MACBETH includes a belief to the effect that its content describes a nonexistent being. It probably also incorporates a host of other evaluative and emotional attitudes toward this content. MACBETH can arouse pity and fear for the violent end toward which the Thane is inexorably headed. One might even feel a measure of sympathy toward him, recognizing that he suffers a self-destructive loss of volitional autonomy not wholly alien to certain of one's own life experiences.

Reasoning as we do about fictive agents and their predicaments, we are bound to have emotional responses akin to those provoked by our cognizance of real persons. Some aestheticians maintain that our feelings for characters are—or, to be rational, ought to be—mere quasi-emotions: to fictional beings and events correspond specifically fictional responses of pretending, imagining, or otherwise making as if we have certain beliefs, desires, and emotions.[19] These theorists doubt that one can have genuine, ordinary emotions about items one knows to be unreal. Rather than a nonentity, though, I take it that the proximal trigger and target of my pity is MACBETH. This item is not a person with problems of his own; nor does it point at such an individual, unlike YACHNIN. But it is a real, causally networked mental furnishing. As such, it is apt to give rise to judgments and feelings—including experiences of pity that seem phenomenologically like those I direct toward living agents. A concept ontology thus lends some support to arguments that cognitive states that are mere thoughts or imaginings, be they narratively- or self-generated, give rise to genuine, garden-variety emotions.[20] Whether my response to MACBETH is rational depends on whether MACBETH describes an agent who merits our pity. Making such judgments is integral to our appreciation of this character and the work in which it is presented.

Notes

1. John Heil's *From an Ontological Point of View* (Oxford: Clarendon, 2003) develops this idea at length.
2. Andrew Kania, "The Illusion of Realism in Film," *British Journal of Aesthetics* 42 (2002): 243–58.
3. Gregory Currie, *Image and Mind: Film, Philosophy, and Cognitive Science* (Cambridge: Cambridge University Press, 1995), 30–42.
4. I closely examine this topic in "The Substance of Cinema," *Journal of Aesthetics and Art Criticism* 64 (2006): 187–98.
5. David Park, *The Fire Within the Eye: An Historical Essay on the Nature and Meaning of Light* (Princeton: Princeton University Press, 1997) introduces readers to the nature and science of light.
6. C. B. Martin, "On the Need For Properties: The Road to Pythagoreanism and Back," *Synthese* 112 (1997); 193–231, at 205.
7. Heil, *From an Ontological Point of View*, 195–207.
8. Proponents of this version of antirealism include Kendall Walton, *Mimesis As Make-Believe: On the Foundations of the Representational Arts* (Cambridge: Harvard University Press, 1990); and Gregory Currie, *The Nature of Fiction* (Cambridge: Cambridge University Press, 1990).
9. Amie Thomasson, *Fiction and Metaphysics* (Cambridge: Cambridge University Press, 1999).
10. Thomasson, *Fiction and Metaphysics*, 35.
11. Peter Lamarque, defending a version of artifactualism in "How To Create A Fictional Character," in *The Creation of Art: New Essays in Philosophical Aesthetics*, eds Berys Gaut and Paisley Livingston (Cambridge: Cambridge University Press, 2003), 33–52, contends that character creation necessitates creation of a narrative.
12. Among the vast philosophical literature on concepts, three recent studies have been especially helpful to me: Jesse Prinz, *Furnishing the Mind: Concepts and Their Perceptual Basis* (Cambridge, MA: MIT Press, 2002); Ruth Garret Millikan, *On Clear and Confused Ideas: An Essay About Substance Concepts* (Cambridge: Cambridge University Press, 2000); Wayne Davis, *Meaning, Expression, and Thought* (Cambridge: Cambridge University Press, 2002).
13. Paisley Livingston, *Art and Intention: A Philosophical Study* (Oxford: Oxford University Press, 2005), 7–8. Livingston's understanding of intentions draws principally upon that of action theorist Alfred Mele, *Springs of Action* (New York: Oxford University Press, 1992).
14. For background on *Throne of Blood*'s literary and theatrical sources, see Keiko McDonald, "Noh into Film: Kurosawa's *Throne of Blood*," *Journal of Film and*

Video 39 (1987): 36–41; Joan Mellen, "On Kurosawa's *Throne of Blood*," *The Literary Review* 22 (1979): 461–71; Donald Richie, *The Films of Akira Kurosawa* (Berkeley: University of California Press, 1973).
15. *Creations of the Mind*, eds Stephen Laurence and Eric Margolis (Oxford: Clarendon Press, 2007) is an excellent introduction to thought about the nature and definition of artifacts.
16. Millikan, *On Clear and Confused Ideas*, 10–13.
17. One might believe that MACBETH refers directly to King Macbeth and describes only that actual historical agent's attitudes and doings.
18. Michael Bristol, "Confusing Shakespeare's Characters with Real People: Reflections on Reading in Four Questions," in the present volume, 19–40, champions just such a view of our engagements with Shakespeare's characters.
19. Kendall Walton, *Mimesis as Make-Believe*; Jerrold Levinson, "Emotion in Response to Art," in *Contemplating Art: Essays in Aesthetics*, (Oxford: Oxford University Press, 2006), 38–55.
20. Noël Carroll, *The Philosophy of Horror or Paradoxes of the Heart* (London: Routledge, 1990), 60–88; Berys Gaut, *Art, Emotion and Ethics* (Oxford: Oxford University Press, 2007), 203–26.

3
Character as Dynamic Identity: From Fictional Interaction Script to Performance

William Dodd

Does it make sense today to talk about dramatic characters in mimetic terms? The materialist critique of the "essential self" of "liberal humanism" brought a breath of fresh air to character criticism by reminding us that *dramatis personae* are verbal constructs and by recasting their apparently unique features as manifestations of social forces. Shakespeare's protagonists, instead of being studied as lifelike, sovereign individuals endowed with agency, were broken down into subject-positions, vehicles of impersonal discourses, *loci* of linguistic capital, products of politeness strategies, and the like. In my opinion, these approaches, which have greatly enhanced our understanding of the plays, are by no means incompatible with a mimetic approach to character—provided we take character as an *effect* and not as an *origin* of speech. Fifteen years ago, Bert O. States made a powerful case for the quiddity of character without ever losing sight of its constructed nature as a textual artefact.[1] In this essay, I argue that one major source of a character's quiddity is the particular way he/she engages in verbal exchanges.

In the first section, I explore how the effect of character is produced dynamically in the interplay between a *dramatis persona*'s pragmatic behavior (what it "does with words" and how it interacts with others) and its semantic attributes (the social, cultural, and moral identity ascribed to it). This dynamic gives rise to what I call a character's discourse biography, exemplified by Othello's verbal behavior in the first three scenes of Shakespeare's tragedy. But what happens when discourse biographies written into the script are performed in Shakespeare's playhouse? In the second section, I discuss some of the theatrical and social conditions that must have affected the realization of the speech actions of Shakespearean characters in early performances. This involves looking at the kind of impact that the social status and stage personae of actors like Burbage, Phillips or Lowin may have had on their characters' fictional utterances and interactions. Then I broaden my scope to some of the so-called "bad" quartos to see what can be gleaned from these about the effect on character of the study- and stage-practices of the London actors. The essay concludes with a glance at how some early modern, popular "purposes of playing" might even reframe fictional discourse biographies like that of Othello.

I

Consider Lynne Magnusson's critique of traditional readings of the "complex speech patterns" of characters like Othello and Desdemona, readings in which divergences from verbal stereotypes tend to be explained as a "particularizing . . . mark of . . . essential character." Magnusson argues that we should learn from Pierre Bourdieu to seek the *raison d'être* of a discourse, not in essential character, but rather "in the socially defined site from which it is uttered." It is important that she still seems to acknowledge a quiddity of character even as she demonstrates how permeable it is to social conditioning. Othello's speech style, she says, is explained by the fact that, as "a person of color and an exotic outsider, [he] might—even without making conscious adjustments—[tend] to mobilize his verbal resources more fully than Venetian speakers."[2] She implicitly ascribes some sort of presiding agency to Othello, something capable of deploying the socially determined elements of his speech and taking responsibility for them. If character is not essential, as Magnusson persuasively argues, then where do we locate our sense of a character's quiddity and agency? I suggest that we locate it in the *dramatis persona's* discourse biography—the unique history of interactions that accrues to its character and is more than the sum of its social determinations. The make-believe game of drama wouldn't work if we weren't able to process discourse events as capable in principle of clinging to characters as well as to contexts and plots.[3] To ascribe dynamically produced character-effects to a *dramatis persona* means to endow it with what Anthony Giddens calls "practical consciousness"—everything "[people] know tacitly about how to 'go on' in the contexts of social life."[4] Verbal interactions adhere to *dramatis personae* and define their relation, moment by moment, to semantic identities. They produce a self to which social and moral identities can be attached or by which they can be challenged.

Othello lends himself to the present discussion because his job depends on maintaining the high public standing of his character. In the Senate scene, his character is literally put on trial, and his life depends on his capacity to produce a winning identity. If he succeeds in establishing a convincing *dynamic* identity, then the negative *semantic* "characters" being thrust upon him will be erased. No other Shakespearean hero is so destructively characterized before his appearance on stage. The audience is thus primed to scrutinize whatever self-image he tries to promote.

Iago's first account of Othello depicts his speech style as "Horribly stuff'd" with "epithets of war" and outmoded vocabulary like "certes" (1.1.12–14).[5] Othello is charactered as one of those swaggering pseudo-veterans that haunt the City of London in Jonson's plays and in the satirical pamphlets. For a contemporary audience, Othello's language resonates with other voices even before he starts speaking. Onto this initial caricature Iago grafts that of an old black ram tupping the white ewe Desdemona, and he constructs Barbantio as the gulled bourgeois father of comedy ("Look to your house, your daughter, and your bags" [1.1.88]). Iago thus stages a racist-paternalist ideologeme as a prelude to our first encounter with the ethnic other.[6]

When Othello appears together with Iago in the next scene, his discourse history is thus bemired from the start by calumnies and stereotypes that cling to him whether he likes it or not. He will combat them with his own preferred "gestalt"—memorably condensed in the line "Keep up your bright swords, for the dew will rust 'em" (1.2.71)—the image of a poised, aristocratic soldier unflustered by civilian authority.[7] But he also displays awareness that such a public image requires careful cultivation. When he knows that boasting is an honor, he will "provulgate" his royal origins: "My parts, my title, and my perfect soul, / Shall manifest me rightly" (1.2.35–36). The Globe audience, listening with Iago, may well have discerned the outlandish jargon of contemporary swaggerers in a speech crammed with *recherché* vocabulary like "out-tongue," "provulgate" (Folio [F] "promulgate"), "demerits," "unbonneted," "unhoused," "circumscription" and, in F only, "Seige" in the rare sense of rank.[8] Under the pressure of destructive identifications like that of Barbantio reported by Iago—"he prated / And spoke such scurvy and provoking terms / Against your honour" (1.2.8–10)—will Othello's parts succeed in "manifesting" him rightly? Unlike Hamlet, he has no Horatio to embody and witness his sincerity. His words must pick their way unaided through a Bakhtinian arena of competing voicings.[9] As Magnusson has noted, Othello, being an outsider, has to work harder with language than do the Venetians, hence the slightly strained plenitude. His greeting to Cassio and the officers—"The goodness of the night upon you, friends" (1.2.39)—hints at a need to fortify friendship with generous linguistic handouts. His discourse biography is conditioned from the start by the hostility in his environment. The stage is carefully set for a trial scene in which Othello will have to negotiate his public identity in a minefield of negative semantic representations. As he tries to steer clear of these he defines the space of his own character; but, unlike Hamlet, he does not seek to create this space inside himself, in the shape of a private subjectivity. He struggles to maintain a public definition of his identity, thereby making himself singularly vulnerable to "charactering" by others. His character—in the early modern sense of the external marks by which a person's identity is socially construed—is thus placed in jeopardy in every single encounter.[10]

The stately, measured rhythm of Othello's first response to the Senate—"Most potent, grave, and reverend signiors, / My very noble and approved good masters" (1.3.76–77)—and his calculated deployment of forensic rhetoric, lay claim to a dignity deserving the attention of the Signiory. Yet there is a hint of hostility in his determination to stage his identity in his own way. In Othello's evocation of his soldiership, the senators might also hear the arrogance of a man of arms towards a semi-bourgeois aristocracy. Othello's discourse style enables him to hold the floor and control the rhythm of the trial. Three times he offers to tell the true story of his wooing, three times he has to be urged to speak.[11] By deferring his narration, he ensures that he will be given full use of the floor and can hold it until his tale is done.

Othello hints that the ultimate source of Desdemona's elopement is mercantile, bourgeois nostalgia for military heroism. He shifts responsibility for how he characterizes himself onto Barbantio, telling how he "loved me, oft invited me, / Still questioned me the story of my life . . . the battles, sieges, fortunes / That I have passed" (1.3.130–33). Othello both reduces the risk of being heard as a braggadocio and seizes the opportunity to affirm his martial identity. He is acutely aware of the kind of identity Europeans tend to thrust upon him. Indeed, he implies that his adventurous life-story might well have been concocted to satisfy a demand for sensational fiction: "It was my hent to speake," he says, "Of hair-breadth scapes i'th' imminent deadly breach," his chance to spin yarns of "antres vast, and deserts idle," of "Anthropophagi" and monsters of nature (1.3.138–46). His metadiscursive comment—"such was the [F my] process" (1.3.144)—shows how conscious he is that his identity depends on social negotiation. As an outsider in Venice, he can't rest on his military laurels but must labor to carve a public identity from or against the models available to him. Above and beyond his practical consciousness, it is this discursive consciousness that constructs him as a *person* standing outside, or beyond the identities others seek to foist on him.[12] By dubbing his tale "my travel's [F Trauellours] history" (1.3.141), he puts quotation marks around the stereotyped "character" of the bragging adventurer.[13] He thus constitutes himself as an active, even manipulative, agent in the language market, capable of estimating the relative amount of "voice potential" he and his interlocutors have at their disposal.[14] Othello's successful verbal 'maneuvers' before the Senate are objective accomplishments that accrue to his discourse biography.

When Desdemona finally shows up in his account, it is as if Othello sees her as being conjured up by his tales. She is his ideal listener, constructing him as deserving both compassion and admiration: "I . . . often did beguile her of her tears / When I did speak of some distressed stroke / That my youth suffered" (1.3.157–60). Having neutralized the 'traveler' stereotype, Othello can now promote the more prestigious identity of a modern-day Aeneas taking a rest from his sufferings in the arms of a chaste Dido. His pathos-filled narrative provides the Senators with a public justification for absolving him. The Duke is thus able to acquit him even before hearing Desdemona's testimony: —"I think this tale would win my daughter too" (1.3.174). But has he been enchanted *himself*? On the surface, his response endorses Othello's performance of his public identity, but both the audience and Othello are fully aware that the Senate has a vested interest in accepting his self-evaluation. The return of Iago with Desdemona will shortly remind the audience just how precariously poised that identity still is. Soon Iago will be recycling his alternative account of Othello's performances as the "bragging, and telling . . . fantastical lies" (2.1.233–34) of a blustering traveler.

Even at this early stage, Othello's interaction style produces the character-effect of an isolated individual laboring to replace hostile interpretations with a rather obsolete, narcissistic identity of his own making. Highly sensitive to context, he gets caught up in a game of manipulation that risks tarnishing his carefully projected image. If Hamlet hypnotized his enemies with the illusion of an essential self ("that within which passes show"), Othello sets out to dazzle his adversaries with a public spectacle of "character." But this puts him at the mercy of the arch-iconoclast Iago, who will soon scrawl the character of a cuckold over Othello's self-portrait. With Othello, as with Hamlet, then, the specific interactive style used to combat threatening identifications is instrumental in producing our sense of the quiddity and uniqueness of their characters. Othello's discourse biography reveals him to be a more self-conscious manipulator of discourse than has traditionally been recognized.

II

But how would this interaction style, these dynamic character-effects, come across in the Globe playhouse? We can never retrieve the original performance conditions, of course, but we can pinpoint some factors that would affect an audience's uptake of Othello's speech acts, especially as these were voiced by Burbage.[15]

Much of Othello's self-construction and speech management will acquire metatheatrical overtones. The obvious example is: "Were it my cue to fight, I should have known it / Without a prompter" (1.2.89–90). Burbage's recent performance biography might well qualify Othello's claim as a shaky attempt to bolster himself up, given that since 1601 the actor has personated a Shakespearean character famous for *not* seizing his cue to fight, despite prompting by his father's ghost. Certainly, Othello chooses neither the right time nor the right target when he takes arms against his own sea of troubles. This is not the first time that Othello has claimed to know better than others what to perform and when. A little earlier, when invited by Iago to 'go in', he responded:

> Not I, I must be found,
> My parts, my title, and my perfect soul,
> Shall manifest me rightly.
>
> (1.2.35–36)

"Going in" takes an actor offstage into the tiring house; but for Othello as for his actor this is the wrong cue: to be manifested rightly they must remain onstage, in public view. Like Burbage, who is "perfect" in his "part" and has "title" to a leading role, Othello insists on performing—*now*. And he has already laid claim to a rhetorical sense of timing:

> 'tis yet to know,
> Which, when I know[16] that boasting is an honour,
> I shall provulgate, I fetch my life and being
> From men of royal height.
>
> (1.2.21–24)

Othello's self-constituting performatives—authoritative speech acts aimed at establishing him as a public figure *entitled* to perform them—thus get enmeshed with the ambiguous social position of early modern actors. For Burbage, to voice such performatives is to merge this fictional outsider's discourse position with his own. Othello's public standing has interesting parallels with that of Burbage and his fellows. Like an actor, he is a mercenary of dubious social status whose labor can earn him the good will of his patrons. He uses his professional skills—the power of his performance—to rise above his "natural" place. He knows when and when not to appear. He can materialize a role from "aery nothings," and *pre-exist* that role as a person. Or at least he can try. Because his problem, like the actors', is getting his new clothes to *fit*. The precariousness of Othello's dynamic character would thus be colored by Burbage's own social predicament—that of an actor almost as indispensable to London and the Court as Othello was to Venice and its Senate, but one for whom (and for whose fellows) there was no proper niche in the hierarchy, no ultimate refuge from antitheatrical prejudice.[17] The ill-fitting robes of so many major political figures in Shakespearean drama (Richard III, Richard II, Hal/Henry V, Hamlet, Lear after abdication, Macbeth)—perhaps all created for and by Burbage—are symptoms of a widening gap between place and person that the early modern actor is in a strategic position to represent. Othello differs from the rest in that his acting style is more indebted to the formal rhetorical tradition than to theatrically interactive modes of character-construction like those recently epitomized in Hamlet. It is now Iago, not Othello, who exploits the potentials of the *platea*-position. For Burbage, to embody Othello's outdated mimesis was to make visible the Moor's distance from the actor's most accomplished stage practice, opening a rift between Othello's self-image and the Globe audience's perception of it. A rift into which Iago, the virtuoso of *theatrical* role-building, will gleefully insinuate himself. This discrepancy must also have affected the audience's perception of Othello's attempt to parry hostile stereotyping by presenting himself as a modern-day Aeneas. Othello subscribes to the same heroic tradition that inspired another tragic emulator of Aeneas, the recently executed Earl of Essex—especially when he displays a warrior's condescension towards the mercantile Senate. A noticeably obsolete style of self-presentation would thus reinforce the impression of the hero's cultural anachronism, giving a topical slant to his discourse biography.

But Burbage also had a history of comic roles. He probably played Othello's near-anagram, Thorello, the jealous husband of *Every Man In His Humour*. Various links between the two plays suggest that Shakespeare expected audiences to have a shadow-scenario of imagined cuckoldry in the back of their minds. Up to 1.3, this is only a potentiality; but it will soon become a powerful item in Iago's bag of tricks. Spoken by Burbage, Othello's opening concession to the Senate—

> That I have ta'en away this old man's daughter,
> It is most true: true, I have married her;
> The very head and front of my offending,
> Hath this extent no more.
>
> (1.3.78–81)

—might easily associate the deceived father motif with the motif of cuckoldry, whose emblem's typical location is precisely the "head and front."

Clearly, the Iago actor's *habitus* must also have affected the unfolding of the Moor's character.[18] The foregrounding of the Vice inheritance in Iago's soliloquies would, in itself, influence an audience's response to Othello. The Moor's confident assertions could easily be perceived as the posturings of a theatrically encircled victim rather than as masterful self-constituting performatives. David Grote argues that Shakespeare initially conceived Iago's role for the actor who probably played Mercutio, Bobadilla, Cassius, Claudius, and Pistol, characters who, for all their differences, have something of the fast-talking, personable rascal. Grote's candidate is Augustine Phillips. If Phillips as the madcap Mercutio had already out-talked Burbage's Romeo, and, as the lean and hungry Cassius, had outmaneuvered Burbage's Brutus, Shakespeare would have expected this further pairing to have highlighted Othello's vulnerability from the start. However, Phillips probably retired before the play was completed and seems to have been replaced by Richard Lowin, a stouter actor adept at playing bluff soldiers and winning rogues. The fact that Iago specifies his age as "four times seven years" suggests that Shakespeare rejuvenated his character to fit the twenty-eight-year-old Lowin. This adjustment would help explain how the Janus-faced Iago could have been successful at the Globe in projecting his public image as a plain-speaking army man.[19]

Lack of substantial contemporary records prevents us from firming up conjectures about how theater conditions and actors' performance biographies interacted with the discourse biography of fictional characters. But it is clear that "character" as Shakespeare the playwright conceived it necessarily inhabits this interface, and that we ignore its theatrical dimension at our own risk. It is worth stressing, however, that a character's discourse biography is not entirely subject to the contingencies of

70 *Character as Dynamic Identity*

actual performances. This aspect of character is constrained by the overall "fictional interaction script," which is what holds a play together.[20] In a play script, the outcomes of verbal (and non-verbal) interactions become the basis of subsequent actions, thereby acquiring objective existence. Later interactions retrospectively select a limited range of acceptable executions and uptakes of speech acts. The actors' performance and the audience's interpretation of these must somehow be woven back into the sequence of interpretations built into the fictional script, or they will drop off like dead branches. Suppose one afternoon, on a whim, Burbage performed Othello's greeting to Desdemona on landing in Cyprus *merely* as bloated, self-regarding rhetoric, and that his quick-witted boy retaliated by delivering Desdemona's response ("The heavens forbid, / But that our loves and comforts should increase, / Even as our days do grow" [2.1.203–5]) as a sarcastic put-down. Their rendering of the exchange would soon be "corrected" by the scripted words of Iago (hardly the type to pass up an opportunity to smear his General) when he grudgingly concedes that "The Moor . . . / Is of a constant, noble, loving nature" (2.1.279–80). Also, if we consider how Shakespeare's actors studied their parts and prepared for performance, it should become clear that this interaction script had a special responsibility for holding the performance as such together.

Tiffany Stern has shown that London theater actors had hardly any time for collective rehearsal and conned their separately transcribed parts in relative isolation.[21] Since 1990, Patrick Tucker's Original Shakespeare Company has been presenting performances in which the actors have seen only their own parts and come into dramatic contact with their interlocutors only at the première.[22] Identifying and experimenting with the constraints placed on actors by part-based learning in early modern repertory companies has led Stern and Tucker to some striking insights into the nature of characterization on such stages. An actor who studied his part separately would clearly have a fairly monadic sense of his role. His major focus would be on identifying the particular "passions" encoded in his lines, in order to produce "action" and "pronunciation" that was immediately intelligible to the audience and to the other actors on stage.[23] However, the preparation of Shakespeare's actors may have been less blinkered than Stern and especially Tucker seem to think. The sharers in the Chamberlain's/King's Men lived elbow to elbow during the season and would surely have seized every opportunity to swap information about their roles. Stern herself recognizes that the boys, especially, would get individual instruction from the sharers they were apprenticed to.[24] Still, actors could not have had a sense of the coherence of the fictional interaction comparable with that of a modern actor equipped with the full text. Nor would they have much chance to rehearse their pragmatic interplay in, say, a set of wit. The part-system thus places a considerable burden on the interaction script mapped out in the promptbook. Since this script is pieced together, mosaic-fashion, by each actor's utterance, it must be able to shepherd interactions along even if the actors focus primarily on "passionating" their individual parts. There is a little evidence that some actors switched off when they had uttered their monadic chunk and simply awaited their next cue, and that others bypassed their fictional addressees by playing directly to the audience for applause.[25] On the other hand, Burbage, according to Flecknoe (1664), "so wholly transform[ed] himself into his Part . . . as he never (not so much as in the Tyring-house) assum'd himself again until the play was done . . . never falling in his Part when he had done speaking, but with his looks and gesture maintaining it still unto the heighth."[26]

Such contrasting behaviors may imply a tension between the (relative) coherence of the interaction script and the (relatively) monadic part-study of the actors. There is evidence, I believe, in some of the "post-performance" Shakespearean quartos, with their precious traces of staging and speech practices, that many actors set out to bridge this gap by adapting their words to the flow of what I will call the "stage interaction plot."[27] We regularly detect them stitching up the seams between speeches, transposing scripted behavior into something like *real* communication behavior—however *sui generis*—between actors on stage. The character's discourse biography thus gets welded to the stage interaction plot, helping to produce "character" as a stage-figure, a hybrid of character and actor.[28] Traces of this plot can be found in the phatic signals (especially characteristic of oral discourse) that are interpolated or "naturalized" by actors as they speak their lines. I use "phatic" rather broadly to cover various language items that ease communication and help maintain contact: for instance, by requesting the attention or response of the listener (*sir, come, dost thou hear?*), indicating the logical link between the upcoming speech and the previous one (*why! nay, then*), showing uptake or subjective evaluation of the previous speaker's speech acts (*marry! alas! tut!*), or expressing degrees of cooperation and (im)politeness (e.g. address terms: *your Grace, sirrah*).[29] The play script already contains a rich array of such signals, representing the characters' practical consciousness of the mechanisms of oral interaction. But the moment they are uttered by an actor, phatic signals draw attention to the here-and-now of *performance*. They become amphibious, serving to bond fictional dialogue to the contingencies of stage interaction, and to root the latter in actor-audience communication. If actor A's intonation suggests that he's expecting to surprise actor B, B may use an interjection like "say you?" to convey his uptake of this to the audience. The remarkable amount of phatic variation suggests that such signals are continually attuned to the pragmatics of social intercourse as actors perceived this. Of course, even texts like Quarto 1 (Q1) and F *Othello*, which do not carry performance traces, are written *by* an actor *for* actors. They contain a blueprint for phatic signaling which promises a close fit between fictional and stage interaction. But quartos like Q1 *Romeo and Juliet* (1597) and Q1 *Hamlet* (1603) demonstrate that this dimension refuses to be fossilized in a promptbook, since it is the essence of the here-and-now of performance. Compared with authorial Quarto 2 (Q2) or Folio texts, these and other post-performance quartos are brimful of interpolations and variations affecting the kind of phatic features illustrated above.

Often, however, phatic items already supplied by the author get omitted—presumably because they didn't come "trippingly on the tongue."[30] Such variations attest to the stage-figure's active participation in an evolving communication that is at once fictional and theatrical. Greg once deplored an Elizabethan actor's addition of "Yar a welcome man sir" to a challenge penned in high-flown style.[31] But the actor presumably felt the need for a phatic signal that would evoke contemporary interaction-ritual prior to crossing swords, as well as alerting his colleague that a foil-thrust was imminent. Many interpolations probably reflect impromptu seam-stitching by actors who had studied their parts in relative isolation. The Q1 speeches of Romeo and especially Hamlet show a marked increase in phatic activity compared to the "good" quartos, and may well carry traces of Burbage's performance habits.[32] Presumably, Burbage would have been equally keen to anchor the complexities of Othello's scripted discourse tightly to the ongoing stage interaction. But for him to engage vigorously in phatic tuning in the "temptation scene" with Iago would mean making Othello play even more visibly into the hands of that master of interaction as personated by the company's fastest-talking actor.

In the "bad" quartos we also find countless examples of reordering and paraphrasing—traditionally blamed on the faulty memory of the two or three actors held guilty of the "memorial reconstruction" of these texts. More recent scenarios of actors collaboratively dictating their parts to a scribe from memory and/or from their scroll—though needing further research—suggest that these short quartos may carry clues that actors often resorted to conceptual rather than verbatim memory, rephrasing or improvising when convenient.[33] This appears to have happened in many of Romeo's later, less patterned speeches as well as in Hamlet's soliloquies.[34] It implies that Shakespeare would expect at least the more accomplished sharers to hammer out their "character" in the here-and-now of performance, thereby involving the audience actively in its creation.[35]

Nevertheless, Q1 *Romeo and Juliet* and *Hamlet*, despite huge differences from the "authorial" second quartos, reveal how sturdy the scaffolding of the fictional interaction script is. Episode after episode is abridged, speech after speech gutted and/or paraphrased, but the sequences of speech acts and uptakes remain surprisingly close to those of the longer texts. This is not simply due to the fact that cutting and rephrasing for performance often took place in the middle of speeches, leaving openings and cue lines relatively intact, and reducing the need for the revision/relearning of adjacent parts. In Q1 *Romeo* and *Hamlet* there are numerous instances where whole cue-lines found in Q2 are eliminated, yet there are virtually no signs that this disrupted the interaction. This suggests that the leading actors tended—as Flecknoe implies—to interiorize their parts, to become fluent in their character, as it were. They could generate their speeches anew by reassembling the vocabulary supplied by Shakespeare. It also suggests that they had developed techniques for getting the illocutionary force of their lines across clearly to their colleagues, encouraging them to respond to pragmatic summonses rather than (simply) to their cues. A possible example: towards the end of Act 5, Scene 1 in modern editions, after starting a speech almost verbatim, Burbage/Romeo in Q1 inverts the order of three elements compared with Q2 and F, and omits his final injunction:

Q1

Rom: Art thou so bare and full of pouertie,
And doost thou feare to violate the Law?
The Law is not thy frend, nor the Lawes frend,
And therefore make no conscience of the law:
Vpon thy backe hangs ragged Miserie,
And starued Famine dwelleth in thy cheekes.
Apo: My pouertie but not my will consents.

(Sig. I 4)

Q2

Rom. Art thou so bare and full of wretchednesse,
And fearest to die, famine is in thy cheekes,
Need and opression starueth in thy eyes,
Contempt and beggerie hangs vpon thy backe:
The world is not thy friend, nor the worlds law,
The world affoords no law to make thee rich:
Then be not poore, but breake it, and take this.
App. My pouertie, but not my will consents.

(Sig. L 1)

Some details of Romeo's speech get blurred in Q1, but it makes sense, despite the inversion. Presumably the illocutionary force of "therefore make no conscience of the law" was successfully sustained by the actor's intonation throughout the retarded motivations, since the Apothecary, though cheated of his cue, gets his line in on time and appropriately. Another glimpse of how actors' ears were attuned to the contingencies of the preceding speaker's delivery is perhaps to be found at the beginning of the same scene:

Q1

(*Rom:*) If she be well, then nothing can be ill.
Balt: Then nothing can be ill, for she is well.

(Sig. I 3)

Q2

(*Rom.*) For nothing can be ill, if she be well
Man. Then she is well, and nothing can be ill.

(Sig. K 4)

In Q1 Burbage/Romeo puts the cart before the horse but the Balthasar actor salvages the shared chiasmus by inverting his half to match.[36]

Let's glance, to conclude, at how fictional interaction scripts and discourse biographies might be affected by those other "purposes of playing" to which, as Robert Weimann has untiringly reminded us, Shakespeare's theater catered. In the public playhouses, humanist mimesis rubbed shoulders with popular traditions of misrule, play, and sport. Whatever we make of Kemp's replacement by Armin, the first Globe continued awhile to host these other purposes of playing.[37] Even in *Othello*, Shakespeare's nearest approach to an Aristotelian tragedy, popular forms of play have a powerful impact upon the mimetic dimension, for example in clowning routines and scurrilous sets of wit. Iago's banter with Desdemona and Emilia in Act 2, Scene 1 is a "quips upon questions" routine just like those published by Armin in 1600. We might imagine Armin listening approvingly as his "trainee" turns the class tables on Desdemona and upstages the courtly Cassio. A pimple on the smooth skin of Aristotelian mimesis, this episode was long considered "one of the most unsatisfactory passages in Shakespeare'.[38] Yet it enables Shakespeare to release theatrical energies that vastly enrich and complicate the fictional narrative. Though scripted, it thrives on the Elizabethan clown's refusal to be engulfed by classical mimesis. It was, rather, the fictive worlds of humanist writers that tended to be annexed by popular horseplay and sport. Iago, after claiming: "my invention / Comes from my pate, as birdlime does from frieze" (2.1.137–38), fires off salvo after salvo of "improvised" rhyming couplets to put down Desdemona. She speaks close to home when she says, "These are old paradoxes, to make fools laugh i' the alehouse" (2.1.150). In fact, Iago has served up the typical fare of city-tavern Fools. By exploiting the subversive energies of clowning, the Iago actor can twist a rope of theatrical skills round the neck of a speaker like Othello, who is committed to a classical rhetoric of self-presentation. This carefully fashioned lead-up to Othello's landing forewarns the Globe audience that the General's heroic gestalt will never be a match for his Ancient's malice. Iago has learnt the clown's knack of riding the rapids of theatrical exchange—be it between characters, or between stage-figure and audience. His accomplishment retrospectively diminishes Othello's rhetorical success in the Senate scene, reframing his discourse biography in preparation for his defeat in the "temptation scene." What we see, then, is a complex dialectic between the individualizing process inscribed in Othello's scripted discourse biography and the distancing, typifying process to which he is subjected by the circumventing world of cruel theatrical play.

Notes

1. Bert O. States, *"Hamlet" and the Concept of Character* (Baltimore and London: Johns Hopkins University Press, 1992).
2. Lynne Magnusson, *Shakespeare and Social Dialogue* (Cambridge: Cambridge University Press, 1999), 167, 171.

76 *Character as Dynamic Identity*

3. See Kendall L. Walton, *Mimesis as Make-Believe* (Cambridge MA): Harvard University Press, 1990).
4. Anthony Giddens, *The Constitution of Society* (Berkeley and Los Angeles: University of California Press, 1984), xxiii. Locating dynamic identity (initially) at the level of practical consciousness means that it can be documented from the surface phenomena of interaction, without having to posit, *a priori*, inwardness or an unconscious.
5. All *Othello* quotations, unless otherwise stated, are from *The First Quarto of Othello*, ed. Scott McMillin (Cambridge: Cambridge University Press, 2005).
6. For this sense of ideologeme see Louise Schleiner, "Voice, Ideology, and Gendered Subjects: The Case of *As You Like It* and *Two Gentlemen*," *Shakespeare Quarterly* 50, no. 3 (Fall 1999): 285–309.
7. Cf. James L. Calderwood, *The Properties of "Othello"* (Amherst: University of Massachusetts Press, 1989), 24: "Crude images of old black rams tupping white ewes ... do not readily wash away despite the sponging motions of the Senate scene." In *"Hamlet" and the Concept of Character*, States discusses the way "circumstantial insinuations" attach to Ophelia's character (131ff.). He uses "gestalt" to refer to "a kind of tonal chord, a denotative center of energy (in word, gesture, manner, etc.) that announces a range of connotations to come" (19).
8. Simon Palfrey, *Doing Shakespeare*. The Arden Shakespeare (London: Thomson Learning, 2005), 52, makes a similar point about Othello's language.
9. For a subtle Bakhtinian reading of Shakespearean character see James R. Siemon, *Word Against Word* (Amherst and Boston: University of Massachusetts Press, 2002).
10. Stephen Greenblatt, in *Renaissance Self-fashioning* (Chicago: University of Chicago Press, 1980), notes that "his identity depends upon ... an embrace and perpetual reiteration of the norms of another culture" (245).
11. I owe this observation to a former student, Valentina Papini.
12. See Giddens, *The Constitution of Society*, 45: "Discursive consciousness means being able to put things into words." Robert Y. Turner, in *Shakespeare's Apprenticeship* (Chicago and London: University of Chicago Press, 1974), discusses the effect of making characters capable of self judgment: "Different from 'characteristics,' it creates the impression of a substance underlying and containing the characteristics" (235).
13. In Thomas Lodge, *Wits Miserie, and the Worlds Madnesse* (London: Adam Islip, 1596), Sig. F 2, one of these "travailers," whose name is "Lying," had plundered the very Plinian materials from which Shakespeare (or Othello himself?) has built this passage.
14. For this use of "voice potential" see Magnusson, *Shakespeare and Social Dialogue*, Chapter 7.
15. "Uptake" is used in J. L. Austin's sense of the hearer's identification of the speech act intended by the speaker. Clearly, the illocutionary force of an actor's utterances will be much affected by how an actor is costumed, where he looks and how he moves while speaking—aspects I have no space to tackle here. On the visual and kinesic dimensions, see Bruce R. Smith, "E/loco/com/motion," in *From Script to Stage in Early Modern England*, ed. Peter Holland and Stephen Orgel (Basingstoke: Palgrave Macmillan, 2004), 131–50; and Palfrey, *Doing Shakespeare*, Chapter 10.

16. Q1 appears defective here; McMillin has integrated it from F.
17. See John Earle, *Microcosmography* (London, 1628), in *English Professional Theatre, 1530–1660*, ed. Glynne Wickham, Herbert Berry, and William Ingram (Cambridge: Cambridge University Press, 2000), 186: "[The player's] profession has in it a kind of contradiction, for none is more disliked, and yet none more applauded."
18. For the concept of an actor's *habitus* see Andrew Hartley's essay in this volume.
19. See David Grote, *The Best Actors in the World* (Westport, Connecticut, and London: Greenwood Press, 2002), 130–34, and Shoichiro Kawai, "John Lowin as Iago," *Shakespeare Studies (Japan)* 30 (1992): 17–34. Lowin played Bosola in *The Duchess of Malfi*, and probably Falstaff, Morose, and Volpone (See Andrew Gurr, *The Shakespeare Company, 1594–1642* [Cambridge: Cambridge University Press, 2004], 233).
20. Richard Ohmann first pointed out that "the action [of a play] rides on a train of illocutions" through which the "movement of the characters and changes in their relations to one another" are expressed (quoted in Keir Elam, *The Semiotics of Theatre and Drama* [London and New York: Methuen, 1980], 159).
21. Tiffany Stern, *Rehearsal from Shakespeare to Sheridan* (Oxford: Oxford University Press, 2000), 52–79.
22. Patrick Tucker, *Secrets of Acting Shakespeare* (New York and London: Routledge, 2002).
23. Stern, *Rehearsal from Shakespeare to Sheridan*, 72 ff. See also Tiffany Stern, *Making Shakespeare* (London and New York: Routledge, 2004), 79ff.
24. See also Scott McMillin, "The Sharer and His Boy: Rehearsing Shakespeare's Women," in *From Script to Stage in Early Modern England*, ed. Peter Holland and Stephen Orgel (Basingstoke: Palgrave Macmillan, 2004), 231–45.
25. See Stern, *Rehearsal from Shakespeare to Sheridan*, 98–99.
26. Richard Flecknoe, "A Short Discourse of the English Stage," in *Love's Kingdom*, (London: 1664), vol. 2 of *Critical Essays of the Seventeenth Century, 1650–85*, ed. J. E. Spingarn (London: Oxford University Press, 1957), 91–96.
27. See Janette Dillon, "Is There a Performance in this Text?" *Shakespeare Quarterly* 45, no. 1 (Spring 1994): 74–86; Laurie E. Maguire, *Shakespearean Suspect Texts* (Cambridge: Cambridge University Press, 1996); Paul Werstine, "A Century of 'Bad' Shakespeare Quartos," *Shakespeare Quarterly* 50, no. 3 (Fall 1999): 310–33. Each have seriously challenged the traditional scenario of how the "bad" quartos were produced through memorial reconstruction. Leah Marcus, *Unediting the Renaissance: Shakespeare, Marlowe, Milton* (London and New York: Routledge, 1996); Peter W. M. Blayney, "The Publication of Playbooks," in *A New History of Early English Drama*, ed. John D. Cox and David S. Kastan (New York: Columbia University Press, 1997), 383–422; and Lucas Erne, *Shakespeare as Literary Dramatist* (Cambridge: Cambridge University Press, 2003) have proposed alternative transmission scenarios such as the collaborative reconstruction of the text-as-performed by dictation to a scribe (from memory and/or written parts) by the actors involved—perhaps for a private patron. In this scenario, variants with respect to a "good" (authorial) text should carry traces of how individual actors actually spoke their parts. Although Werstine rightly insists on the difficulty of demonstrating that specific errors/variants originate with the actor and

not, say, with the scribe or compositor, the sheer number of the phatic variants I discuss below seems to point overwhelmingly in that direction. Maguire, *Shakespearean Suspect Texts*, 135–46 surveyed actors' variants in the BBC TV Shakespeare, and found that they matched the types attributed to early modern actors by W. W. Greg, *Two Elizabethan Stage Abridgements* (Oxford: Clarendon Press, 1923) and others.

28. Cf. Bridget Escolme, *Talking to the Audience* (Abingdon and New York: Routledge, 2005), 16: "Shakespeare's fictional figures undoubtedly have desires and interests that differentiate them one from another," but "Shakespeare's stage figures have another set of desires and interests, inseparable from those of the actor. They want the audience to listen to them, notice them, approve their performance, ignore others on stage for their sake. The objectives of these figures are bound up with the fact that they know you're there." Lesley W. Soule, in *Actor as Anti-Character* (Westport, Connecticut, and London: Greenwood Press, 2000), Chapter 5, shows brilliantly how the "performative plot" provided in *As You Like It* for the boy actor's playful interaction with the audience enters into dialectic with the "mimetic plot" of the cross-dressed Rosalind to produce the richness and complexity of this stage-figure's "character."

29. Scholars usually classify actors' errors or variants syntactically or semantically, whereas the concept of the phatic function of language (see Roman Jakobson, "Closing Statement: Linguistics and Poetics," in *Style in Language*, ed. Thomas A. Sebeok [Cambridge, MA: MIT Press, 1960], 350–77, esp. 355–56), enables us to select out those which serve to stress/maintain/repair communicational contact.

30. I have compared five first quartos (*Richard III* [1597], *Romeo and Juliet* [1597], *Henry V* [1600], *The Merry Wives of Windsor* [1602], *Hamlet* [1603]), widely agreed to show performance traces, with the corresponding "authorial" quarto or Folio text. In those parts of the Q1 texts that are close enough to Q2 or F to allow us pinpoint specific phatic variations, I have made the following, inevitably approximate, count. The absolute numbers of variants (many involving names, or address terms) are: *RIII* 273; *RJ* 337; *HV* 299; *MWW* 385; *Ham* 417. The proportion of such variants to the total number of lines per first quarto varies markedly: *RIII* 8.0 per cent; *RJ* 15.2 per cent; *HV* 18.4 per cent; *MWW* 25.7 per cent; *Ham* 19.4 per cent. *Additions* (interpolation, expansion, repetition) and *substitutions* (replacement, displacement) of phatic items represent about four fifths (79.1–83.6 per cent) of the whole in each of the first quartos; *omissions* constitute the remaining one fifth (16.9–20.9 per cent). There are marked differences in the ratio between additions and substitutions across these five plays, the former ranging from 30.4 (*RIII*) to 54 (*Ham*) per cent, and the latter from 29 (*Ham*) to 48.7 (*RIII*) per cent. These figures are intended only to give a rough idea of the magnitude of this phenomenon here, and will receive more careful analysis in a forthcoming essay.

31. Greg, *Two Elizabethan Stage Abridgements*, 304.

32. For instance, that of reiterating short phrases, of which I have counted sixteen clear examples. Leah Marcus, *Unediting the Renaissance*, 161, notes "Hamlet's nervous doubling of words and phrases in F as opposed to Q2 . . . Many modern critics regard this stylistic quirk as quintessentially Shakespearean, but it is

probably at least partly Burbage—based on the oral 'authority' of the playhouse rather than the written authority of the author's text."
33. On conceptual versus verbatim memorizing, and on occasional improvisation by early modern actors, see Marcus, *Unediting the Renaissance*, 160ff., and Maguire, *Shakespearean suspect texts*, 113ff.
34. Similar flexibility can be detected in the fluent style of the Mercutio actor and, in Q1 *Henry V*, of the Fluellen actor. Evidence of habitual improvisation by clowns and other comic actors is, of course, widespread. See David Wiles, *Shakespeare's Clown* (Cambridge: Cambridge University Press, 1987).
35. For examples of modern players actively constructing their character in collaboration with the audience, see Tucker, *Secrets of Acting Shakespeare*; Escolme, *Talking to the Audience*; Jonathan Holmes, *Merely Players?* (London and New York: Routledge, 2004).
36. Response adaptations of this kind could possibly have occurred during the dictation process itself. It will obviously need a more thoroughgoing examination of evidence than I have space for to substantiate this kind of claim.
37. See Wiles, *Shakespeare's Clown*; Grote, *The Best Actors in the World*; Gurr, *The Shakespeare Company*; Richard Preiss, "Robert Armin Do the Police in Different Voices," in *From Performance to Print in Shakespeare's England*, ed. Peter Holland and Stephen Orgel (Basingstoke: Palgrave Macmillan, 2006), 208–27.
38. *Othello*. The Arden Shakespeare, ed. M. R. Ridley (London and New York: Methuen, 1979), 54n.

Part II History

4
Personnage: History, Philology, Performance

André G. Bourassa

> Like actors who, trained not to show any shyness on the face, wear a mask, so too I, at the moment of entering onto the stage of the world where until now I lived as a spectator, go forward masked.
> —René Descartes, *Larvatus prodeo*, 1618[1]

René Descartes' depiction of the world as a stage inhabited by characters echoes Shakespeare's Jaques: "All the world's a stage, / And all the men and women merely players; / They have their exits and their entrances, / And one man in his time plays many parts" (*As You Like It*, 2.7.139–43).[2] The similarity of these metaphors reveals a common idea in early modern France and England. In effect, over time, the words *theatrun mun*, with the common alternatives *amphitheatrum* and even *globe*, took on the meanings of a meeting place for performance; but also as a global vision, whose textual realization was a series of compendia, the first of which was Pierre de Launay's anthology of European poetry, *Theatrum mundi*.[3]

This chapter begins with a diachronic analysis of character through the use of the French terms *personnage*, *caractère*, *tragique*, and *comique*, tracing the development of the terminology of character from Ancient Greece to the Renaissance. This new philological, diachronic interpretation of *personnage* provides the foundation for a critical reassessment of the modern idea of theatrical character. The discussion then shifts to a synchronic study that examines the formal and functional dimensions of the theatrical performance of character, and it concludes by considering the multivalence of any character, especially the need to take more fully into account the transmutation of theatrical character from one production to another.

84 Personnage: *History, Philology, Performance*

The evolution of the French word *personnage* is remarkably complex. It comes from the Latin *persona*, meaning "mask," but has three possible etymologies. Latinists have suggested *personare*,[4] meaning "to resonate" or "to retain," which would make *persona* a resonator, a wooden or leather mask behind which the actor's voice vibrates. However, according to the *Dictionnaire étymologique de la langue française*, the term comes from the Etruscan *pharsus* or *farsus*, meaning, in Latin, "full" or "stuffed," which is the source of the extended meaning of farcical theater.[5] This word refers to *persomai* [περσομαι], a passive from *pertho* [περθω], meaning "to turn over," "to pull down," derived from *per-* [περ-] , "with force," and *tithèmi*, "to place" or "to lay down." This etymology refers as much to the recumbent statues of tombs as to the ghosts of mystery plays, and it corresponds better than the two others to the attributes of *persona*, which is closely related to *sôma* [σωμα], a "dead body," then a "living body," and finally a "human person," following the same metaphoric trajectory as *persona*.

The use of *persona* in Latin to designate a human being effectively signified no more than an image for a long time. *Persona* finally took on the sense of "person" in the classical period.[6] The Latin Church used it as of the second century to designate the persons of the Trinity, while refusing the Greek Church the right to do the same with *prosôpon* [προσωπον], "something covering the face," which nonetheless also had the sense of "mask."[7] Strangely enough, the Church chose to designate the "nature" of these three invisible persons with the word *hypostasis* [υποστασις],"that or he who stands underneath," which is related to another theatrical term, *hypocrite* [υποστασις], "he who replies, who 'criticizes,' from underneath [the mask]." The notion of the mask remains present in the vocabulary of Greco-Roman mystery plays to signify the invisible; it was common practice to employ the words *face*, *figure*, and *visage* to designate the person of God. Still today, the anthropomorphic faces of the Father and the Son are described as symbols, each being perceived as a *persona*.[8]

The concept of "person" is thus derived from public theater. The concept of *personnage* developed in an opposite direction. To play a role, that is, "to wear a mask," was expressed as *personam induere* (to assume, to take on), as in Descartes, or *personam agere* (to act, to manage).[9] This last expression yielded *personage*, which appeared in 1250 to designate a personality, a distinguished person; that is, someone who played a noteworthy role in a milieu. By a curious reversal, this term, having entered common usage, returned to the theater.

The use of *character*, the English equivalent of *personnage*, is more recent; the French *caractère* is recorded in 1274 and the English *character* in 1314.

Derived from the Greek *karakter* [καρακτερ], both describe an engraved letter. By analogy, they can also designate the traits of an individual, which allowed the development of the literary portrait, as in Theophrastus' *The Characters*. In English, as in French, the term was long deprived of its literary value, which it didn't regain until Shakespeare's time:

> This category of texts constituted a true genre in Europe in the 17th century following the translation from Greek in 1592 of Theophrastus' *The Characters* (c. 319 BC) by the erudite Genevan Calvinist Issac Casaubon, refugeed in England after the assassination of Henri IV, later translated into English from Casaubon's version in 1593 by John Healey. Theophrastus' brief text (probably incomplete) offers in fragments a gallery of portraits that illustrate condemnable social behaviours ("The Disguised," "The Arrogant," "The Slanderer") or faults ("The Gossip," "The Lout"). As the beginning of the fragment on "The Disguised" foretells, it is about . . . showing a character in action.[10]

English literature was slow to use the word *character* in the sense of *personnage*. Rather, *nature* was used, undoubtedly due to the dispute that led the Latin Church to choose *natura* (rather than *substantia*) to translate *hypostasis*. Shakespeare himself scarcely uses *character* (37 times), giving the term, circa 1590-91, the sense of inscription, of a material sign, extended metaphorically to a moral sign.[11] Perhaps once, in *Coriolanus*, 1607-8, we recognize a meaning close to *personnage*.[12] He sometimes used, circa 1600, forms of the verb *personate*,[13] proposed by Florio to translate the Italian *personare*, "to personify" (1598). John Marston also did so in 1602 in *The History of Antonio and Mellida*, while Francis Bacon used *personation* in the sense of personification in 1622. All three writers thus endow *persona* with its literal meaning.

Forms

If we approach *personnage* in terms of its formal, functional, and virtual dimensions, we observe a slippage between the character of the written dramatic text, with open forms, according to the formula of Volker Klotz, and that of the performance, whose formal aspects are often closed off by its onstage interpretation, resulting in a loss of virtual potentiality.[14]

The word *personnage*, taken literally, refers first of all to masked acting, but it means more than "mask" since its complete source is *personam agere*; that is, to lead, to manage the mask, which refers to *agens*, the agent or actor. The *personnage* is thus seen as the principal "carrier of meaning." In fact, the relationship between the mask and its carrier was a subject of Hellenistic illustrations in which actors hold their mask in their hand and contemplate it as if to impregnate themselves with its character before wearing it.[15]

The scenic *personnage* is essentially a form constructed for performance. It only exists in reference to another form exterior to the text or the scene, even in the case of contemporary improvisation. Theater as we now know it has existed since spectators have understood that they were part of a convention and in the presence of a representation, not a presentation. Unlike in the mystery plays of old, actors no longer tried to make spectators believe that they were confronting their gods or ancestors, but rather *representations* of gods or ancestors—by agents or disguised actors wearing masks. The forms of the mask were a necessary step in differentiating between the pretend truth of ritual and the confessed verisimilitude of theater. The *personnage* of the dramatic text is an image analyzable in these terms; the *personnage* of the scenic text though is both an image and an image carrier that is capable, because he is essentially active, of manipulating the meaning of the acting.

The first *personnages* were of a trivial nature or form, born on fairground trestles erected at crossroads on market days. Customers were confronted with a generally crude representation arising from the wine harvest that the Greeks named "trugedy" [τρυγῳδια], "a truculent ode." "Trugedy" was often burlesque and remained so for the Etruscans: personifications of animals, clownery by banquet entertainers named "parasites"; performances by laughable "characters" (misers, cuckolds, serfs, masochists); apparitions from above in the form of lemurs and larva; that is, disembodied spirits. This last word, *larva*, monopolized the sense of mask, and perhaps Descartes was unaware of the burlesque aspect of the word *larvatus*, "disguised as larva (or spirits)," when he used it to describe his entrance on the world scene.

The form of *personnages* is closely tied to the form of the play in which they act. Patrice Pavis goes so far as to affirm that "they coincide with their speech . . . They take their meaning from their relative place in the actuary configuration."[16] But must we suppose that the form of a play derives necessarily from the political and social system that incites or allows it? Art sociologist Pierre Francastel affirms that "[p]ainting, art, and theater in all its forms visualizes for a certain time not only literary terms and legends but also social structures. It is not the form that creates the thought or the expression, but the thought, the expression of common social content of a period, that creates the form."[17] Francastel's vision coincides with the progressive emergence of dramatic forms, such as trugedy, tragedy, and comedy, which I present here in light of a revised etymology.

Tragedy [τραγῳδια], "an initiating ode," was born under the reign of the first tyrant, Cleisthenes, and entered the Great or City Dionysia during the last tyranny.[18] Tragedy presents aristocrats who consider themselves equal to gods and who cannot sin except by "excessive virtue," that is, by excessive power. An analogous social link exists in comedy [κωμῳδια], the "urban ode."[19] Comedy acquired respectability under the first democratic reign, denouncing citizens who violated civil rules and who sin by "excessive vice"; by weakness powerless to play their social role.[20] The same holds true of the drama that reappeared during the Enlightenment and which immediately set in parallel masters and servants in order to show that either one could be protagonists of high or low actions. Shakespeare, however, often escapes this formal categorization due to his tendency to include comic and even burlesque episodes in his tragedies according to an oppositional system. From one period to another, the formal aspects of characters seem to be marked by the forms of theater and the socio-political milieu into which characters are inserted.

In the eighteenth century, we find a strange character, Nemo, whose name means "nobody" or "no man," who challenges the socio-political forms of his time. Nemo, who appeared at the time of François Villon, was born of the imagination of law students of the Basoche; this character has the quality of having no qualities, despite being associated with contesting and transgressing forms due to his refusal of any reference to a known exterior form:

> "This 'character' born of the excessive use of negation reappeared frequently as an empty signifier that could be reinvested with new signs in the secular theater of the late Middle Ages where he was codified in a series of utopian demands. Primitively derived from a university prank, Nemo became the hero who gave hope to the deprived before being cleverly recuperated by humanists."[21]

This "nobody" seems to be the counterpart—and simultaneously the mirror image—of the character of Peter Van Diest, *Le Miroir de la félicité*, which surfaced in the Antwerp Chamber of Rhetoric in 1485 and was translated as *Everyman* in England and *Jedermann* in Germany. Whether they were nobody or everybody, these characters from a new genre were confronted with the choice of seeking or refusing to seek to enter the theater of the world. In Descartes' sense, the mask was the sign of a nomination.

88   Personnage: *History, Philology, Performance*

With the Renaissance, *personnage* often took the form imposed by the suggestion of a "character" or a fixed "type"—another word of typographic origin used to designate "characters." Commedia dell'arte, of course, had all these stock types, such as Ingenue, the young lover, the *senex iratus*, all the "zannis," *Jean-qui-pleure* and *Jean-qui-rit*, who played on public stages.

Next to these stock characters derived from improvisational playing, there were more subtle ones arising from new writing. On the French stage between 1550 and 1615, there were figures other than those of biblical inspiration. Numerous writers offered up "characters"; these included Claude Billard de Courgenay, Roland Brisset du Sauvage, George Buchanan, Cosme de Châteauvieux, François Du Souhait, Hélie Garel, Estienne Jodelle, Robert Garnier, Jacques Grévin, Jean de Hays, Pierre Mathieu, Anthoine de Montchrestien, Nicholas de Montreux, and Marc-Antoine Muret. Notably, they redrew portraits of historic and legendary couples, such as Albion and Rosamund, Clotaire and Radegund, Antony and Cleopatra, Massinissa and Sophonisba, Roland and Angélique, and Romeo and Juliet. They did not fear putting on stage political personalities as recent as the admirals André de Brancas and Gaspard de Coligny, the Dukes of Guise and Nemours, the kings and monarchs Edward and Elizabeth of England, Catherine de Medici, Henri III and Henri IV of France, and Mary Stuart of Scotland.

England would do the same. Some playwrights, such as John Bale, Robert Greene, Christopher Marlowe, and Shakespeare, also dared to write about kings such as Edward II, James I, John, Henry IV, V and VI, or Richard II and III. Buchanan, a Scot exiled for many years in France, staged the Queen, Mary Stuart. These writers recognized the relative closeness of "quality" and "character" of these characters to those of Antiquity; they also recognized in them a lineage derived from legendary royal and chivalric "characters": Gawain, Arthur, and Lancelot, as well as Charlemagne, Angélique, and Roland.

Next to these suggestions of heroes renowned for their historical and even mythic accomplishments, a tradition of "characters" developed. The genre begun by Theophrastus had been replaced by the *Lives* of Lucian of Samosata, a Roman-Syrian rhetorician of the Greek diaspora whose texts were used in college curricula and highlighted a particular trait in a character. In less than a decade, from 1572 to 1579, Charles Estienne's *Les Abusz*, Jean de la Taille's *Saül le furieux*, Jean de Larivey's *Le Jaloux* and *Le Morfondu*, and Pierre Le Loyer's *Le Muet insensé* all appeared. Ten years later, Roland Brisset translated *Baptiste, ou La Calomnie*, a neo-Latin play by George Buchanan. But it is possible that hiding behind this often moralizing practice was a ruse to justify the theater in social terms, especially since France was in the middle of its Wars of Religion (the St Bartholomew's Day massacre took place in August 1572).

Lucian's work must have been known to Shakespeare and his English contemporaries because he staged one of his "characters," the misanthrope Timon of Athens. Similar fixed characters appear in *The Taming of the Shrew* (c. 1593) and *The Merry Wives of Windsor* (c. 1596–7), but Shakespeare's characters do not have the fixedness of the miser in Plautus, the masochist in Terence, or the different stock types in commedia dell'arte. The fixed character nonetheless triumphed in Molière, who created *personnages* whose names referred to stock types that have now entered into language as common names: a Don Juan, a Harpagon, or a Tartuffe. For a period of twenty years, from 1653 to 1672, Molière's titles referred to a dozen different characteristics: jealousy, absent-mindedness, vexation, stylistic affectation, inappropriateness, imposture, Don Juanery, misanthropy, greed, gentlemanliness, treachery, and hypochondria.[22] He preceded Jean de La Bruyère's *Caractères* (1688) by twenty years.

The *personnages* evoked until now—except Nemo and his avatars—are often closed forms to the extent that they move within highly coded literary forms. These forms play significantly on the identification of the person with the *personnage*, rather than the inverse. Since Georg Büchner's *Woyzeck* (c. 1837), the contemporary *personnage* has leaned instead towards open forms more generally free from heavy literary conventions. There was indeed a period of epic forms susceptible, due to their succinctness, of better supporting the social function, but the current trend is rather towards the rupture of discourses and transfers between disciplines.

Functions

Antiquity left behind epics and myths that served as models for the first tragic *personnages*. Pottery, fresco paintings, mosaics, and sculptures from the period indicate that artists put forward a practice that contributed to defining visually the character of *personnages* by associating them with an animal or a symbolic object. The main *personnage* of the world's most ancient dramatic text, Gilgamesh, is represented as a symbolic lion; and Rabinal Achi, the most ancient *personnage* of the Americas, is associated with the figure of the Mayan king "Shield-Jaguar" of the city of Yaxchilan; this was a means of indicating their function.

In semiotics, we sometimes speak of the actantial functions of a text, which is a hypothesis that the text can be read like a structured sentence with a subject, an action, and an object.[23] Dramatic *personnages* thus appear in a network that can help clarify the line of action desired by the author. On stage, though, the *personnage* is not only acting but an actor, and sometimes he finds himself in a position to modify functions, to "interpret" them, or to suggest his own reading or that of the director.

Functions are related to forms. Tragedy, comedy, and, notably, drama, whose forms outlasted the situations that gave rise to their emergence, continue to offer a particular type of action to the subject / object relationship of their *personnages*. Authors and directors during a regime change have paid the price of a change in civil structures. For example, Aristophanes was obligated to excuse himself publicly for having imitated and ridiculed a politician in front of outsiders; *Tartuffe* was censored for doing the same to courtiers who supported Jesuit casuistry; Voltaire's *La Mort de César* was banned in Lower Canada because it defended the republican system. Of course, Shakespeare was not forbidden from staging the death of English kings, but his *personnages* did not have the function of denouncing the monarchical system.

Let us examine three functions specific to the very notion of *personnage*: making images, supporting the action, and doubling.

Aristotle's function of mimesis [μιμησις] translates as "to make an image" rather than "to imitate," although both words are from the same root. Today actors are trained to construct a *personnage* and they find themselves working towards the imaginary rather than mere imitation. Today's theater is certainly an art of representation, but in the sense that it presents the spectator with a postponed, reconstructed real, and not a simulacra or a false-resemblance. Antonin Artaud refuted the idea that theater was a double or an ersatz version of life; for him it is actually a new manifestation, as if it was theater that found in life its own double. Aristotle's notion of "verisimilitude" is often confused by readers with an idea about pretending to be like life. Today actors never pretend to be other than themselves. They pretend not to be kings or gods but rather the revived image of kings and gods; spectators know this since they know actors by their name. The Greek and Latin terms from which we acquired "image" and "imitation" can equally signify a *persona*, phantasm or ghost of the stage. This imitation or reflection often tells us more about reality than reality itself. As Henri Bergson wrote: "Art has no other object than to set aside practically useful symbols, conventionally and socially accepted generalities, and anything that hides reality in order to place us face to face with reality itself."[24]

Modernists and surrealists have raised important questions about figurative painting. Some advocate ways of giving the scenic painting a third dimension; others demand room for a new dimension—that of the unconscious. For example, one could evoke literary cubism, the rupture of linear sentences begun by Guillaume Apollinaire in his plays *L'Enchanteur pourrissant* (1909) or *Les Mamelles de Tirésias* (1917). One could also mention the automatism of Claude Gauvreau and the "dramatic objects" of his *Les Entrailles*, short plays in which acoustic images have as much importance as visual images.[25] Both challenged figuration and the construction of the *personnage* as much as the scenery. Samuel Beckett also gave us *personnages* without character, moving in *Endgame* according to a paradoxical interpretation of Aristotelian rules of non-action, non-time, and non-place.[26]

The second function, support of the action, is tied to the notion of *personnage* as a motor of action, as a *personam agens*. It is simultaneously mask and support of the mask, *prosôpon* and *hypostasis*. It is the motor and the mobility of this action, hence the name *actor*. The *personnage* is programmed, engraved with a character, but the actor is the agent of this program that he must complete. For the spectator, the actor is a metaphor or a metonymy of a god, a man or an animal, through his costume, his gestures, and his voice. He is thus a living sign, an auto-motor.

In the theater, the audience is faced with a living spectacle whose *personnages* are not reducible to cartoons. It is certainly not in this sense that one could speak of "virtuality." They are signs, but in the broad sense of "character," which is why philosophers from the second and third centuries borrowed *hypocrite*, or rather *hypostasis*, as an analogy of the person, seat of the action and of the reason that determines the action. In fact, Hannah Arendt wrote, without a direct allusion to theater but in borrowing its terminology, that "the act only takes on a meaning through the speech in which the agent identifies himself as an actor."[27] In one way or another, the art of *hypocrite*, to designate the actor's work by its Greek name, is often perceived as the misrepresentation of the real by a lie. Theater, for those who do not see in some *personnages* who incarnate evil a suggestion for good by inversion, is often perceived as fabrication, even false representation, whereas it is actually action, as is still suggested by the name of Spanish mystery plays (*auto sacramental* in which *auto* means *act*) used to designate the main division of Western plays.

The third function is the doubling of the *personnage*. The *personnage* can be approached from the point of view of metatheatricality, acting to the second degree. This type of acting brings a perceptible distance in the double disguise when not only the *agens*, the actor, hides behind the *persona*, but the *persona* itself hides behind another. In the Romantic stratagem of recognition, one finds in the other a father, a lost child. But we also find a doubling split in conflicts about social condition, in the trickery of gods, and disguised princes whose doubling is often known to the audience. In Hellenistic theater, for example, the incarnate gods were identifiable by their white mask.[28] Disguises are part of Marivaux's proceedings in *Le Jeu de l'amour et du hasard* (1730) with the premonitory role change between masters and servants.

Doubling is only one way to place the *personnage* in front of himself, and to provoke this consciousness of individuality and the relationship of the self to the self that is at the origin of personhood. Metatheatrical doubling was already part of Greek tragedy when *personnages* like Oedipus were unaware of themselves, or in comedy when an author like Aristophanes staged other authors like Aeschylus and Euripides in *The Clouds* (247 BCE). This reflexivity can be found in Terence's *Heauton Timorumenos (The Self-Torturer)* (163 BCE) with this thought on the *personnage* of the person: "I am man and nothing human is foreign to me." The secularity of the *personnage* can be found in many forms in Shakespeare's works—notably *Hamlet*, not only in the scene with the traveling actors to whom Hamlet gives advice about playing, but also in the scenes with the Ghost of his father and in his thoughts on the skull of the royal fool.

The dramatic literature of Québec consists of some works that put a *personnage* in *mise en abyme*, such as Normand Chaurette's *Provincetown Playhouse, juillet 1919, j'avais 19 ans* (1981) or Michel Marc Bouchard's *Lilies [Les Feluettes, ou la Répétition d'un drame romantique]* (1988). There are also plays in which authors become *personnages*, such as André Gagnon and Michel Tremblay's *Nelligan* (1990), and Jovette Marchessault's *Saga of the Wet Hens [La Saga des poules mouillées]* (1981).[29] This phenomenon of ancient authors inscribed as *personnages* in recent works is a sign of maturity, both from the point of view of the writing and that of Québécois culture in general. The phenomenon allows the playwright to take a step back from his own works and at the same time allows the spectator to situate the *personnages* in the repertory.

Virtualities

When the *personnage* moves from the dramatic text to the scenic text, there is a passage from the latent to the patent, from the implicit to the explicit. In the construction of the *personnage*, nothing is absolutely predetermined by the author, no matter what the lines and the precepts, except some inescapable actantial functions. Virtuality is what Volker Koltz calls an open form.

The staging of a text is a "reading."[30] One can, for instance, imagine a *Hamlet* that is romantic in its love relationship, reformist in its vision of the kingdom, existentialist in its reflection on being, oedipal in its relationship to the mother; and one can give the play as many different orientations to which the text is open. The author's text offers virtual forms that only become real on stage, that are only actualized by the actor, by virtue of certain choices.

What is true about the relationship of the actor to the *personnage* and to *personnages* among themselves is also true of the relationship of *personnages* to the space, since the transition from virtual to real also takes place from dramatic space to scenic space. In reading Paul Claudel's *The Satin Slipper* [*Le Soulier de satin*] (1929), one can imagine many Spanish castles, even though there would be only one on stage, unless practicable scenery is used, as was the case in Jean-Louis Barrault's production in Montréal in 1967, in which the scenography reserved a power of virtuality and each spectator could build his own mental castle.

Moreover, as Gilbert Turp has observed, a "third space of theatricality" is created between the real spaces of the stage and the audience, and this third space is only perceivable at the moment of production:

> Since art allows us to understand an affective experience, the envelopment of the theatre constitutes . . . the third space of theatricality, by analogy with the third genre of knowledge of Spinoza. It is the space in which the affective attachment operates. It is a chaotic space, a field of energy in which an infinity of affects circulates. It is a space of desire, the space in which knowledge enters our very body.[31]

In effect, the actor, "the mask wearer," is master of the "character" whose role has been given to him. When he learns this role, he prepares in relation to a presumed, ideal spectator. The spectator enters the theater with more or less conscious expectations about the *personnage* with whom he will be in contact. Throughout the show, however, both must mentally and physically negotiate the performance, each journeying part way into the no man's land between the stage and the audience:

> Plato also speaks of a third space, the *chora*, that is neither the space of the speaker nor the space of the performance, but a surface-space, an imprinted-space marked by affects that recall and remember; a memory-space.

The third space is . . . the perceptible body onto which all theatrical affect imprints itself. The first work to be done when we do theatre is to arouse this belonging to the third space by opening in the performance a depth that can envelop the stage, the theatre, the actors, and the spectators.[32]

The professional actor will not stumble easily from the construction of the *personnage* that was agreed upon during the rehearsal, but in theater everything is a convention; that is, an agreement which is constantly negotiated between the stage and the audience. In any case, even the actors often negotiate their text according to the director's readings and the audience's reception.

The mask of words

The *personnage*, especially in tragedy, is born from the personification of dead people and their gods, gods who are perceived as strays searching for a *hypostasis* or a *hypocrite*. The *personnage* thus moved from the status of a typical mask and its support to that of the atypical unmasked actor whom we find in Beckett's works. "Characters," for their part, undoubtedly date from the beginnings of the stage, but we know when masks, make-up, and costumes fixed certain famous traits. Theater is obviously not the only art to have recourse to "characters," but theater is the only art to confide the personification to an intermediary actor. In contemporary theater, this acting gives us many rewritings of plays. *Antigone* and *Electra* are plays and *personnages* that are renegotiated across the centuries in relation to new actions and receptions.

Contemporary theater has constantly tested the dramatization and theatricalization of the *personnage*. Some of the most convincing examples can be found in *Endgame*. The audience could well wish to negotiate the action, but the play is so paradoxical that it literally respects the classical conventions at the same time that it is true to none. In the third virtual space where, for such a play, conventions are negotiated, the audience confronts non-*personnages* (they are "nobody") in a non-action in a non-place in a non-time. It is a perfect unity in the absence of any conventional unity, without any possible recourse to the protection of the predetermined or the hallowed costume. The *personnages*, even those of ancestors enclosed in their amphora, like with the Etruscans, are presented in all their nudity and all their human frailty.

A new philological approach has dissected the original meaning of the words *personnage* and *character*. The present sense of a word cannot owe anything to its past: the word *spirit*, which today signifies that what is immaterial, used to mean in Sanskrit, Greek, and Latin *breath*, which is material and measurable. In examining ancient texts like those of Shakespeare, it is essential to know the discursive context that produced and continues to produce these words. According to Ferdinand de Saussure, the entrance into a language resembles the entrance into a game of chess that has already begun; one knows where the pieces are but not where they came from. The linguist concedes to the departing player the privilege of having had strategic intentions, but in the spatio-temporal movement of a language, writers also have creative intentions.[33] Remarkably, all the words discussed here have moved from a first meaning to a metaphorical meaning by modifying the movement: *character, personnage, trait, truculent, type, style*. The actor who gives an innovative face to his *personnage* is also a creator of meaning: he must take the *personnage* where the author placed him and make him move. The actor and the *personnage* function as in in the initial self image that Descartes and Shakespeare gave us; they advance on the stage of the world with the costume, the theater, and the scenery that are provided to them, without really knowing what happened before the fragment of history whose role was confided to them, while still hoping to play their role well and in keeping with the way this moment of life will unfold in front of the public. André Bourassa's essay was translated from the original French by Jennifer Drouin.

Notes

1. Translated from René Descartes, *Premier Registre*, in *Oeuvres*, ed. Charles E. Adam and Paul Tannery (Paris, Vrin: 1996), X, 213.
2. All Shakespeare quotes are from *The Riverside Shakespeare*, 2nd ed., textual editor G. Blakemore Evans (Boston: Houghton Mifflin, 1997).
3. For "amphitheatrum," see Charles Scribanus, *Amphitheatrum honoris in quo Calvinistrarum in Societatem Iesu criminationes iugulatae* (Tongres, formerly *Palaeopoli Aduaticorum* (Belgium): Verheyden, 1606); for "globe," see Simon Girault, *Globe du monde* (Langres: Des Preyz, 1592).
4. The infinitive *personare* means "to personate, to act or play the part of any person," according to John Florio, *Queen Anna's New World of Words, or Dictionarie of the Italian and English Tongues* (London, 1611).
5. From *farcio*, to stuff, to cram. An Etruscan inscription links *farsus* to mask.
6. "*Sine personis atque tempoiribus*" [without regard for persons or circumstances]. Cicero, *De Oratore / On the Making of an Orator* I–II, trans. E. W. Sutton (Cambridge, MA: Harvard University Press, 1959), 134.
7. See Maurice Nédoncelle, "*Prosopon et persona dans l'antiquité classique: Essai de bilan linguistique*," *Revue des Sciences Religieuses*, 22 (1948), 277–99.
8. See Roger D. Haight, *Jesus: Symbol of God* (New York: Orbis Books, 1999).

9. As in *"gerere personam civitatis"* [to represent the state], in Cicero, *De Oficiis*, trans. Walter Miller (Cambridge, MA: Harvard University Press, 1961), 126–27.
10. Marcel and Claude de Grève, "Caractère / Character; Feature," *Dictionnaire International des Termes Littéraires* <http://www.ditl.info/art/definition.php?term=1160>.
11. "I do conjure thee / Who art the table wherein all my thoughts / Are visibly character'd and engrav'd." *The Two Gentlemen of Verona*, 2.7.2–4.
12. "I paint him in the character," *Coriolanus*, 5.4.26.
13. *Twelfth Night* (2.3), which was performed in 1602; *Timon of Athens* (1.1) (1607); *Cymbeline* (5.5) (1612).
14. Volker Klotz, *Geschlossene und offene Form im Drama* [Closed and Open Form in Drama] (Munich: Hanser, 1960).
15. See André G. Bourassa and Frédéric Kantorowski, *Chronologie générale du théâtre* <http://www.theatrales.uqam.ca/chronologie/chrono2.html>.
16. Patrice Pavis, *Dictionnaire du théâtre* (Paris: Messidor / Éditions sociales, 1987), 175.
17. Pierre Francastel, *La Réalité figurative* (Paris: Gonthier, 1965), 237–38.
18. See Paulo Scarpi, *Le religioni dei misteri* (Milan: Mondadori, 2002), vol. 1.
19. See Henry G. Liddle and Robert Scott, *Lexicon: Abridged from Greek-English Lexicon* (London: Oxford University Press, 1963), 402, 719. The term "comedy" is thus related to kwmoi, farandole, a Provençal dance.
20. Pierre Berthiaume, *"Trugoidia: le chant de la lie. À propos de la fonction sociale de la comédie ancienne,"* *L'Annuaire théâtral*, 15 (1994), 22–33.
21. Jelle Koopsmans and Paul Verhuyck, *Sermon joyeux et truanderie (Villon—Nemo—Ulespiègle)* (Amsterdam: Rodopi, 1987), 6.
22. *A Jealous Husband* [*La Jalousie du barbouillé*], *The Scatterbrain* [*L'Étourdi*] (c. 1653–54), *A Lovers' Quarrel* [*Le Dépit amoureux*] (1656), *Affected Young Ladies* [*Les Précieuses ridicules*] (1659), *The Nuisances* [*Les Fâcheux*] (1661), *Tartuffe* [*Tartuffe*, ou *L'Imposteur*] (1664), *Don Juan* (1665), *The Misanthrope* [*Le Misanthrope*, ou *L'Atrabilaire amoureux*] (1666), *The Miser* [*L'Avare*] (1668), *The Would-Be Gentleman* [*Le Bourgeois gentilhomme*] (1670), *Scapin's Schemings* [*Les Fourberies de Scapin*] (1671), *The Hypochondriac* or *The Imaginary Invalid* [*Le Malade imaginaire*] (c. 1672–73).
23. Some analysts established an absolute system that Gremias presented as a research intuition: "hypothesis of an actantial model envisioned as one of the possible principles of the organisation of the semantic universe . . . If we wanted to question the possible uses, as a structuring hypothesis, of this operational model, we would have to start by one observation: wanting to compare the syntactical categories to the inventories of [Vladimir] Propp and [Étienne] Souriau obliged us to consider the relationship between the subject and the object . . . as a more specialized relationship consisting of a heavier semic investment of 'desire', transforming, at the level of demonstrated functions, into 'quest.'" Algirdas J. Greimas, *Sémantique structurale* (Paris: Larousse, 1966), 174, 180–81.
24. Henri Bergson, *L'évolution créatrice* (Paris: PUF, 2001), 120.
25. See Ferdinand de Saussure, *Cours de linguistique générale*, ed. Tullio de Muro (Paris: Payot et Rivages, 1995), 32.

26. See Gérard Piacentini, "*Le référent philosophique comme caractère du personnage dans le théâtre de Samuel Beckett,*" *Revue d'histoire du théâtre* 42 (1990): 323–70, esp. 357.
27. Hannah Arendt, *Condition de l'homme moderne* (Paris: Calmann-Lévy, 1988), 235.
28. Bourrassa and Kantorowski, <http://www.theatrales.uqam.ca/chronologie/Phlyaques3.html>.
29. André G. Bourassa, "*Quand les poètes deviennent personages,*" *Lettres québécoises* 26 (1982): 46–48.
30. Bertolt Brecht, *Petit Organon pour le théâtre*, suivi de *Additifs au Petit Organon* (Paris: L'Arche, 1978), 92.
31. Gilbert Turp, "*Le troisième lieu de la théâtralité: Essai sur la représentation de l'immanence et l'expérience affective de la connaissance,*" *L'Annuaire théâtral* 19–20 (1996), 24–71, quote at 32.
32. Turp, "*Le troisième lieu de la théâtralité,*" 34.
33. Saussure, "*Cours de linguistique générale,*" 127.

5
The Properties of Character in *King Lear*

James Berg

> I wepte much, because no man was found worthy to open and to reade the Booke, neither to looke thereon.
> *Revelation 5:4*[1]

How can we best capture what "character" meant to Shakespeare? Consider a description, in *King Lear*, of the letter-carrier Oswald by Lear's loyal servant Kent, now playing the part of the letter-carrier Caius: "What dost thou know me for?" asks Oswald. Kent replies:

> A knave, a rascal, an eater of broken meats; a base, proud, shallow, beggarly, three-suited, hundred-pound, filthy, worsted-stocking knave; a lily-livered, action-taking knave, a whoreson, glass-gazing, super-serviceable, finical rogue; one-trunk inheriting slave; one that wouldst be a bawd in way of good service, and art nothing but the composition of a knave, beggar, coward, pander, and the son and heir of a mongrel bitch, one whom I will beat into clamorous whining if thou deniest the least syllable of thy addition.
>
> (II.ii.13–21)[2]

In its lexical emphasis, this description of Oswald harks back to the Renaissance sense of character as "the fashion of a letter, mark, or stamp"—though it is not to be confused with the slightly later seventeenth-century revival of the ancient Theophrastan "character sketch."[3] Kent is not *writing* character; he is *reading* character already written. He is *declaiming* (literally "shouting away"), copying in sound what nature has already shouted away in things ("nature disclaims in thee" [II.ii.48]). For Kent, Oswald is already character; some thing, or set of things, waiting to be parsed in syllables. Kent confirms Oswald's status a few lines later by calling him a "whoreson zed," an "unnecessary letter" (II.ii.55). The letters that might comprise words, however, are only metaphors for the elements of Oswald, whom Kent is rendering in syllables through fierce declamation. Some of Oswald would today be called objects: orts, suits, stockings, mirror, and trunk. Those are not all the elements of his character, of course. There are also his attributes: rascal, knave, whoreson, rogue, beggar, coward, and pander. But because everything about him is *reading material* for Kent, the distinction between *Eigenschaft* (property as in "characteristic") and *Eigentum* (property as in "possession") falls away, as do legal distinctions between kinds of things owned.[4] Possessions themselves become character: they are symbolic. Their joining together in a relation of belonging occurs as Kent sounds them out, and this relation constitutes Oswald's "addition," which constitutes Oswald, whose very character is property—stuff comparable to the most important kind of stage property there was for Shakespeare. As Kent adds, "a tailor made thee" (II.ii.55)

In *King Lear*, all "character" is like that. All character *is* property, where property represents not just what persons seem to own, but the *things* that properly belong *with* them. And all property is character, symbolic *reading material*. Of course, I am generalizing from a feeble example. Kent is talking about a shallow and unnecessary letter-carrier, not character with depth—not his beloved Lear, not the noble Edgar, not the true Cordelia, not himself. But feebleness at the core of formidable persons is for me the play's central theme: these persons are, at bottom, versions of Oswald, though the bottom is harder to sound in some than in others. When the soundings stop, the play has helped us to feel what it is like to be the stuff of an Oswald in the shape of a Lear—a collection of symbolic belongings. Contrary to what it may speak, such character can never effectively deny its addition. Once character, consisting of belongings, is sounded out, it cannot be *un*-sounded out, changed though its subsequent impressions may be. "Does any here know me? This is not Lear" (I.iv.185), insists the king when he thinks his land is no longer attached to him because he has surrendered ownership. Edgar, dispossessed of his inheritance, says "Edgar I nothing am" (II.iii.21). Neither statement is true; the old man and his kingdom divided are the character comprising Lear. The firstborn son of a great landowner and his stolen inheritance and his disguise as Poor Tom are the character comprising Edgar. True, Edgar does not comprehend his character. But read in context it amounts to Edgar, Edgar's denial attesting to the limits of his lexical prowess.

Many studies of Shakespearean impersonation rely on a later and more immediately literary and person-related understanding of "character" than my logic assumes. Leanore Lieblein's chapter in this volume, for instance, associates Shakespearean character with the seventeenth-century Theophrastan character sketch, and with Thomas Heywood's description of the performed role as "person personated." Such beginnings can produce brilliant results. But also to be considered, in the context of Shakespeare, is a sense of "character" as any *thing* in the world (not just on a page or stage) to be *read*—a sense prevalent in English before the revival of Theophrastus, yet also recalling the ancient Greek χαρακτήρ (engraved mark), which came, especially in English, to mean "letter" or "figure."[5] Admittedly, the rubric to which I refer is broad; from the providentialist perspectives that repeatedly captured Shakespeare's interest, such "character" could encompass all Creation, not just fictional persons. Still, it is crucial to the liveliness of Shakespeare's impersonations, since it implies a reading consciousness: "subjectivity," as it were, parsing *properties* and *persons* syntactically, determining how they *belong* and *make sense* together. The conning of lines and rehearsing of plays on the Jacobean stage no doubt involved a similar struggle writ small, facilitating thespian triumphs of verisimilitude—the struggle by an actor to comprehend a *part* or *role* in terms of the unknown *whole* of a play shadows the larger dilemma of reading one's life. For character *not* on stage, character *in life*, to read itself in the context of its properties—parsing itself amidst the syntax of *things*—would be an impossible contortion. That does not, however, rule out the tragically self-assertive (or self-dismantling) struggle to do so.

Understanding character in this way allows us again to appreciate the wonder of many of Shakespeare's impersonations in the process of reading them as expressions of material history.[6] Margreta de Grazia rightly and brilliantly reads *King Lear* as an "anti-early-modern" text that "blocks the mobility identified since the nineteenth century with the Modern—through its locking of persons into things, proper selves into property." Yet she insists that her focus on "objects" yields insights radically different than would a focus on "character." "When character is dominant, Gloucester's plight seems more like Lear's: both old men are suffering at the hands of their children. Once objects are admitted . . . Edgar's story makes a more compelling counterpart: both men are detached from their possessions."[7] Subjected to the rigors of materialist history, it seems, *King Lear* differs in its very structure from the *King Lear* known to students of character. As I shall propose, however, character in the *Shakespearean* sense is inseparable from the play's representation of deep "historical actants" and "cultural formations"—from its apprehension of a post-"feudal" crisis in property relations as expressed in its treatment of what we call "objects."[8]

My argument will amount to more, I hope, than a trick of definition. For despite large differences, the "character" I have identified has much in common with the "character" that names literary impersonation.[9] True, in Shakespeare's time, a "character" did not necessarily correspond, in a one-to-one ratio, to an individual impersonation. A single body could feature many characters, as when Marlowe's Tamburlaine says to Theridimas, "Art thou but captain of a thousand horse, / That by characters graven in thy brows, / And by thy martial face and stout aspect, / Deserv'st to have the leading of an host?"[10] But such examples have much to tell us about the composition of modern literary character. Modern characters in books, after all, are no more individuals than Shakespeare's "character." The very term "character" threatens to reveal that they *are* text, "elements of a linguistic structure, lines in a drama, and, more basically, words on a page," as Stephen Orgel puts it.[11]

One might see such literally textual character as an offshoot of the kind of character constituting the larger text of Creation. As seventeenth-century physician Thomas Browne says, "There are mystically in our faces certaine characters . . . wherein he that cannot read A, B, C, may read our natures." This is because "[T]he finger of God hath left an inscription upon *all* his workes, not graphicall, or composed of letters, but of their severall formes, constitutions, parts, and operations."[12] The concept to which Browne refers surely has roots in the hermeneutical habit of reading *res*, as well as *verba*, allegorically—a tradition dating back to Augustine, who applied it in his insistence that the very *things* described in the "Old Testament" figured what was in the New.[13] This habit was pervasive in the seventeenth century; in his illness, poet and preacher John Donne says to his God, "Neither art thou . . . a *figurative, metaphoricall God* in thy word only, but in thy workes too. The *stile* of thy works, the *phrase* of thine actions, is *metaphoricall*."[14] From such a perspective, the world is not only stage but text—all "objects" stage properties, all persons impersonations, all persons *and* things *character*, the stuff of signification. Yet if being character means being grouped with *things*, it does not mean being an unsympathetic "object" (it is thanks to the poststructuralist emptying out of the signifier that we are prone to see signifying material, even when human, as unfeeling, or lacking a "self"). The sentient sign—the reading consciousness that must suffer itself to be read in the context of its things, is *pathetic* in the truest sense of the word. "To be a slave," according to Lisa Freinkel, "is to be a sign." The things described in the Old Testament (including persons) are slaves to the things in the New.[15] On the Jacobean stage, Shakespeare emphasized that *things* were character, that persons were among them, and that the inscrutable intention of Providence determined how, where, and when they might belong to each other. "Symbolic economies" and "material economies" were "inextricably intertwined."[16]

So if a modern novelist elicits empathy for characters by hiding that they consist of character, Shakespeare elicits empathy through the close-up experience of what it is like to *be* character, aware that one's substance is stuff of signification and striving vainly, through divestments of belongings, to read it. "There is a kind of character in thy *life*," as Vincentio says to Angelo in *Measure for Measure*, "[t]hat to *th'observer* doth thy history / Fully unfold. Thyself and thy belongings / Are not thine own so proper, as to waste / Thyself upon thy virtues, they on thee."[17] In *King Lear*, staged a year later, the character in life is precisely what, perhaps in reaction to the commodification occurring around Shakespeare's theater, locks "persons into things, proper selves into property."[18] This character consists of persons *and* belongings, as the person of Kent is inseparable from the land of Kent, the person of Albany from the land of Albany. In such a context, the movement of property—the bestowal of coxcombs, the alienation of land, the disbursement of goods, the endowment and marrying off of children, the shaking of the "superflux" of royal pomp to the poor to "show the heavens more just" (III.iv.35–36)—is a declamation of the character of persons and things in the form not only of speech but also of action, a parsing, or sounding out, of the character of things *in action* to communicate meaning. But persons, embedded in what they hope to declaim, cannot do the parsing. Without comprehension, try though they may to declaim by disclaiming (as Lear does when he divides his kingdom), they cannot sound out the text in which they are written. The "disowner" of belongings acts only as character on paper speaks, by a predetermined ventriloquism from beyond the text. Confining neither person to the category of "subject," nor belongings to the category of "object,"[19] the movement of property in *King Lear* reveals both person and belongings as constituting character, the pathetic linguistic sign, conscious, at best, that it is a sign but too deeply embedded in the Providential text of things to grasp itself. This discovery is indeed worthy of great tragedy; St John the Divine, as the epigraph of this chapter indicates, wept over the impossibility of reading *things*, a task requiring the help of Christ.

As critics observe, in fact, images from St John's vision—its eclipses, heavy precipitation, and shifting of real estate forcing kings and great men to hide in "dennes"—pervade *King Lear*.[20] In quoting Revelation,

I would add, the play reproduces St John's lexical perspective on history, which treats as a declamatory reading, by the "Lamb" of God, the very courses of events that blossom with the breaking of the seals of the great scroll of judgment.[21] Where Revelation imagines the unscrolling of *things*, Shakespeare's famously apocalyptic tragedy imagines property movement as unfolding. Frequently, the revelatory images involve sartorial dismantling, from Lear's metaphor for the division of his kingdom ("now we will divest us both of rule, interest of territory, cares of state" [f.I.i.45]); to Edgar's rifling the pockets of Oswald's corpse for letters; to Lear's final "pray you, undo this button" (V.iii.283), a tiny gesture of unfolding, before he dies. As if to help spectators identify the lexical connotations of its unfoldings, the play relies, for the structure of its plot, on the circulation of hand-written letters, most of which are unfolded and read onstage, creating analogies with the expropriative transactions they accompany. "To know our enemies minds," says Edgar, about to open a letter intercepted from Regan, "we rip their hearts. / Their papers is more lawful" (IV.v.248–49).

Understood in this context, Lear's division of the kingdom itself reveals profound lexical associations. Like the Lamb's declamation in Revelation, Lear's division is a public reading, and in positioning himself as declaimer, as parser of lands with daughters and sons-in-law into a statement of love, he asserts Providential lexical authority. In commanding a *speaking* of total love of *himself*, he has less interest in finding out who loves him most than in showing how effectively he has deciphered this meaning. He will be the one to make sense out of his daughters by characterizing them with land: "Which of you shall *we say* doth love us most, / That we our largest bounty may extend / Where nature doth with merit challenge? Gonerill, our eldest born, *speak* first" (I.i.47–49).[22] The verbs cast the extension of bounty as equivalent to *saying*. Lear himself will "say" his daughters' natures; *his* reading will *be* the extension of bounty, sounding out meaning by parsing bounty with person.[23]

Emblematic of such lexical expropriation—alienation of property as explication of character—is the casting of the division as a distribution of dowries. The dowry that "comes with" the bride corroborates Lévi-Strauss's notorious estimation of bride as token of exchange.[24] To endow one's daughter with a portion is to assert her one-ness with the portion, yet also to remove the portion from her control. The dowry is a qualifier that, translated into Gonerill and Regan's speech, *modifies* them: "of all these bounds, even from this line to this . . . we make thee lady" (I.i.58–61). Lear *makes* Gonerill "lady" by modifying her with real estate, which also turns her into one of his providers, with "champagnes riched" (I.i.60) and "plenteous rivers" (I.i.59). Endowments thus articulate a daughter's character—what she *is* and what she *says*—when put in motion. Nor do such endowments merely consist of commodities. Cordelia's response of "nothing" (I.i.82–84) to her father's challenge, "What can you say to draw / A third more opulent than your sisters?" (I.i.80–81) does not lose her all endowment. That is apparent not only in the language Lear uses to cast her off to Burgundy ("dowered with our curse" [I.i.198]), but also in the language with which France responds:

> Is it but this? A tardiness in nature
> Which often leaves the history unspoke
> That it intends to do? My Lord of Burgundy,
> What say you to the lady? Love's not love
> When it is mingled with regards that stands
> Aloof from th'entire point. Will you have her?
> She is herself a dowry.
>
> (I.i.230–36)

France indeed sees Cordelia as endowment, politely offering Burgundy a last chance to "have" her. What, then, *is* "the entire point" from which Burgundy's love that is "not love" stands "aloof"? Cordelia's capacity as property to characterize her husband and the land with whom and with which she is to belong—"Queen of us, of ours, of our fair France." Through action, nature declaims in her. As character she will signify in *deed*, not word, since nature "often leaves the *history* unspoke that it intends to *do*." "Nor are those empty-hearted," as Kent says earlier, "whose low sounds reverb no hollowness" (I.i.146–48). No re-verbing. No re-iterating nature (God's language) in words.

Lear's frustration with non-verbal charactering contradicts his very agenda in dividing the kingdom. He pretends to declaim not just words but things. What can it mean that he says, from the start, "we have divided / in three our kingdom" (I.i.32–33) when the division is *about* to take place; that the play opens with Kent and Gloucester's conversation about the division (I.i.1–6) *before* Lear has publicly parsed the territories; and that Lear has reserved, for Cordelia, a "third more opulent" than "her sisters" (I.i.80–81) *before* she speaks? Such enigmas advertise Lear's ability to read *things*: he purports *already* to know which lands belong with whom, and so already to know what the daughters speak, collectively, when properly parsed—that Cordelia's nature challenges with most merit; that she loves Lear most.[25] The kingdom Lear divides has allegedly already parsed, already sounded out daughters' love. The "contrived" or "staged" feel of the contest enhances this illusion; what the superb notes in the Cambridge edition call "the pretence of the contest," is actually, I think, the pretence of *no* contest. "Speak," Lear commands a character (I.i.49, 81), for he has already parsed her; seen which destined livery of land suits her: "shadowy forests . . . champains riched . . . plenteous rivers and wide-skirted meads" (I.i.59–60). Lear advertises, *avant la lettre,* the paradox of the hermeneutic circle: the daughters' speech paraphrases the *whole* of Lear's statement, that which "we" shall "say"; the lands and daughters are the character he reads, fragments of his statement, whose proper joining brings them to life to speak the whole. To make the character speak, one must know how the kingdom parses; to know how the kingdom parses, one must know what the character says. Lear casts all speaking as repeat performance reflecting prior grasp not just of the things belonging to him but of what they *mean.* "We have this hour a constant will to *publish* / Our daughters' several dowers" (I.i.38–39). In its supposed redundancy, the love "test" is syntactical analysis—explication of something already declaimed via parsing of lands.

From this parsing Lear tries to inoculate himself, casting it as a semiosis of everything (the kingdom) and everyone (Albany, Cornwall, Gonerill, Regan, Cordelia, France) *except himself.* In the first words of the play, even Kent is confused about how to read Lear, evidently shaken in his notion that "the king had more affected"—had more natural attachment to—"the Duke of Albany than Cornwall" (I.i.1–2). For "now," Gloucester adds, "*in* the division of the kingdom"—*in* the articulation of land, the act-speech that *says* "which of the dukes he values most"—"qualities are so weighed that curiosity in neither can make choice of either's moiety" (I.i.3–6). *In* the division is a statement of the qualities, a *characterismus,* of the Dukes. But Lear remains safely illegible, evidently separate from such parsing. Gloucester discusses "the division of the kingdom" in the passive, with phrasing that obfuscates its perpetrator's status as character. Lear's use of the royal "we," from his first appearance (I.i.31) exactly until the moment he collides with Cordelia's "nothing" ("Here I disclaim all my paternal care, propinquity and property of blood" [I.i.107–8]), has a similar effect. "Know that we have divided in three our kingdom" (1.1.3–4). Who is this "we"? The pronoun casts the divider as unattachable to any human time or body. In the words, "while we / Unburdened, crawl towards death" (I.i.35–36) are connotations of multiplicity in the famous dictum, "the king is dead; long live the king," which, in turn, associates the dividing agency with the aeveternal scope of providential history.[26]

Cordelia's obtrusive failure to speak what Lear thinks he has figured out in land undermines his pretense to have parsed *things*, in "actions real," prior to verbal translation. It brings to the fore the devastating question haunting the parsing-test from the start: if Lear has already declaimed the character constituting his daughters by parsing daughters with lands, why the translation into words? Why not let things speak for themselves? Gonerill and Regan, humoring Lear's delusion that he has parsed *things*, try to make their speech look as if it extended beyond words. Gonerill puts the inadequacy of words *into* words ("Sir, I love you more than word can wield the matter . . . a love that makes breath poor, and speech unable"[I.i.50–55]); Regan says Gonerill "names" her "very deed" of love, apparently devoting her whole body or life ("the most precious square of sense") to her father (I.i.66–69). But Cordelia's "nothing" *truly* lets things speak for themselves.[27] What *can* she say to "draw" the opulent third of the thing represented on Lear's map? She can declaim no *thing*; she can only declaim words, indicating the thing that is her "bond," letting it characterize itself: "I love your majesty according to my bond, no more nor less" (I.i.87–88). The grotesque image she uses to describe the thing-speech expected of her ("unhappy that I am, I cannot heave my heart into my mouth"[I.i.85–86]), suggests she has endowments that will speak, but *she* cannot be the agent of their speech, nor can Lear be this by parsing them with land. Such things (land and hearts) take more time to speak than Lear allots for words. The fact of incompletion is one of the most important, and neglected, points Cordelia makes. Note the obtrusive enjambments, particularly the one that divides her "I" in time:

> Good my lord,
> You have begot me, bred me, loved me, I
> Return those duties back as are right fit,
> Obey you, love you, and most honor you.
> Happily, when I shall wed,
> That Lord whose hand must take my plight shall carry
> Half my love with him, half my care and duty.
> Sure I shall never marry like my sisters.
>
> (I.i.89–98)

For *now* Cordelia obeys, loves, and honors her father wholly, not because of his command but because this behavior signifies his fulfillment of his paternal duties; again she points to her bond. Then she provides a tentative scenario (the possibility of marrying a man who captures her devotion) to show why she can say no more. The meaning of "Happily" is "by hap" or—better yet—"providentially" (as the wordplay connoting "in happiness" suggests). The operation of the orbs, incomprehensible to Cordelia or to Lear, will articulate *things*—Cordelia and her heart, her husband's "hand," "the vines of France," the "milk of Burgundy" (I.i.79), Lear's lands. The course of events through which Cordelia's heart speaks is incomplete, and the syntax of things belies Lear's hurried paraphrase, revealing him as the pattern of all impatience. His problem is not that he thinks his youngest daughter loves him least. His problem is that the parsing of land and children does not *say* she loves him most.

What it *helps* to say are things beyond the grasp of the pre-Christian King. It *helps* to say what other chronicle plays (*Gorboduc, Locrine, Woodstock*), and chronicles themselves, say. Kingdom-division brings calamity, as expressed in stories of these kings, and divisions among Saxons prior to the Norman Conquest.[28] But without a larger context, it cannot speak in full. The historical lessons from chronicles, political tracts, and didactic plays and poems hover in the margins, beyond the scope of the play—as if Shakespeare were deliberately presenting a perspective too small in context to allow the reading of such lessons. Kent, in the Folio, demands of Lear, "Reserve thy state" (I.i.143), as if dividing it would destroy it, but, in his prior conversation with Gloucester, seems content with division. A coronet is divided on stage—an emblem of the destruction of the kingship, but the king still wears his crown: the coronet, confusingly, is Cordelia's. The meaning of royal land-division is far more accessible in *Gorboduc*, which concludes with a promise of fifty years of civil war.[29] Lear's division of the kingdom does result in political division, but, as Kent says, "the face of it is covered" [III.i.12]). In the quarto, Kent explicitly observes that the division has opened Britain to invasion ("From France there comes a power / Into this scattered kingdom" [III.i.22–23]). But in both versions the invader is his ally Cordelia, so that he represents invasion as good news. (The brutally unified front that Gonerill and Regan show to Lear may also make division seem desirable.) Indeed, so effectively does the play mimic the difficulty of *reading* historical lessons by interpreting the disposition of property that it has tempted even modern critics to see Lear's impulse to divide the kingdom as political wisdom.[30] Shakespeare offers clues of his patron King James I's retrospective reading of kingdom-division, as articulated in the *Basilicon Doron* ("by deuiding your kingdomes, yee shall leaue the seed of diuision and discord among your posteritie").[31] But he creates the sense that human character gropes vainly in search of such truths.

Lear's parsing is a tiny phrase in a clause of semes so extensive that, from up close, the character involved in it has no chance of reading it.

For the phrase—the foolish parsing of a kingdom—to add up from the historical distance of Jacobean England, Lear himself must embody certain properties or characteristics. He must be a "very Foolish, fond" *senex* (V.i.57), not in his "perfect mind" (V.i.60), impatient, doting, dwarfed in wisdom by his own Fool. Cordelia's "nothing" unfolds these features. "Come not between the dragon and his wrath," Lear warns Kent—unveiling himself as both dragon and Wrath. "*I* loved her most and thought to set my rest / On her kind nursery" (I.i.116–7). "What would'st thou do, *old man*" (I.i.140) cries Kent, having read his master in relation to himself, now an emblem of rude plainness alliteratively joined to the character of the king: "Be Kent unmannerly / When Lear is mad" (I.i.139–40). Like Oswald, Lear consists in properties that make providential sense, syntactical elements not fully parsed in his own time: love, age, madness, majesty, folly, impatience, *and land.*

If one separates owner from commodity, that last item violates parallel structure; it does not belong under the rubric "characteristic." But in this play, *things* are syntactical elements inseparable from persons, not objects removed from subjects. Lear's parsing of land with daughters unfolds into a "character" of himself—as an attachment to the very land he surrenders. Before the division we see him looking at a cartographic representation of the kingdom ("Give me the map there" [I.i.32]). But the act of division stretches him out on the rack of his tough world, in perpetual travel all over Britain "by monthly course" (I.i.126). From scene to scene he moves over land, north to Albany, south to Gloucester, towards Cornwall, but then, unwelcome in any house, out *onto* the land, and to the southeastern verge of the kingdom in Dover. Unlike his counterpart in Holinshed, he can never separate himself from Britain.[32] "Am I in France?" Shakespeare has his Lear ask Cordelia, eliciting her poignant answer, "in your own kingdom, sir" (IV.vi.75). His attachment is irrevocable. As *character to be read*, he seems, as in Paul Yachnin's description of Othello, possessed by his own possessions.[33] At his moment of greatest patience, when he himself *is* a "patient" (the scene of his reunion with Cordelia and momentary emergence from madness), he himself appears to understand this. "I am mainly ignorant / What place this is: and all the skill I have / Remembers not these garments . . . Do not laugh at me, / For, as I am a man, I think this lady / To be my child Cordelia" (IV.vi.62–67). For a moment, things—daughter, clothes, land—appear to Lear as properties *with which* he comes. Even somatic endowments reveal themselves as unpossessed attachments. "I know not what to say: I will not swear these are my hands" (IV.vi.52). He is himself a dowry.

Once recognized as declamation of character rather than separation of subject from object, Lear's division patterns out a lexical dilemma shared by others in the play, who pervasively take up the challenge of putting *things* into motion to parse them. Doing so means unfolding one's story as *character*, as *figure* in "the middest," as Frank Kermode says, of things.[34] The division of the kingdom makes this challenge palpable in the vastness and persistence of real estate. But the play has a rich store of ways to make it felt. Hence, Albany's schizophrenic oscillation between sense-making in invoking "the wages of virtue and . . . the cup of . . . deservings" and bafflement in "O see, see!" (V.iii.278), as the unfathomable fact of Cordelia's hanging and Lear's grief unfolds like one of the appalling images emerging from the opening of the seals in the great scroll in Revelation, with the numinous directive, "Come, and see."[35] The imagery of unfolding seems to elicit a compulsion, on feeling declaimed, to declaim. The unfolding, against Lear's will, of his human outfit of knights (which Lear defends by comparing it to Gonerill's "gorgeous" clothing [II.iv.261–62]), finds answer in Lear's willful unfolding of clothes upon seeing Edgar's "presented nakedness" (II.iii.11): "Off, off, you lendings! Come, unbutton here." (III.iv.97). And Edgar's nakedness, in repeating, as if originally, the action by which he *has been* stripped of inheritance, epitomizes his effort, throughout, to position himself as an authoritative interpreter of things. "Think," he commands his blind, suicidal father Gloucester, having drawn entirely in words a vast cliff at Dover and then pretended to watch the old man jump and survive, "that the clearest gods, who make them honours / Of men's impossibilities, have preserved thee" (4.5.73–74).

But words cannot translate the character of things, as Gloucester has discovered in struggling to parse things by reading the conspiracy letter that Edmond has forged. Gloucester sounds out words easily, but the very questions he asks ("My son Edgar, had he a hand to write this? A heart and brain to breed it in? When came this to you? Who brought it?"[I.ii.53–55]) require him to parse things, the hardness of which finds powerful expression in his desperate reliance on "character" as letters *alone*. The very narrowness of his usage, in his fateful question of Edmond, "Know you the character to be your brother's?" (I.ii.58), signals his problem. The Vice, impishly flaunting his ability to fool his father even while hinting at the truth, lets us know that Gloucester's vision of all "character" as handwriting is only a tiny part of the "kind of character" that is in one's "life." He answers, "If the *matter* were good . . . I durst swear it were his, but in respect of that, I would fain think it were not" (I.ii.59–60). Gloucester's "It is his" (I.ii.61) elicits "it is his hand, my lord, but I hope his *heart* is not in the contents" (I.ii.62–64). The character Gloucester should parse encompasses not *just* the writing but the heart of Edgar, the brain, the circumstances of the letter's delivery and presentation by Edmond, the *matter* of the letter. Gloucester's *literal*-mindedness derives not, I think, from failure to see that things mean, but from impatience with the hardness of their meaning. So does his bad reading of the cosmos as he exits: "these late eclipses of the sun and moon portend no good to us . . . This villain of mine comes under the prediction—there's son against father. The King falls from the bias of nature—there's father against child" (I.ii.91–98).

Hence, Shakespeare conveys a sense of the "kind of character" in life not just by using character on the page as a synecdoche for it, but by emphasizing palpably how painfully, if ephemerally, such synecdoche—like Borachio's villain "deformed"—mangles the full course of things. Gloucester's misparsing is, like Lear's division of land, a discursive *doing* that results from the error of treating mere human writing as the universe of God's character. This error cascades into total mis-parsing of things, corrected only when the judicial combat between Edgar and Edmond *does* let things speak for themselves. Gloucester's hasty reliance on written words results in a pre-*judicial* declamation, in action, of *things*—a hasty *decision* that the thing that is the handwriting must parse with the heart of Edgar, so that it is, indeed (in deed), "his." As the one of whom Gloucester can say "it is his," Edgar is not Edgar ("know, my name is lost" [V.iii.111], he says before his trial-by-combat with Edmond). But then Edgar is always Edgar, because the handwriting is never appropriate to him, despite the imposition. It is and is not his, as the inheritance of an earldom is and is not Edmond's during the same parenthetical period (the herald announcing Edgar's challenge to Edmond calls Edmond "supposed Earl of Gloucester" [V.iii.103–4]). As Stephen Booth says, "[The] identities of the characters in *King Lear* are both firm and perfectly fluid."[36] Likewise, with regard to "Edgar's" "character," the Quarto registers the question of belonging with a question mark ("It is his?"), revised by the Folio into a period, after Gloucester's "it is his." The Folio's period suits Gloucester's impatience; the Quarto's "it is his?" signifies uncertainty that a reader *should* feel in parsing things.[37]

Ultimately, Gloucester's mis-parsing unfolds, like Lear's, into a reading of himself; or, more precisely, a parsing of himself with his eyes. (The text draws distinct parallels, in fact, between Gloucester's eyes and Lear's lands, as when the Fool taunts Lear about the division of the kingdom by explaining that ones nose "stands ith'middle on's face" . . . "to keep one's eyes on either side's nose, that what a man cannot smell out, he may spy into" [I.v.16–19]). The blinding has the force of a declamatory exercise, linked to Cornwall's earlier unfolding of an incriminating letter to Gloucester from France, intercepted with the help of Edmond. Cornwall identifies the punishment as revenge, but it takes the shape of interrogation, forcing character to "speak"(III.vii.56). "Come sir," demands Gonerill. "What letters had you late from France?" Yet as interrogation it begins, like Lear's division, at the end. "Be simple answered, for we know the truth" (III.vii.42–43). In the absence of hope for news, the interrogation highlights the nature of revenge as a restatement *of* things *in* things.

Revenge is mine, says the Lord. The human struggle to take it always involves lexical impatience, over-hasty parsing of the Providential character of things. When Regan tears his beard, Gloucester ridiculously chastises her by suggesting the seized fibers will speak: 'These hairs, which thou dost ravish from my chin / Will quicken and accuse thee" (III.vii.38–40). And with the prophesy that immediately occasions his blinding ("I shall see / The wingèd vengeance overtake such children" [III.vii.64–65]), he pathetically misreads what is happening. Nor do the vindictive "children" themselves know what their deed really *says*. Does it say Gloucester is a spy? Does it speak Cornwall and Regan's cruelty, as Regan later worries? ("It was great ignorance, Gloucester's eyes being out / to let him live. Where he arrives he moves / All hearts against us" [IV.iv.11–12]). Edgar reads the blinding as a statement, expressed somatically, of Gloucester's adultery: "the dark and vicious place where thee he got / Cost him his eyes" (V.iii.162–63). His reading, then, denies the power of declamation to the human agents of Gloucester's blinding, attributing it to the "just" gods, who "of our pleasant vices, make instruments to plague us" (V.iii.161–62). As critics have suggested, the symbolism of castration surrounding the event strongly suggests that the blinding expresses the adultery.[38] But the perpetrators cannot comprehend this; it comprehends *them*. Poignant in this regard is Regan's unwitting echo of Gloucester's earlier allusion to the female pudenda ("do you smell a fault" [I.i.13]), with the jeer that Gloucester might now "smell / His way to Dover" (III.vii.93–94). The allusion pushes providential declamation beyond the consciousness of the character that constitutes it—even when this character forms a person.

The highest state of consciousness achievable in such a circumstance may be consciousness of *unconsciousness*, evidenced by the resignation— the forced patience—that Gloucester seems to have developed just before his death. Blinded so that he cannot read words, he learns by analogy that he cannot read things, as he shows when the mad Lear tries to engage him in a declamatory challenge:

Lear: . . . Read thou this challenge; mark but the penning of it.
Gloucester: Were all thy letters suns, I could not see.
Edgar: [Aside] I would not take this from report; it is,
  And my heart breaks at it.

Lear: Read.

Gloucester: What—with a case of eyes?

Lear: O ho, are you there with me? No eyes in your head, nor no money in your purse? Your eyes are in a heavy case, your purse in a light; yet you see how this world goes.

Gloucester: I see it feelingly.

(V.iii.132–43)

Seeing things "feelingly" is *not* reading, *not* seeing how the world "goes," but seeing how it *is* (even Edgar registers tastes of that, both in his interjection here and in his advice, concluding the play, to "speak what we feel, not what we ought to say" [V.iii.298]). Surely Gloucester's imagining of the letters he cannot read as "suns" itself suggests a pun: he once tried to read his sons *literally* in a letter; he *cannot* now make the same mistake.

Still, the great achievement of the blinding derives not from what it can mean as one's view of the context widens, but from its immersion of spectators and readers into the very *texture* of character, which defies comprehension. The graphic corporeality and temporality of the figure, in other words, both demand and daunt a reading of it. The obstacle to reading is never more overwhelming than when Cornwall, concerned with the practical problem of how to dig his feet into Gloucester's eye sockets, instructs, "Fellows, hold the chair" (III.vii.66); or when a servant's challenge interrupts the blinding process, only to prolong its agony; or when Cornwall addresses the other eye as a mass of "jelly" to be ex-pressed onto the ground (III.vii.82). Though spectators and readers are reminded that such belongings (bodily *things*) *speak* ("one side shall mock another," says Gonerill, parsing the eyes or eye sockets in speech [III.vii.70]), they are also reminded that words cannot wield this matter; that persons, themselves composed of character, can barely begin to apprehend significance beyond its texture.

Today, when things can be thought as *mere* texture, mere *objects* produced or consumed by human *subjects*, "character" finds itself chained to page or stage or screen. "Character" has taken on the meaning of fictional person, serving to distinguish textual persons from "real." And since the real person is the modern "subject" defined by separation from commodified "object," anything that locks the fictional person into fictional things may remind us she is character. "Realism" requires distinction between "character" and *thing* on page or stage; "character" in its most distorted form denotes a literary illusion of inner "mind" divorced from objects. This separation began long ago. One can see its seeds, for example, in William Hazlitt's early nineteenth-century *The Characters of Shakspeare's Plays*:

> The mind of Lear, staggering between the weight of attachment and the hurried movements of passion, is like a tall ship driven about by the winds, buffeted by the furious waves but that still rides above the storm, having its anchor fixed at the bottom of the sea.[39]

For Hazlitt, Lear's "mind" looms large, ready to come unmoored from its oceanic context. But if such descriptions of "mind" mark the origins of literary character, they also partake of what precedes them. Whatever Hazlitt's intention, the passage leaves doubt as to whether "the mind of Lear" encompasses Lear's character. The mind is the "tall ship" *above* the storm of passions, while the character might include not only the tall ship but also the storm, and the anchor reaching to the deeps. Hazlitt provides little detail about this "weight of attachment", but surely it involves Lear's appurtenances: land, title, bonds. As things inherited and bequeathed, these extend beyond "the mind of Lear" in time and space, evoking a vast text of history and lending the mind belonging with them providential meaning past the wit of any character to speak. From such a perspective, to which Hazlitt still seems half committed, one can perhaps see what "depth of character" might really mean for Shakespeare's Lear: not depth of *a* character Lear, but the *O Altitudo!* of the character of things shaping Lear's person—*depth of character* formed by locking person into things, proper self into property.

Notes

I am grateful to the following, whose comments on drafts helped and encouraged me with this essay: Rebecca Berg, Michael Bristol, Susan Carlson, William Dodd, Barbara Hodgdon, Joseph Porter, Julie Solomon, Edward Tayler, Marion Wells, Laura Winkiel, Martha Woodruff, and Paul Yachnin.

1. *The Bible*, translated from the Hebrew and Greek (London, 1599).
2. Citations from *King Lear* refer generally to *The Tragedy of King Lear*, ed. Jay Halio (Cambridge: Cambridge University Press, 2005), based on Shakespeare's 1623 folio. I have also consulted *The First Quarto of King Lear*, ed. Jay Halio (Cambridge: Cambridge University Press, 1994).
3. See Robert Cawdry, *A Table Alphabeticall, conteyning and teaching the true writing, and vnderstanding of hard vsuall English wordes* (London, 1604). The first collection of Theophrastan character sketches in English was Joseph Hall's *The Characters of the Virtues and Vices* (London, 1608). This appeared three years after the first performances of *Lear* (see Halio's introduction to *The Tragedy*, 1).
4. Marx distinguishes between these concepts, arguing that their conflation amounts to a mere "bourgeois play on . . . words" falsely naturalizing private property. On the Shakespearean stage, predating the firm establishment of the self-owning individual, such conflation occurs, I suspect, to *opposite* effect. Karl Marx and Frederick Engels, *Collected Works*, vol. 5 (New York: International Publishers, 1976), 231.
5. "character, *n*," *Oxford English Dictionary*, 2nd Edition, 1989, *OED Online*, 3 December 2007 <http://dictionary.oed.com/cgi/entry/50036832>. See all of section I, "literal senses."
6. This essay is not the first to pursue such an agenda with *King Lear*. See, for instance, William Dodd's, "Impossible Worlds: What Happens in *King Lear*, Act I, Scene I?" *Shakespeare Quarterly* 50, no. 4 (1999): 477–507, as well as Richard McCoy's, "'Look upon me, Sir': Relationships in *King Lear*," *Representations* 81 (2003): 46–60.
7. Margreta de Grazia, "The ideology of superfluous things: *King Lear* as period piece," in *Subject and Object in Renaissance Culture*, ed. Margreta de Grazia, Maureen Quilligan, and Peter Stallybrass (Cambridge: Cambridge University Press, 1996), 17–42; 21.
8. The terms are from Richard Halpern, *The Poetics of Primitive Accumulation: English Renaissance Culture and the Genealogy of Capital* (Ithaca and London: Cornell University Press, 1991), 218. Halpern's and de Grazia's are perhaps most prominent among a host of "materialist" readings that treat *King Lear* as symptomatic of the transition from "feudalism" to "capitalism."
9. Harold Fisch, "Character as Linguistic Sign," *New Literary History*, 21, no. 3 (1982): 592–606.
10. Christopher Marlowe, *Tamburlaine the Great, Part I* in *Doctor Faustus and Other Plays*, ed. David Bevington and Eric Rasmussen (Oxford: Oxford University Press, 1995), I.ii.168–71.
11. Stephen Orgel, "What is a Character?" in *The Authentic Shakespeare and other Problems of the Early Modern Stage* (London: Routledge, 2002), 8.
12. *Religio Medici*, in *The Major Works*, ed. C. A. Patrides (London: Penguin, 1976), 135–36; emphasis mine. For similar examples, see Ernst Robert Curtius, *European Literature in the Latin Middle Ages* (Princeton: Princeton University Press, 1973), 319–26.
13. *On Christian Doctrine*, trans. D. W. Robertson, Jr. (Indianapolis: Liberal Arts Press, 1958).
14. John Donne, *Devotions upon Emergent Occasions*, in *The Complete Poetry and Selected Prose of John Donne*, ed. Charles M. Coffin (New York: Modern Library,

1952), 446–47. This passage came to my attention in Edward W. Tayler's unforgettable chapter on *Paradise Lost* in *Milton's Poetry: Its Development in Time* (Pittsburgh: Duquestne University Press, 1979), 60–104; 103.
15. *Reading Shakespeare's Will: The Theology of Figure from Augustine to the Sonnets* (New York: Columbia University Press, 2002), 17.
16. Natasha Korda, *Shakespeare's Domestic Economies: Gender and Property in Early Modern England* (Philadelphia: University of Pennsylvania Press, 2002), 11.
17. *Measure for Measure*, in *The Riverside Shakespeare*, ed. G. Blakemore Evans (New York: Houghton Mifflin, 1997), I.i.27–31; italics mine.
18. For discussions of commodification and the stage, see Jean-Christophe Agnew, *Worlds Apart: The Market and the Theater in Anglo-American Thought, 1550–1750* (Cambridge: Cambridge University Press, 1986) and Douglas Bruster, *Drama and the Market in the Age of Shakespeare* (Cambridge: Cambridge University Press, 1992).
19. The terminology derives from Burckhardt (who, as de Grazia says, writes of an "individuated subject . . . cut off from objects" [17]) and Marx, (who describes a "commodified object . . . cut off from subject" [17]). On the development of these terms, see de Grazia's synopsis (17–21), a wonder of trenchancy and erudition. Also see William Kerrigan and Gordon Braden, *The Idea of the Renaissance* (Baltimore and London: Johns Hopkins University Press, 1989); and Julie Robin Solomon, *Objectivity in the Making: Francis Bacon and the Politics of Inquiry* (Baltimore and London: Johns Hopkins University Press, 1998).
20. For the quotations, see Revelation 6:12–17. For critical studies on the play's allusions to Revelation, see Frank Kermode, *The Sense of an Ending* (Oxford: Oxford University Press, 2000); and Joseph Wittreich, *"Image of that Horror": History, Prophesy, and Apocalypse in "King Lear"* (San Marino: The Huntington Library, 1984).
21. *Revelation 5: 2–4.*
22. In this quotation and all subsequent quotations of *King Lear*, italics are mine.
23. For an impressive discussion, from a different perspective, of the hermeneutic dimension of Lear's division, see Dan Brayton, "Angling in the Lake of Darkness: Possession, Dispossession, and the Politics of Discovery in *King Lear*" *English Literary History* 70, no. 2 (2003): 399–426.
24. Levi-Strauss, *Elementary Structures of Kinship* (Boston: Beacon Press, 1969), 496. Karen Newman's "Portia's Ring: Unruly Women and the Structures of Exchange in *The Merchant of Venice*," *Shakespeare Quarterly*, 38, no. 1 (1987): 19–33, referred me to this source.
25. Shakespeare gets the idea of a pre-division from Edmund Spenser (*The Faerie Queene*, 2nd ed., ed. A. C. Hamilton [Harrow, England: Longman, 2001], II.x.27–28), but connects the land more intimately to speech.
26. Ernst Kantorowicz, *The King's Two Bodies* (Princeton: Princeton University Press, 1957), 273–91, 446–50.
27. For an inspiring meditation on "nothing" in *King Lear*, see Tayler, "*King Lear* and Negation," *English Literary Renaissance*, 20, no. 1 (1990): 17–39.
28. See the preface to Raphael Holinshed, *The Chronicles of England from William the Conqueror . . . until the year 1577* (London, 1587).
29. Thomas Norton and Thomas Sackville, *Gorboduc; or Ferrex and Porrex*, ed. Irby B. Cauthen Jr. (Lincoln: University of Nebraska Press, 1970). See "The Order and Signification of the dumb Show Before the Fifth Act."

30. See, for instance, Harry Jaffa, "The Limits of Power," in *Shakespeare's Politics*, ed. Allan Bloom (New York: Basic Books, 1964), 113–45.
31. *Basilicon Doron*, in *Political Writings*, ed. Johann P. Sommerville (Cambridge: Cambridge University Press, 1994) 42.
32. *The Historie of England*, 20.
33. Anthony B. Dawson and Paul Yachnin, *The Culture of Playgoing in Shakespeare's England: A Collaborative Debate* (Cambridge: Cambridge University Press, 2001), 111–30.
34. Kermode, *The Sense of an Ending*, 8.
35. *Revelation 6: 1,3*, and *7*.
36. *King Lear, Macbeth, Indefinition, and Tragedy* (New Haven: Yale University Press, 1983), 46.
37. In *The First Quarto*, Act I.ii.59, Halio emends the period to a question mark. For the original punctuation, see the *True Chronicle Historie of the life and death of King Lear* (London, 1608), sig. C1v.
38. Halio, "Gloucester's Blinding," *Shakespeare Quarterly*, 43, no. 2 (1992): 221–23.
39. William Hazlitt, *The Characters of Shakspeare's Plays* (New York: Wiley and Putnam, 1845), 101.

6
Embodied Intersubjectivity and the Creation of Early Modern Character

Leanore Lieblein

> *Playes are in vse as they are vnderstood,*
> *Spectators eyes may make them bad or good.*
>
> (F2v)[1]

According to Thomas Heywood in his *Apology for Actors* (1612), theater takes place in a place between—between the performance and the spectator as the above suggests, but also, as he elsewhere makes clear, between the performer and the performed; or, to use his words, between the "personater"[sic] and the "person personated" (B4r; C4r). The challenge, however, is to establish how persons were conceptualized, and by what process the person personated became, in a sense that both early moderns and we today might understand, a character. In addition, if it is, as Heywood suggests, spectators' eyes that make a play bad or good, how are we to describe the contribution of the spectator to a discussion of character on the early modern stage?

Early modern persons to be personated were understood to exist in the world while characters, etymologically speaking, were a product of writing. Nevertheless, characters existed not only on the page but on the stage, though the word to describe them as such made its first appearance only in 1664.[2] Heywood suggests that the process of personation was experienced in theatrical terms as a physical as well as an imaginative process in which, in the course of personation, the person personated, the personating actor, and the perceiving spectator participated in a process of mutual transformation. Or, as Edward Burns felicitously puts it in *Character: Acting and Being on the Pre-Modern Stage*, "Character is a two-way process ... [,] a transaction between two human subjects. Conceived of in this way, character is a creative perception, which constructs both observer and observed as its subjects."[3] In this essay, I draw upon early modern sources as well as the vocabulary more recently generated by Maurice Merleau-Ponty to propose a notion of early modern character as the product of a physically informed communication that results from the actor's embodiment and the spectator's experience of the person personated.

Body-subjects

The tradition of phenomenology as developed by Merleau-Ponty and others offers a theory of the human being that insists on corporeality and intersubjectivity as elements of consciousness. Potentially productive for a theory of character are phenomenological concepts of "being-in-the-world" and "embodied subjectivity." Although I start by describing these concepts generally, I situate them ultimately with respect to the three poles of my discussion: the person personated; the actor; and the spectator.[4]

There are two parts to "being-in-the-world." One is the "being" subject, or the experiencing person; the other is the "world" being experienced. The subject of experience, which may be an actor or a spectator as well as a person to be personated, is, according to Merleau-Ponty, an *embodied person,* rather than a mere "mind."[5] "[What] we mean by a 'world' is not something we merely contemplate but something we *inhabit.*"[6] Our understanding of the world is affected by our experience of being in it.

What this view insists upon is the importance of corporeality for both subjectivity and perception. Perception, for example, is not just the impact of the world upon the senses of the perceiver. What and how that world is perceived is colored by the bodily experience of the perceiver. We could not look at a pool of water and mistake it for a writing desk,[7] even if visually we perceived an undisturbed flat surface, because we not only experience it sensorily, but also corporeally. Even if we are not touching it, due to our corporeal history we experience it as lacking the firmness and resistance required for a writing desk. Similarly, we perceive a wheel, if it is lying on the ground, differently from a wheel bearing a load, because our perception takes into account the force being exerted upon, and supported by, the wheel. Thus the same phenomenon perceived by two identically placed perceivers may differ as a result of their different histories of embodiment. A candle flame experienced by a child who is drawn to it by its animation and brightness will be experienced differently by another child who has once been burned by a candle's flame.[8] Therefore, to use the example cited by

Eric Matthews, we as human subjects are not "in-the-world" in the same way as, say, biscuits, are "in" a biscuit tin.[9] As perceiving subjects we are *within* the world that we perceive, and perception is only possible as a relationship to a world. To "be-in-the-world" is to both find and create meanings in the world.[10]

Subjectivity thus exists in an interactive relationship of the body in dialogue with its world.[11] As Monika M. Langer writes: "[I]deas are never absolutely pure thoughts but rather, cultural objects necessarily linked to acts of expression whose source is the phenomenal body itself as already primordially expressive. In short, phenomenology must awaken us to an awareness of consciousness as incarnate in a body and inhering in a world."[12] For this multi-faceted agent of experience—the experiencing person in the world—Merleau-Ponty uses the term "body-subject." The body-subject (i.e. a person in the world) exists in time, and, as in the case of the child's experience of the candle flame, it is a product of both present perceptions and past experiences.[13]

This conception of an individual as a corporeally experiencing subject has important implications for our understanding of actors, spectators, and, I would argue, characters as a product of the communication that takes place among them. In the sections that follow, I begin by focusing on the early modern sense of character as a form of writing in order to stress the distinction between persons and characters. I then go on to consider the rhetorical concept of *actio* as a writing on the body and its implication for the relationship among the early modern actor, the person he personates, and the personated person. Finally, I consider the embodied spectator as a participant in an intersubjective process whereby personated persons, corporeally generated and experienced, can be thought of as characters.

Persons personated

As early as the thirteenth century, according to the *OED*, the word "person" refers to "an individual human being; a man, woman, or child."[14] In contrast, it is only two hundred years later that the word "character" is used to refer to a person, and even then only as "a person regarded *in the abstract* as the possessor of specified qualities; a personage, a personality."[15] In other words, characters in Early Modern England are not persons in the world. André G. Bourassa elsewhere in this volume distinguishes etymologically between persons and characters. The word character comes from the Greek word for an instrument for marking or engraving—an impress, a stamp, or a distinctive mark—while the word person derives from the classical Latin *persona*, or the mask used in theatrical performance.[16] One emphasizes the process of creation, while the other focuses on its product. Their etymologies can help us understand the distinction and relationship between the two terms.

The prose genre of Theophrastan "Characters," widely popular in the Jacobean period, while far removed from dramatic characters as we find them in the work of Shakespeare and his contemporaries, invites us to think of early modern characters as related to but different from persons in the world. Persons are not characters. An entry in the ninth (1616) impression of the Overburian Characters, called "What a Character is," while referring to narrative character, offers us a way of thinking about dramatic character as well. The entry relates the term to the Greek word, and goes on:

> Character is also taken for an Egiptian Hierogliphicke, for an impress, or shorte Embleme; in little comprehending much.
> To square out a Character by our English level, it is a picture (real or personal) quaintly drawn in various colors, all of them heightened by one shadowing.
> It is a quick and soft touch of many strings, all shutting up in one musical close; it is wit's descant on any plain song.[17]

There are several elements of this definition that deserve our attention. First of all, a Character in this context is something that is not found but made. Secondly, a Character is a form of writing, not only of stylus on papyrus but also of chisel on stone. It comes from a word that means "to engrave or make a deep impression" and, indeed, the examples given involve a transformation of materials—of a surface by colors, of strings by plucking. Joseph Hall also describes the writing of Characters in terms of metaphors of drawing and engraving. Classical authors, he writes in the "Premonition of the Title and Use of Characters" that introduces his *Characters of Virtues and Vices* (1608), "bestowed their time in drawing out the true lineaments of every virtue and vice, so lively, that who saw the medals, might know the face . . . Their papers were so many tables, their writings so many speaking pictures, or living images . . ."[18] In other words, a Character is both a product of technical skill and a work of art. It produces, as the Overburian text tells us, a synthesis, the various colors "heightened by one shadowing" and the touch of many strings, "all shutting up in one musical close (cadence)." A Character offers an interpretation, "in little comprehending much." In conclusion, "it is wit's descant on any plain song."

A Character is therefore a transformation of elements in the world. The Theophrastan Character is a crafted artefact, not a reproduction of a person who exists in the world. Though it bears a recognizable relationship to persons in the world, it tends to single out a social or moral quality or aspect of persons and develop that as the Character. This process of abstraction produces a generalization which may be idealized or satirized but nevertheless remains a category or a type. Examples from the Overburian *Characters* include "A good Woman," "A Dissembler," "A Courtier," and "An Affectate (i.e. affected) Traveler." Therefore, the Theophrastan Character is not an individual. However bizarre, eccentric, or seemingly *sui generis*, or on the contrary however rooted in a specific social context, the Theophrastan Character remains a hypothesis.

A dramatic character, too, is a form of writing, a transformation of materials, a synthesis, and an interpretation. However, the writing is accomplished by the actor's process of performing a part, and the material transformed is the actor's body. Unlike Theophrastan Characters, persons on the stage are embodied by the actor. Indeed, it is what he calls personation that for Heywood in the *Apology* distinguishes theatrical performance from other modes of representation:

> Oratory is a kind of a speaking picture, therefore may some say, is it not sufficient to discourse to the eares of princes the fame of these conquerors: Painting likewise, is a dumbe oratory, therefore may we not as well by some curious *Pigmalion*, drawe their conquests to worke the like loue in Princes towards these Worthyes by shewing them their pictures drawne to the life . . . A Description is only a shadow receiued by the eare but not perceiued by the eye: so liuely portrature is meerely a forme seene by the eye, *but can neither shew action, passion, motion, or any other gesture, to mooue the spirits of the beholder to admiration.*[19]

The musician and the visual artist accomplish their creation through the plucking of strings or the application of paint. The actor in contrast transforms the material of his own body:

> *Tully* in his booke *ad Caium Herennium*, requires fiue things in an Orator, *Inuention, Disposition, Eloquution Memory,* and *Pronuntiation,* yet all are imperfect without the sixt, which is *Action*: for . . . without a comely and elegant gesture, a gratious and a bewitching kinde of action, a naturall and a familiar motion of the head, the hand, the

body, and a moderate and fit countenance sutable to all the rest, I hold all the rest as nothing.[20]

It is through his physical embodiment of the person personated that the actor can "shew action, passion [and] motion (i.e. emotion)." Through this act of embodiment—"a comely and elegant gesture, a gratious and a bewitching kinde of action, a naturall and a familiar motion of the head, the hand, the body"—the actor articulates a relationship to the person personated and precipitates a response in the spectator ("mooue[s] the spirits of the beholder to admiration").

In this way, the dramatic character differs from the Theophrastan character, which always remains at a third-person distance from its narrative voice. Even when the quality which defines the Character is firmly situated in a physical body, as in the case of John Earle's "discontented Man," the Theophrastan character is a person described but not personated:

> His composure of himselfe is a studied carelesnesse with his armes a crosse, and a neglected hanging of his head and cloake, and he is as great an enemie to an hat-band, as Fortune. He quarrels at the time, and vp-starts, and sighs at the neglect of men of Parts, that is, such as himselfe . . . Hee neuer drawes his own lips higher then a smile, and frownes wrinckle him before fortie.[21]

The discontent is reflected in the body language of his pose, expression, gesture, and costume. But these physical qualities are described, not performed, and they are mediated by the voice of the describing author. When they are performed, they are transmuted by the corporeal history of the actor.

Similarly, persons in the world are not characters until they have been personated; that is, until they too have been mediated by the imagination and body of an actor in interaction with other similarly corporeal actors in the presence of an audience. André Bourassa reminds us of Hellenistic illustrations in which an actor holds up and contemplates the mask (i.e. the *persona*) he will wear in performance, as if to familiarize himself with it. But as David Wiles argues in his recent *Mask and Performance in Greek Tragedy*, the Greek actor does not become the mask, any more than the early modern actor becomes the person personated, but transforms and is transformed by it: "[T]he primary function of the tragic mask is not to seal and fix a character type, but to transform a wearer," and it is only when the wearer is so transformed that it can "take power over an audience."[22]

The person personated, like the mask, may of course be recognizable as a familiar "type" or an existing or possible individual in the world, but it is only when personated or filtered through the body of the performing actor who is himself transformed by it that that individual can be thought of as a character. In other words, the early modern actor is, in Merleau-Ponty's terms, a body-subject. His perception of the person to be personated, whether a person in the world or in a dramatic text, is informed by his own corporeal history, just as the reception of that personated person is similarly informed by the corporeal history of the spectator. In the section that follows, I suggest that early modern sources invite us to look at personation as an intersubjective process in phenomenological terms.

Between mask and face

Joseph Roach in *The Player's Passion* suggests that central to the desire to understand the nature of acting in the seventeenth century was the ultimately unsuccessful attempt to "bridge the distance between mask and face, a character's persona and the actor's body."[23] While I do not propose to resolve the problem articulated by Renaissance rhetoricians, I do wish to revisit it in order to explore the way in which a person through personation is transformed into a character by the embodied subjectivity of the actor. In this section, I am trying to argue two things. The first is that acting is neither a replication of nor an identification with the person to be personated. Secondly, rhetorical theory of the early modern period also suggests that the process of personation is understood as an intersubjective relationship between embodied subjects.

To begin with the first, according to Heywood, the measure of an actor's performance is his capacity "to qualifie euery thing according to the nature of the person personated."[24] For B. L. Joseph, in a still valuable 1964 study of Elizabethan acting, the word "identification" describes this process: "The actor was identified [with his character]; he behaved as if he were the imaginary character come to life; when he was successful this is how he was accepted by his audience." Among the evidence Joseph cites are the passages from Heywood's *Apology*, quoted above. He also quotes from the Character of "An Excellent Actor" attributed to John Webster—"what wee see him personate, wee thinke truely done before vs"—as well as from comparisons of actors, including Edward Alleyn and Richard Burbage, to Proteus, the mythological figure who could change his shape.[25]

However, it is possible to read that evidence differently. The process of personation does not necessarily involve the effacement of the actor.

After all, performance of a variety of roles on successive days was part of an actor's conditions of employment, and actors seem to have drawn upon established social and performative traditions to convey specific situations and emotions.[26] Robert Weimann suggests that an actor's relationship to the role he was performing depended upon its dramatic function.[27] And, according to Susan Cerasano, a player "did not attempt to *become* a character, but to *represent* a character, to convey emotion in such a way that the spectator could relate to a character's joy or grief."[28] Personation is a product of an actor's performance, and the image of the Protean actor suggests not so much the disappearance of the actor in his role as admiration for the accomplishment of the actor who achieves multiple personations.

Nevertheless, though personation may be functional, Heywood, like Shakespeare before him, recognizes that it should not be mechanical:

> [T]his is the action behoouefull in any that professe this quality, not to vse any impudent or forced motion in any part of the body, no rough, or other violent gesture, nor on the contrary, to stand like a stiffe starcht man, but to qualifie euery thing according to the nature of the person personated: for in oueracting trickes, and toyling too much in the anticke habit of humors, men of the ripest desert, greatest opinions, and best reputations, may breake into the most violent absurdities.[29]

Heywood is an enemy not only to "oueracting trickes" (what Hamlet calls sawing the air, tearing a passion to tatters, or out-Heroding Herod), but also to under-acting—standing like "a stiffe starcht man" [3.2.1–16] (what Hamlet would call being too tame).[30] The gestures and expressions of which he disapproves are formulaic. Because they do not proceed from the corporeal agency of the actor as a body-subject, they result in a performance of the actor that is, in our modern understanding of the word, artificial rather than artful. Such "impudent and forced" excesses are potentially a consequence of the advice offered to the boy players in the Induction to John Marston's *Antonio and Mellida*, who know their own lines but not what roles the others play:

> O, ho; then thus frame your exterior shape
> To haughty form of elate majesty
> As if you held the palsy-shaking head
> Of reeling chance under your fortune's belt

In strictest vassalage; grow big in thought
As swoll'n with glory of successful arms.

(Induction. 7–12)[31]

Alberto's instruction to the actor playing the role of Piero, Duke of Venice, offers the equivalent of an Overburian Character, and to the young actor seems easy enough to follow. But while a palsy-shaking head or the framing of one's exterior shape to haughtiness will "read" Old Duke, until they have not only been imitated by the body of the actor but also informed by his own corporeal history in interaction with other dramatis personae similarly transformed by the corporeal agency of their actors, they will be insufficient on their own to turn the old Duke from a Theophrastan Character into a dramatic character.

While, as we have seen, there was a distance between the personating actor and the person personated, there was also a relationship, and it is the absence or failure of such a relationship that Heywood criticizes. Early modern sources suggest we need to resist what Robert Weimann has described as "the traditionally over-emphasized distinction between 'formal' and so called 'naturalist' styles of acting."[32] Both Hamlet and Heywood use the word "nature." The word is an abstract noun ("the modesty of nature" [3.2.19]), and a property that inheres in persons ("the nature of the person personated"); both meanings are present as early as the twelfth century, according to the *OED*.[33] The "nature of the person personated" is made manifest in the "nature" of the personating person, the body-subject who is the actor by whose corporeal agency the person personated is created and transformed. Spectators could thus be both impressed by the skill of the actors as actors and moved by the emotional impact of their performances. It was the performing body, as Heywood suggests, that was the vehicle of that emotional impact. Rhetorical theory of the early modern period, in which the roles of the rhetor and the actor are often intertwined, articulates the relationship between emotion and performance and sees performance as an act of communication. The rhetorical concept of *actio* is described as a writing on the body, and the process of personation is understood as an intersubjective relationship between embodied subjects.

The expressiveness (indeed, for anti-theatricalists, the seductiveness, as Philip Stubbes recognized)[34] of the performing body is widely commented in the early modern period. Montaigne, for example, in the *Apology for Raymond Sebond* (1595) speaks of the power of gesture to signify.[35]

Also on the continent, the *Hieroglyphica* of Pierio Valeriano (1602) interprets the human body as a repertoire of hieroglyphs, in which each part has potentially multiple significations.[36] And, for John Bulwer in England, "chirologia," the language of the hand, is, after Babel, "the only speech and general language of human nature."[37] The body of the actor was perceived as a sign and at the same time imbued with the capacity to affect the physical space and the bodies of others around him.[38]

The discipline of rhetoric articulates and draws upon the emotional and imaginative agency of the performing actor as a model for the rhetor. Andrew Gurr writes, "In the sixteenth century the term 'acting' was originally used to describe the 'action' of the orator, his art of gesture."[39] And Joseph Roach points out that "the rhetorical concept of *actio* was the nexus of the seventeenth-century ideal of theatrical eloquence."[40] The language of gesture, contrary to some modern characterizations of it, was not a rigid and mechanical system of signs. The delivery the rhetoricians strove for was "natural," "familiar" and "lively" (the words most often used); and it was the actor, in fact, who was taken as the model of such communication.[41] However different oratory is from acting and the rhetorician from the actor, it is from the practice of acting that the rhetoricians draw their examples, and upon which they base their arguments. Quintilian, for example, who was widely cited by Renaissance rhetoricians, suggests that the reader of his *Institutio Oratoria* "draw a parallel from the stage, where the actor's voice and delivery produce greater emotional effects when he is speaking in an assumed role than when he speaks in his own character."[42] As we see in the Character of "An excellent Actor," the relationship was reciprocal: "Whatsoeuer is commendable in the graue Orator, is most exquisitly perfect in [the actor]."[43]

The complementary terms *pronuntiato* and *actio*, which were used to refer to the vocal and corporeal elements of the orator's communication, were also at the heart of the actor's process of personation. For Quintilian, vocal delivery and bodily movements were part of a continuum. *Pronuntiatio* (delivery) was perceived as a physical act, to be performed by the body as a whole.[44] Thomas Wright in *The passions of the minde in generall* (1604) defines action as an "externall image of an internall minde."[45] For the rhetoricians, the movements of the body were intimately related to the experience of emotion. As Wright says, "[T]he passion which is in our brest must be the fountaine and origen of all externall actions. . . . [B]y mouth [the actor] telleth his mind; in countenance he speaketh with a silent voice to the eyes; with all the universal life and bodie he seemeth to say, Thus we move, because by the passion thus we are moved."[46] Similarly, John Bulwer in *Chirologia* speaks of the hand in performance as "receiving good intelligence of the pathetical motions of the mind."[47] Or, in the words of Joseph Roach: "What orators and stage players do, then, is to discover the passions of the mind with their bodies—larynx, limbs, torso, and head together—thereby transforming invisible impulse into spectacle and unspoken feeling into eloquence."[48]

Here we see, in Renaissance terms, the actor as a "body-subject." It is in his body that he feels and articulates his emotions and thoughts, and within it that he experiences the emotions and thoughts of other persons. How he experiences other persons, and how he personates them, is a product of his own embodied subjectivity. For an actor, persons personated exist both in his experience of people in the world and in the lines of a dramatic text. His experience of people in the world will inform his reading of the dramatic text. And his experience of reading texts, as well as his personal history, will inform his perception of the *dramatis personae*. Rhetorical theory of the early modern period suggests that the process of personation is understood as an intersubjective relationship between embodied subjects in what today are phenomenological terms.

B. L. Joseph, as we saw above, argues that the actor informs his expression of the lines by identification with an imagined speaker. "Identifying," he claims, is feeling and expressing the emotion attributed to this imagined speaker. The emotion is signaled by the author's language, most especially by that given to the person to be personated, and communicated by the rhetorical tropes the speaker is given in the text. The recognition of such tropes, part of the education of all Elizabethan schoolboys, is a familiar process. The emotion in turn calls forth appropriate gestures in a process widely employed and disseminated by rhetoricians.[49] There are two problems with this approach. The first is with claiming that personating is equivalent to identifying. The second is with establishing the relationship between the idea of a "person personated" and a character. Joseph assumes that the rhetorical tropes in the dramatic text were transparent and that the shared gestural vocabulary of actors would have led them to similar interpretations of the role: "I suggest," he writes, "that when the author was alive, when the language was contemporary, and when the ingeniousness of the language was fitted to the person, each actor had the same character-image of the same role, although he had his individual method of embodying it in performance."[50] This assumption does not take into account the variability of the actor's experience of performing and the variability of the audience's ability to respond to a performed text. For example, not all spectators, certainly not the women or the trades people among the spectators, would have had the same education as the Elizabethan schoolboys he repeatedly mentions. Joseph also imposes upon Elizabethan performance an idea of personhood that speaks more of Stanislavski (whom he explicitly invokes) than it does of Shakespeare.

William Worthen, in *Shakespeare and the Authority of Performance*, offers a critique of this hypothesized ability of a universalized, naturalized actor to intuit character as "author-ized":

> Actor training [today] assumes an integrated and organic "subject" which can be discovered through the body, beneath the blockages and obstructions of culture. The [contemporary] theater requires this body, though, in part because it regards the production of character as the actor's principal task, and takes "character" as the transparent mimesis of human being in the world, rather than, say, as an interested, rhetorical representation of subjectivity, a limited model of agency.[51]

Joseph wants to use Renaissance rhetoric in the service of a static notion of character which he claims is universal. I would like to underscore Worthen's notion of character as an "interested, rhetorical representation of subjectivity," and substitute for Joseph's "identification" the rhetoricians' more dynamic sense of "imagination." Quintilian draws upon an Aristotelian precept that "a strong imagination begets the event itself."[52] According to Roach, Sir Francis Bacon, in his "Experiments . . . touching transmission of spirits and the force of imagination" (*Works* 2:641) "divide[s] the power of the imagination into three categories: first, over the 'body of the imaginant'; second, over the objects of inanimate nature, including corpses; and third, over 'the spirits of men and living creatures.'"[53] Through imagination, or, in more contemporary terms, the corporealized perception of the body-subject, the body is acted upon to transform and be transformed by that which it perceives as being external to it. The perception of the imagined embodied other is informed and expressed by the actor's own corporeality. Thus the personation of the same *dramatis persona* will differ from actor to actor and indeed may differ in the same actor's performance on different occasions.

The experience of embodied intersubjectivity is illustrated in *The Spanish Tragedy*, a play in which a performance is actually used to communicate suffering to an on-stage audience. Hieronimo's experience of an Old Man's grief is informed by his own similar history:

> Ay, now I know thee, now thou nam'st thy son;
> Thou art the lively image of my grief:
> Within thy face my sorrows I may see.
> Thy eyes are gummed with tears, thy cheeks are wan,
> Thy forehead troubled, and thy muttering lips
> Murmur sad words abruptly broken off
> By force of windy sighs thy spirit breathes;
> And all this sorrow riseth for thy son:
> And selfsame sorrow feel I for my son.
>
> (3.13.162–69)[54]

These lines, were they written in the third person, would be the equivalent of a Theophrastan Character of "A Grieving Man." The description certainly guides an actor's performance of the role of the Senex. But the lines also testify to the powerful impact body-subjects have on one another. The Old Man's grief is transformed by Hieronimo's own experience of it in his own suffering body. Similarly, the actor playing Hieronimo brings his own corporeal history to the performance of the role. We may contrast this with the absence of intersubjectivity seen above in the advice given to the boy actor in the Induction to *Antonio and Mellida*.

At the same time, the actor whose performance is informed by his own corporeal experience of the imagined corporeality of the person to be personated does not become that person. It is only "as if the Personater were the man Personated."[55] "As if." These are the critical words that Heywood in the *Apology for Actors* uses to distinguish between the actor and the person personated. It is that "as if" that distinguishes the actor's body from his mask, and that is the source of the actor's art and his ethical distance from the person he personates. In the *Apology*, Heywood, with ambivalence, tells the story of Caesar performing the role of Hercules: "yet was Caesar so extremely carryed away with the violence of his practised fury, and by the perfect shape of the madnesse of Hercules, to which he had fashioned all his actiue spirits, that he slew him [i.e. the actor playing Lycus] dead at his foot, & after swoong him . . . about his head."[56] Although Caesar's acting is cited as an example of the participation of even kings and emperors in what he calls "Tragedies naturally performed" (i.e. performed to life), Heywood prefers the "better manner" in which royal participation has more recently taken place.[57] The actor is enriched by his personation, but not effaced by it. He is able to experience and communicate the violence, but does not replicate it.

The embodied spectator

Spectators also have their own corporeal histories. As Edward Burns writes, "The issue of character is the issue of the construction of the subject in spectatorship as well as in performance."[58] The spectator, too, is a body-subject who is transformed by his or her embodied experience of the actor's performance. Roach points out that according to classical and Renaissance physiology, the link among the actor, the person personated, and the spectator was a literal and physical one:

> The rhetoric of the passions that derived from pneumatism endowed the actor's art with three potencies of an enchanted kind. First, the actor possessed the power to act on his own body. Second, he possessed the power to act on the physical space around him. Finally, he was able to act on the bodies of the spectators who shared that space with him.[59]

Thus it is not only the actor, but also the spectator who is corporeally affected by the actor's performance of his role. The physical connection between the actor and his spectators is described in the Overburian Character of "An Excellent Actor": "[S]it in a full Theater, and you will thinke you see so many lines drawne from the circumference of so many eares, whiles the *Actor* is the *Center*."[60]

According to Heywood, this physically transformative impact of theater is potentially morally transformative as well:

> [W]hat English blood seeing the person of any bold English man presented and doth not hugge his fame, and hunnye at his valor, pursuing him in his enterprise with his best wishes, and as beeing wrapt in contemplation, offers to him in his hart all prosperous performance, as if the Personater were the man Personated, so bewitching a thing is liuely and well spirited action, that it hath power to new mold the harts of the spectators and fashion them to the shape of any noble and notable attempt.[61]

Once again we must note the "as if." The "personater" does not become the man personated but he creates him as a persuasive and moving character through the mediations of his own embodied subjectivity. The performance, which illustrates the capacity of the actor to appropriate and be transformed by the person he is personating, also demonstrates the corporeality of the spectator's response. The spectator is described as experiencing the personation of the "bold English man" in his own body by "hugging" his fame, "honeying" at his valor, and "pursuing him in his enterprise." Furthermore, the personation has the power to "new mold the harts of the spectators and fashion them to the shape of any noble and notable attempt." In other words, the spectator, morally transformed by the physical and ethical impact of the performance, is potentially emboldened to emulate by enacting them the virtues of the performed person.

Hamlet's encounter with the Ghost illustrates the power of telling to transform its listener viscerally. First, the Ghost describes the potential effects of the story he is not allowed to tell:

> I could a tale unfold whose lightest word
> Would harrow up thy soul, freeze thy young blood,
> Make thy two eyes like stars start from their spheres,
> Thy knotted and combined locks to part,
> And each particular hair to stand an end,
> Like quills upon the fearful porpentine.
>
> (1.5.15–20)

The Ghost does tell, however, of the poison that "bark'd about, / Most lazar-like, with vile and loathsome crust / All [his] smooth body" (1.5.71–73), and in doing so does elicit from Hamlet a corporeal response: "O fie, hold, hold, my heart, / And you, my sinows, grow not instant old, / But bear me [stiffly] up" (1.5.93–95).[62] The Ghost's tale is chilling, but its effect on others—say Horatio and Marcellus, were they listening—would not be the same as its effect on Hamlet. Hamlet's own relationship to his father, his mother, and his uncle "in-forms" the physical response that will potentially spur him to his revenge, and creates for him in his own way the Ghost as a character. The same is true of spectators in the Globe Theater, whose own experiences will inform their embodied experiences of both the Ghost and Hamlet as characters.

Hamlet draws upon the principle of embodied response in his decision to stage 'The Mousetrap' in order to test the innocence of Claudius: "Hum—I have heard / That guilty creatures sitting at a play / Have by the very cunning of the scene / Been strook so to the soul, that presently / They have proclaim'd their malefactions" (2.2.588–92). Heywood, in the *Apology*, offers similar examples of spectators moved by their own histories to respond physically to the actor's personation with confessions of hidden guilt. He cites, to take just one of his examples, a performance in Norfolk by the Earle of Sussex's Men. The play, "the old History of Fryer Francis," performed the story of a woman who, having secretly murdered her husband in order to enjoy her young lover, was haunted by his ghost. "As this was acted," Heywood writes, "a townes-woman (till then of good estimation and report) finding her conscience (at this presenment) extremely troubled, suddenly skritched and cryd out Oh my husband, my husband! I see the ghost of my husband fiercely theatning and menacing me."[63]

This is an extreme example of a spectator's embodied experience of an actor's performance, but it serves to suggest that a dramatic character in performance is not necessarily either unitary or static. Rather, the early modern experience of dramatic character suggests that it is a product of an intersubjective communication among the person personated, the actor, and the spectator.

Notes

1. Thomas Heywood, *An Apology for Actors* (London, 1612). Transcriptions from Heywood's *Apology* are taken from the printable full text version of the 1612 edition in *Early English Books Online*, http://eebo.chadwyck.com/home. Signature numbers, and italic typeface when it appears, have been taken from the document images. All early modern sources are taken from the *EEBO* site unless otherwise indicated.
2. *OED Online*, http://dictionary.oed.com/entrance.dtl. "character, *n*." 17. a: "A personality invested with distinctive attributes and qualities, by a novelist or dramatist; also, the personality or 'part' assumed by an actor on the stage" (hereafter cited in text as *OED*).
3. Edward Burns, *Acting and Being on the Pre-Modern Stage* (New York: St. Martin's Press, 1990), 2.
4. Thomas J. Csordas, "Introduction: The Body as Representation and Being-in-the-world," in *Embodiment and Experience: The Existential Ground of Culture and Self*, ed. Thomas J. Csordas (Cambridge: Cambridge University Press, 1994), 1–24, explores the applicability of the Merleau-Ponty model to other disciplines, especially anthropology and ethnology. I see the present essay as working in a similar mode.
5. Eric Matthews, *The Philosophy of Merleau-Ponty* (Montreal: McGill-Queen's Press, 2002), 55.
6. *The Philosophy of Merleau-Ponty*, 45.
7. *The Philosophy of Merleau-Ponty*, 54.
8. *The Philosophy of Merleau-Ponty*, 60.
9. *The Philosophy of Merleau-Ponty*, 53.

10. *The Philosophy of Merleau-Ponty*, 54.
11. *The Philosophy of Merleau-Ponty*, 56.
12. Monika M. Langer, *Merleau-Ponty's Phenomenology of Perception: A Guide and Commentary* (Tallahassee: The Florida State University Press, 1989), xv.
13. *The Philosophy of Merleau-Ponty*, 60.
14. *OED* "person, *n.*" 2.a; In the sixteenth century "person" can refer as well to "a role or character assumed in real life, or in a play," see also, "person, *n.*" *OED* I.1.
15. *OED* "character, *n.*" 16.a; my emphasis.
16. André G. Bourassa, "*Personnage*: History, Philology, Performance," trans. Jennifer Drouin, in *Shakespeare and Character*, ed. Paul Yachnin and Jessica Slights (London: Palgrave Macmillan, 2009), 84–85.
17. Sir Thomas Overbury, "What a Character is," in *Sir Thomas Ouerbury his Wife. With addition of many new elegies vpon his vntimely and much lamented death. As also new newes, and diuers more characters, (neuer before annexed) written by himselfe and other learned gentlemen* (London, 1616), S2v–S3r. Herschel Baker, *The Later Renaissance in England* (Boston: Houghton Mifflin, 1975), 711, points out that the definition of the character as a literary form in the seventeenth century was very loose, and often bordered on the essay, the moral treatise, the aphorism, and the epistle.
18. Joseph Hall, *Characters of vertues and vices* (London, 1608), A5r.
19. Heywood, *An Apology for Actors*, B3v; my emphasis.
20. Heywood, *An Apology for Actors*, C4r.
21. John Earle, *Micro-cosmographie, or, A peece of the world discovered* (London, 1628), number 6, B12v–C1r.
22. David Wiles, *Mask and Performance in Greek Tragedy: From Ancient Festival to Modern Experimentation* (Cambridge: Cambridge University Press, 2007), 225. Ironically, etymologically speaking it is the French word *personnage* which, according to Bourassa, "means more than 'mask' since its complete source is *personam agere*, that is, to make act, to manage the mask, which refers to *agens*, the agent or actor," which carries the sense I am attributing to the early modern potential of the word "character." In English, however, the word "personage," in the early modern period as in our own, is closer to the word person and therefore, unlike the early modern sense of the word "character", refers to an individual who might exist in the world.
23. Joseph R. Roach, *The Player's Passion: Studies in the Science of Acting* (Newark: University of Delaware Press, 1985), 56.
24. Heywood, *An Apology for Actors*, C4r.
25. Sir Thomas Overbury, "An excellent Actor," *New and choise characters, of seuerall authors together with that exquisite and unmatcht poeme, The Wife* (London, 1615), M2v. B.L. Joseph, *Elizabethan Acting*. 2nd edition (Oxford: Oxford University Press, 1964) 1. Joseph, 3–5, even goes so far as to find in Hamlet's description of the Player's Hecuba speech the equivalent of Stanislavski's "magic 'if'." While Hecuba is nothing to the Player, nor she to him, the Player has been able to "force his soul so to his own conceit" and in doing so produce Hecuba's emotion.
26. Roach, *Player's Passion*, 42; Arthur F. Kinney, *Shakespeare by Stages: An Historical Introduction* (Malden, MA: Blackwell, 2003), 58.

134   Embodied Intersubjectivity and the Creation of Early Modern Character

27. Robert Weimann, "The Actor-Character in 'Secretly Open:' Action Doubly Encoded Personation on Shakespeare's Stage," in *Shakespeare and Character*, ed. Paul Yachnin and Jessica Slights (London: Palgrave Macmillan, 2008), 177–93.
28. Cited in Kinney, *Shakespeare by Stages*, 56.
29. Heywood, *An Apology for Actors*, C4r.
30. William Shakespeare, *The Tragedy of Hamlet, Prince of Denmark. The Riverside Shakespeare*, ed. G. Blakemore Evans et al. (Boston: Houghton Mifflin, 1974). Quotations from *Hamlet* are from this edition.
31. John Marston, *Antonio and Mellida. The First Part.* Ed. G.K. Hunter (Lincoln: University of Nebraska Press, 1965).
32. See Weimann, "The Actor-Character," in this volume.
33. The *OED*, "nature, *n.*" suggests the link between the two: "[A]ctive force that establishes and maintains the order of the universe, group of properties or characteristics that define objects (early twelfth century)" and "attributes, innate disposition of a person (late twelfth century)."
34. Phillip Stubbes, *The anatomie of abuses contayning a discouerie, or briefe summarie of such notable vices and imperfections, as now raigne in many Christian countreyes of the worlde: but (especiallie) in a verie famous ilande called Ailgna: together, with most fearefull examples of Gods iudgementes, executed vpon the wicked for the same, aswell in Ailgna of late, as in other places, elsewhere. Verie godly, to be read of all true Christians, euerie where: but most needefull, to be regarded in Englande* (London, 1583), L8r–L8v.
35. Michel de Montaigne, *An Apology for Raymond Sebond*, trans. and ed. M.A. Screech (London: Penguin Books, 1987), 18–19.
36. Pierio Valeriano, *Hieroglyphica* (Lyon, 1602; repr., New York: Garland, 1976).
37. John Bulwer, *Chirologia: Or the Natural Language of the Hand and Chironomia: Or the Art of Manual Rhetoric* (1644), ed. James W. Cleary (Carbondale: Southern Illinois University Press, 1974), 6.
38. Roach, *Player's Passion*, 27.
39. Cited in Kinney, *Shakespeare by Stages*, 56.
40. Roach, *Player's Passion*, 32. Among the most widely read discussions of rhetoric in England were Thomas Wilson, *The arte of rhetorique* (London, 1553); Abraham Fraunce, *The Arcadian rhetorike: Or The praecepts of rhetorike made plaine by examples.* (London,1558); and Thomas Wright, *The passions of the minde in generall* (London: 1604), Book V.
41. Joseph, *Elizabethan Acting*, 6.
42. Cited in Roach, *Player's Passion*, 24.
43. Overbury, *An Excellent Actor*, M5v.
44. Roach, *Player's Passion*, 32.
45. Wright, *Passions*, 176.
46. Wright, *Passions*, 174, 176.
47. Cited in Joseph, *Elizabethan Acting*, 8.
48. Roach, *Player's Passion*, 32–33.
49. Joseph, *Elizabethan Acting*, 72 et passim.
50. Joseph, *Elizabethan Acting*, 86.
51. W.B. Worthen, *Shakespeare and the Authority of Performance* (Cambridge: Cambridge University Press, 1997), 110.
52. Roach, *Player's Passion*, 25.

53. Roach, *Player's Passion*, 46.
54. Thomas Kyd, *The Spanish Tragedy*, 2nd edition, ed. J. R. Mulryne (New York: W. W. Norton, 1989).
55. Heywood, *An Apology for Actors*, B4r.
56. Heywood, *An Apology for Actors*, E3v.
57. Heywood, *An Apology for Actors*, E3v, E4r.
58. Burns, *Acting and Being*, 121.
59. Roach, *Player's Passion*, 27.
60. Overbury, *An Excellent Actor*, M5v.
61. Heywood, *An Apology for Actors*, B4r.
62. Carol Chillington Rutter, *Enter the Body: Women and Representation on Shakespeare's Stage* (London: Routledge, 2001), xi.
63. *An Apology for Actors*, G1v; Another example Heywood cites took place when a company of English players were performing in Amsterdam a play in which an innocent man is murdered by having a nail driven through his temples: "As the Actors handled this, the audience might on a sodaine vnderstand an out-cry, and loud shrike in a remote gallery, and pressing about the place, they might perceiue a woman of great grauity, strangely amazed, who with a distracted & troubled braine oft sighed out these words: Oh my husband, my husband!" (G2v).

Part III Performance

7
Metatheater and the Performance of Character in *The Winter's Tale*

Paul Yachnin and Myrna Wyatt Selkirk

> Maybe metatheater is the foundation of performance?
> Maybe it is the root of theatrical magic?

This comment about metatheater and theatrical magic comes from Sarah Waisvisz, a young scholar and performer, who took part in a theatrical experiment at McGill University in 2003, in which a group of student actors, directed by Myrna Wyatt Selkirk, explored the lines of connection between metatheater and character in *The Winter's Tale*. In what follows, we say more about the experiment and what we learned from it, and we address Sarah's propositions about metatheater, performance, and theatrical magic. We focus also on character (about which Sarah and her fellow actors also had much to say), and we try to define theatrical magic, or at least try to describe how the magic of performance operates and how it might have operated in Shakespeare's playhouse.

We should also tell you something about who we are. Selkirk is an acting teacher, director, and Drama and Theater professor at McGill. She has been an assistant director at the Neptune Theatre (Halifax) and the Shaw Festival (Ontario). At McGill, she has directed numerous productions, including Michel Tremblay's *Bonjour, là, Bonjour*, Shakespeare's *Twelfth Night* and *The Merchant of Venice*, and *The Castle* by Howard Barker. Paul Yachnin is a scholar who has published on theater and early modern culture and society, including the books *Stage-Wrights* and *The Culture of Playgoing in Early Modern England* (with Anthony Dawson). We started working together when Selkirk invited Yachnin to take part in her Theater Lab class. Yachnin provided a set of readings about metatheater, which served to initiate discussion of the topic; in addition to developing their own understanding of the idea of metatheater, the students began to experiment theatrically with the text of *The Winter's Tale*. Naturally, they were looking for indications and also opportunities for metatheatrical performance, and they were also thinking about what those opportunities might add to a staging of the play.

The students learned very early on that, classically, metatheater has been seen as an element of the drama that draws attention to the theatrical practices that underlie and produce the fictional, represented world of the play. James Calderwood, in his 1974 book *Shakespearean Metadrama*, provides a useful definition of the range of the term:

> Shakespeare's plays are not only about . . . various moral, social, political, and other thematic issues . . . but also about Shakespeare's plays. Not just "the idea of the play" . . . but dramatic art itself—its materials, its media of language and theater, its generic forms and conventions, its relationship to truth and the social order—is a dominant Shakespearean theme, perhaps his most abiding subject.[1]

In a particularly bold instance of this dimension of theater, the boy actor playing the famous queen Cleopatra shows his face at a critical moment in her unfolding tragedy (the actor might not have squeaked, but he certainly was a boy):

> The quick comedians
> Extemporally will stage us, and present
> Our Alexandrian revels: Antony
> Shall be brought drunken forth, and I shall see
> Some squeaking Cleopatra boy my greatness
> I' th' posture of a whore.
> (*Antony and Cleopatra*, 5. 2. 216–21)[2]

It is not, of course, that the Queen disappears at this moment, leaving in her place only a boy in women's clothing. It is that she puts herself at risk—or she is put at risk—by the reference to a boy actor playing her as if she were a Roman prostitute. Indeed, if the audience members feel strongly that she is being put at risk by what the text is making her say, then they will apprehend the presence of the playwright as well as the presences of the character and the actor. Later in the essay, we will return to the conjoinment of theatrical risk with the metatheatrical layering of character, actor, and author. We'll consider how metatheater produces theatrical risk and the co-presence of actor and character, because we want to understand just how metatheater helps to produce the particular phenomenon of Shakespearean character, especially in performance and in the presence of an audience. But, for now, let us consider the question in more familiar, more literary terms.

What, then, are we to make of this disclosure of the everyday performance practice (boys taking the parts of women) that stands behind the illusion of a queen contemplating the choice between suicide or the humiliation of being taken to Rome as Octavius' trophy? For over forty years, at least since the publication of Anne Barton's 1962 study *Shakespeare and the Idea of the Play*, the answer to this question, and to many questions of the same kind, has been framed in terms of *meaning*—the meaning of the play as a play, including what the play says about itself and the theater; what it suggests about the truth-value of theatrical performance; and what it sees as the relationship between theater and real life. Barton comments that Cleopatra's speech is of a piece with the play's evocation of the theatricalized "emptiness and deceit" and its representation of theater's "ability to cheapen and degrade." "In the hands of the players," she says, "[Cleopatra's] love for Antony will become ignoble and common."[3]

A particularly strong line within metatheatrical criticism of Shakespeare reads his drama for what it can tell us about the playwright's social and artistic biography. Here the plays address the situation of the playhouse, the actor, and the dramatist in a world that did not at all revere playing or playgoing. This way of reading the self-reflexiveness of the plays runs from Barton to Sigurd Burckhardt's *Shakespearean Meanings* (1968), to Alvin Kernan's *The Playwright as Magician* (1979), and then up through the early phase of New Historicism, with Louis Montrose's rethinking of metadrama in his 1979/80 essay "The Purpose of Playing," to Stephen Greenblatt's reflections, first published in 1984, on the relationship between *King Lear* and the Reformation controversy about exorcism.[4] Between the earlier formalist and the more recent New Historicist versions of metatheater is a shift from an emphasis on Shakespeare's self-reflexive art to a focus on his performative or illocutionary language. Roughly, it is a change from thematic to functionalist criticism—from an interest in what the plays mean to a focus on what they do. For Burckhardt, the plays reflect the writer's struggle as he moves ever closer to the perfection of his art; Montrose and Greenblatt think of Shakespearean metadrama as capable of changing the situation of the theater in its social setting by legitimating the practices and languages of playing. So Burckhardt says that in *The Merchant of Venice*, Shakespeare learns that "his work as a commissioned playwright need not be a servile, money-grubbing prostitution of his talent . . . there was dignity in his trade, truth and worth in the two hours' traffic of the stage."[5] In similar but different terms, Greenblatt shows us how Shakespearean metadrama, by projecting theatrical "emptiness" onto the world itself, is able to create a favorable social and historical space for theater:[6]

> He writes for the greater glory and profit of theater, a fraudulent institution that never pretends to be anything but fraudulent, an institution that calls forth what is not . . . that evacuates everything it represents. By doing so the theater makes for itself the hollow round space within which it survives. The force of *King Lear* is to make us love the theater, to seek out its satisfactions, to serve its interests.[7]

Naturally, and especially in light of what we learned from the work of the theater lab students, we follow the "performative turn" of New Historicism. We ask, "What does metatheater do?" rather than, "What does it mean?" But where both formalist and historicist versions of metatheater tend to read it as a representation of "mere" theatricality, a kind of busy emptiness that Shakespeare must overcome or somehow turn to account, we see theatrical performance itself as full of meaningful opportunities and challenges—there is nothing fraudulent or empty about it—and we see metatheater as functionally integral to the operations of acting, playmaking, and playwatching. Indeed, it is our contention that metatheater is a very nearly ubiquitous feature of Shakespearean dramatic design and also a key element in Shakespeare's achievement as a creator of character.

Our interest in metatheater and character allows us to recapture an important dimension of the topic that figured prominently in Lionel Abel's seminal study *Metatheatre: A New View of Dramatic Form* (1963).[8] Abel centered his thinking about metatheater on character, the element of the approach that has suffered the most marked diminishment in subsequent criticism, especially in materialist versions of metatheater, which have turned away from the category of character as at once too formalist and too essentialist. For Abel, of course, metatheater named a genre rather than a feature of a number of different genres. On his account, metatheater displaced tragedy and indeed made tragedy impossible in the face of Shakespeare's momentous discovery that reality was a foundationless illusion no different in kind from the imagined world of a play like *Hamlet*. While metatheatrical criticism of various kinds has flourished, Abel's thesis has found few followers: for one thing, his definition of tragedy was far too narrow; for another, his theory of genre as something frozen in amber failed to understand the living, contestable law of artistic types (and it was clean contrary in spirit to the antifoundationalist version of the world he found in Shakespeare); third, his thesis was unable to account for the metatheatrical elements in very many plays, including tragedies, going back all the way to antiquity; and, finally, it was of a piece with twentieth-century existentialism, which has given way to the antihumanist thinking of neoMarxism and poststructuralism, which in turn has tended to underwrite more recent, materialist forms for criticism. Sartrian existentialism coupled antifoundationalism and humanism, so that the person found radical freedom, self-consciousness, and commitment precisely because of the made-up nature of the world; Althusserian neoMarxism, to take one example, conjures a personless world where the constructedness of reality now includes within its purview the very people who previously had been described as the radically free creators of the world and themselves.

Abel's particularly resonant insight is that many of Shakespeare's characters are themselves dramatists and so conscious of, resistant to, and creative with the roles that the playwright has assigned them to play. The character Hamlet, who (Abel says) attempts to rewrite the melodrama Shakespeare gave him by pursuing the Universal (i.e. by choosing Death), is the originating figure of metatheater:[9]

> [F]or the first time in the history of drama, the problem of the protagonist is that he has a playwright's consciousness. . . . .[Hamlet] is the first stage figure with an acute awareness of what it means to be staged. How be dramatized when one has the imagination to be a dramatist? After *Hamlet* it would be difficult for any playwright to make us respect any character lacking dramatic consciousness. . . . The problem of author versus character was I think first envisaged in *Hamlet*. From now on—unless there is to be a new culture whose values we can scarcely foresee—no dramatist has the right to set any supposedly self-conscious character on the stage who does not collaborate in his dramatization. In this sense Jean-Paul Sartre was profoundly correct. No one with self-consciousness can ever do anything drastic in life or on stage, with our respect, that is, unless he has agreed to his commitment.[10]

Abel is important for us because he emphasizes character as central to metatheater, even though we are not, of course, developing his interest in the philosophical and cultural meaning of Shakespeare's self-reflexive drama, at least not along the lines he follows. He is important also because he keeps his attention on performance, which is in part a consequence of his character-centered approach but also partly due to his lively interest in the theater for its own sake. Finally, as the passage quoted above suggests, he attends to the ethics of acting and playwatching, more particularly to the ethical relationship between the characters and the playgoers. The character must commit consciously to his role in the play—as it is presented to him and as he is able to shape it—in order to earn the audience's respect. The idea is that there is something of consequence at stake in Shakespeare's characters, in the work of actors in performance, and in the attention that we pay as members of an audience to the unfolding of the drama takes us back to the first chapter of this book. Michael Bristol says that a theory of dramatic character must include also an account of human nature and value if it is to become more than a bare analysis of theatrical technique. Like Bristol, we are seeking to explain both the technical operation of characterization in Shakespearean performance and what that operation can tell us about the broader philosophical implications of performance. In this case, we argue that theatrical technique and human value are inseparable because the metatheatrical performance of character enacts and makes visible the dialogical constitution of personhood and community—how, that is, we make ourselves and each other up as individuals and how those substantial acts of imagining create collectivity.

* * *

We could not have developed our ideas without the Theater Lab students' intelligent and inventive approach to a series of scenes from *The Winter's Tale*, or without their performance of the scenes before a audience of about 100 students, faculty, and members of the public at McGill the evening of 30 October 2003. Our thinking was also stimulated by the discussion that followed that performance, and by discussions among ourselves and with other members of the Shakespeare and Performance Research Team. After both the project and the course were complete, the student actors were asked a series of questions about their interaction with the audience.[11] What started to emerge was that direct address to specific audience members did alter the character from how it had been rehearsed. This direct address was often associated with the obviously metatheatrical moments in *The Winter's Tale*, but that was not always the case, especially as it became clear that the actors/characters were fed and changed by direct contact in general and as it emerged that the text fully supported this. Though the students were not asked directly about common theatrical techniques such as playing an objective or physical action (techniques that spring from the work of Konstantin Stanislavski), it came up frequently in their discussions of actor/audience interaction. They felt that what their character needed from the audience (their goal) and what they did to pursue this goal was integral to the relationship. If we define character as a set of dynamic relationships, then certainly relationship to the audience must be central in the creation and definition of character.

The character of Autolycus is, like Hamlet, one of Shakespeare's dramatists. Roxana Vahed played Autolycus; she said that "Autolycus' character is created through the constant oscillation between the play-life and spectator-gaze. Moving into eye contact with the spectator was a little like asking and confirming character-ship, confirming existence of the play-world and appealing that they buy into it. It serves as a confirmation of their and our participation in the theatrical event." Roxana insisted that the audience was essential in the creation of the character of Autolycus since "the audience is the only group fully aware of who he is, and so [she] felt most in character in the moments when he shares his plans, or gloats while he is pulling some trickery or deciding how to meddle. In these moments, Autolycus is acknowledging both the audience as secret confidants and establishing the 'present' in the play."

Katie Spurgeon, who played Hermione, felt that direct contact with the audience only worked for her when she was able to involve them in her goal. In her appeal to the court, she was "able to use them in this instance as an obstacle or 'other' to try and gain their approval or sympathy while at the same time directing [her] action toward Leontes."

In both of the above cases, the actor spoke of what the character wants from the audience. This is very much the same way that they would discuss what they want from other characters in the play. Katie went on to say that "you must have a particular point of view on the audience's presence otherwise your interaction becomes muddy and general." This often means that actors will decide ahead of time whether the audience collectively is friend, enemy, a part of themselves, an army of soldiers, or a courtroom full of friends or enemies, etc. Actors cast spectators in roles that they don't know they have been given until the moment of interaction. Of course, the audience doesn't necessarily take on the role they are cast in, though many do as an instinctive response. If an actor smiles sweetly at the members of the audience, they know they are a friend, whereas if the actor berates them, they know they are meant to feel ashamed or defensive, and often their response suggests that they have taken on exactly the role for which they were cast.

Sarah Waisvisz, who played the Clown, also spoke of a character goal in relationship to the audience. She noted that "Autolycus in particular aligned himself with the audience, and the Clown at various times asked the audience for help and support." Sarah contended that "the project overall highlighted the vast spectrum between metatheatrical language like Leontes' 'play boy, play' and a character like the Clown who engages with the audience for a crucial purpose like survival or necessity." Her thought was that the distinction is related to stakes—about how badly the character needed to get something from the audience.

Another important issue that came up several times in student comments was complicity with the audience. Autolycus says to the audience:

> How blessed are we that are not simple men!
> Yet nature might have made me as these are,
> Therefore I will not disdain.
>
> (4.4.745–47)

Such a text allowed Roxana, as Autolycus, to rely on the audience as conspirators; and, in such moments, she felt "camaraderie between the spectators and the character in the form of a shared thought and sense of superiority." Sarah noted that "by their participation in the contract of belief or suspension of disbelief, the audience helps to sustain the illusion and permit the continuation of the performance." Both Sarah and Roxanna argued that "metatheater, in performance, affirms the audience's role as active participants" (Waisvisz).

It is interesting to consider Katie's thoughts as she stood as the statue of Hermione: "At moments I almost took on an audience point-of-view of the goings-on myself. I guess you could say that my 'inner dialogue' was aided and abetted by both the audience proximity and the fact that I was made to stand stock still." She described the moment of release as "a brimming over of nervous energy of both the character and the actor. The physical relief was tied to the emotional release of the moment. Having been removed from the scene in such a central way, I could now re-engage as a member of the story stepping back in completely to the character point-of-view. So in this sense, I felt as though I bridged the 'metatheatrical gap' between audience and actor for a time."

Max Woertendyke played Leontes. He said that eye contact with the audience made his Leontes more aggressive and that the surge of energy in the moment of eye contact changed his character. He also asserted that "metatheater helps the actor to avoid becoming a passive actor." He found that audience resistance to contact affected the formation of the character as much as a very giving and open audience member would have. "If I perceived someone was bored, for instance, instead of thinking as an actor about how either that sucks or what I can do about it to spice the performance up—I instead responded as Leontes and it was Leontes who then demanded attention from his viewers by speaking to them directly and making them, not himself, the subject of the speeches." The following passage was played by Max as a direct address to the audience:

> And many a man there is, (even at this present,
> Now, while I speak this) holds his wife by th' arm,
> That little thinks she has been sluic'd in's absence,
> And his pond fish'd by his next neighbor—by
> Sir Smile, his neighbor.
>
> (1.2.192-96)

These words spoken to specific audience members brought out an arresting awkwardness and attention in the audience. This interesting and useful discomfort was multiplied in our case since Max was speaking, in many instances, to people that he knew and some of whom knew each other. Since Max sat with the audience and moved and stood beside people in the audience, there was no doubt to whom he was speaking. This created a more outward-looking—as Max says, a more aggressive—Leontes than if the passage had been muttered to himself. If the lines are played as a private moment, the character might chastise himself, lament, curse, or fret inwardly. When they are played as a public moment, the actor/character plays some of the same actions, but he also mocks and goads and uses the words against the audience in a much bolder way than in a private moment of torment. He wants to see the spectators respond—to make them feel the connection so that he knows that he's not alone in this. He makes them the subject of his speech, which is a very different act from referring to himself and a group of unspecified cuckolds.

All this draws our attention to how direct engagement with the audience changes the style of playing, the action, the character goal, and the nature of the stakes for the actor/character. The stakes are always higher in front of an audience than they are in rehearsal, and direct contact with the audience can be even more potent than the powerful knowledge that you're being watched. Some actors in the project found it hard to stay focused when making eye contact with an audience member. There is great risk in this moment of contact. Roxana dealt with this by being "steeled and ready" and "holding the cloak of character tightly in order to justify the interaction and not to fail." The risk of failure—of exposure—is a potent force that keeps the stakes high.

As noted above, the audience can affect *what* actors do as well as *how* they do it. Autolycus invites the audience to share in his superior knowledge of the situation. The audience is an essential ingredient in the playing of this action: "to invite." If we go back to the idea that character is a set of dynamic relationships, it must follow that character is the sum of the actions played, since each thing you *do* to another character or to the audience is the essential ingredient in how you relate to them. Rather than describing the character with adjectives, we used verbs for the real nuts and bolts of character development. This is common practice in actor training and in many rehearsal processes. For instance, some of the things that Hamlet does throughout his play are: to fret, ponder, plot, criticize, chastise, appeal, trick, and flirt. It is less useful for us as theater practitioners to describe him as moody, conniving, lost, or lonely. Playing an action is the most basic thing an actor can *do*. Actions can be played without pretense so the character and the actor are one and the same in that moment. It is in the choice of actions that the actor and character split. One particular actor in life may interact with people mostly by teasing, flirting, or boasting, but the character that he or she is playing may be defined better by verbs such as complain, accuse, or threaten, which are things that actor may rarely, if ever, do in life. Each can be defined by the sum of their actions.

Each action has many subtle nuances and *how* each action is played moves into a conversation about style—another important part of character. The *how* is affected by the audience since the energy generated from audience interaction, of which all the actors spoke, and the sense of complicity with the audience affect *how* the action is played. An open, engaged look from an audience member may elicit a gentle appeal, whereas a look of hostility might make the appeal more harsh and demanding. Or it may change the action completely—an appeal can turn into a demand or even a reproach if not well received. All this is played in the present tense.

It's hard to rehearse audience interaction—in rehearsal, actors talk to their audience of one—the director. Sarah noted how wonderful it was finally to engage with the audience "who aren't expecting anything, who don't know the jokes already." She went on to talk about "the willingness of the audience to accept and to 'participate the actor' which made it very comfortable to pursue metatheatrical engagement."

In "Performance and Participation" Anthony Dawson asserts that "the actor, by participating his body, creates his part, constructs the person he represents; the audience participates the actor, exchanging its hold on ordinary reality for an embodied, but also of course impersonated, passion."[12] Yet the audience doesn't need continuous illusion in order to be able to participate. "Metatheatrical theatre in fact pushes the argument to the most extreme level: the members of the audience are aware of the artifice and yet, or maybe because of it, they are nevertheless compelled to participate, engage, and be enticed" (Waisvisz).

To draw attention to the artifice, we staged *The Winter's Tale* project in a large open classroom with regular fluorescent lighting, which meant that there was no light to focus the audience's attention. We set up alley seating with the two sections of the audience facing each other. The actors continued to set up in the space and greet the audience as they arrived. A few of the actors found this a fairly uncomfortable time, particularly as some of them had family members, friends, and fellow students coming to see the performance. These intimates made it essential for them simply to be themselves. A good deal of high school and university theater (and still a lot of professional theater) does focus on representational rather than presentational forms of playing, so this fear is understandable. Actors who have trained extensively in clown and mask seem to be much braver in this regard. On the other hand, a number of actors adapted well to audience interaction. For instance, Sarah was surprised at how easy it was to swing between greeting the audience as herself, making sure to play her flute when required, and jumping into her clown scene. She found that it was actually easier to play to the audience than it would have been to perform as if with a "fourth wall".

Though there was a need to be able to snap in and out of character between scenes, the actors somehow managed within the scenes to use audience interaction as part of the life of the characters. That was never an expectation or requirement, but it is the main thread that ran through the response sheets. Rather than dropping in and out of character, the actors simply found a character goal to relate to the audience. This nourished the character, changed, and strengthened it. Actors love being "in" character and when they bought into the risk of eye contact with the audience, they actually went deeper into it rather than being drawn out of it. The power of make-believe allowed them to create the audience just as the audience was helping to create them.

* * *

The students' reflections, along with the experiment itself, suggest a way of thinking about Shakespearean metatheater very differently from how Calderwood, Kernan, or Greenblatt do. The moments where the plays explicitly reflect on their own theatrical artifice—moments of thematic attention-getting that have, naturally, drawn the most literary-critical notice for the past fifty years—are something like nodes in the plays' whole cloth deployment of metatheater in a theatrical project of characterization and audience formation. Hamlet on "actions that a man might play," or Cleopatra on squeaking Cleopatras boying her greatness, or Leontes' obsessive use of the word "play" ("Go play, boy . . . Thy mother plays, and I / Play too" [1.2.187–88]) are of a piece with a larger and more ubiquitous dimension of the plays that points to the competitive and collaborative practices of actors with each other and with the members of the audience, and it also tells us something about Shakespeare's practices as a writer for the theater. As we have noted, this dimension of performance is supported—not merely allowed—by the text. Sarah as the Clown was able to straddle the line between herself as actor and herself as character in order to solicit the audience's backing at the very moment that Roxana as Autolycus seemed to have all the advantages that superior knowledge, the practice of speaking in asides (called for in the text), and the putting off of a false beard (also called for) could give her. The effect of their exchange was to reveal how many metatheatrical playing opportunities the text could actively support (even at moments where it did not seem at first to call for them).

The scene comes after Polixenes' discovery of Perdita's cross-class romance with Florizel and the young couple's flight from Bohemia. Autolycus, very much connecting with the audience, revels in the rewards that are falling upon him. "Sure the gods do this year connive at us," he says, "and we may do any thing extempore" (4.4.676–77). He spots the Shepherd and his son, decides to take advantage of them, stands aside, eavesdrops on them, changes costume, confronts them. In reply to his challenge, the Clown says, "We are but plain fellows, sir" (721). Playing with the phrase "to give the lie," which means primarily "to challenge someone by accusing him of lying" and, secondarily, "to tell a lie," Autolycus extends his attack on them:

> A lie; you are rough and hairy. Let me have no lying. It becomes none but tradesmen, and they often give us soldiers the lie, but we pay them for it with stamped coin, not stabbing steel, therefore they do not give us the lie.
>
> (722–26)

The Clown's rejoinder, which cued Sarah's engagement with the audience, plays also with the key phrase: "Your worship had like to have given us one [i.e. the lie], if you had not taken yourself with the manner" (727–28). *Riverside* explains the line thus: "[Y]ou almost told us an untruth (i.e. that the tradesmen had *given* you the lie). But you caught yourself in time. *With the manner* = in the act." Sarah gave the line a more straightforward reading that connected with a more complex characterization of the Clown. "You almost accused us of lying," Sarah's Clown seemed to say, "but only tradesmen do that, and you bore in mind your disguise as a courtier."[13] Sarah played the line knowingly to the audience, as if her character knew something about Autolycus that he did not know she knew, something that she could not have known as the Clown but that could have come to her only because she was also an actor who knew the text. Sarah's metatheatrical reading of the line thus released a meaning that had been obscured by literary commentary, gave the Clown a more sophisticated grasp of Autolycus' challenge and his language, allowed the Clown a moment of competitive knowingness (seeking complicity with the spectators to rival Autolycus' connivance with them), and, importantly, suggested how the text is designed to promote a fluid and flexible metatheatrical performance style that invites actors to be themselves and their characters at the same moment so as to engage the audience more effectively and to deepen the characters they personate.

* * *

Metatheater deepens character in two ways. One is that it seems to cast off theatricality as an inferior or questionable representational mode so that what is being acted is given the status of non-theatrical representation. Cleopatra is really there because "she" can express disdain for boy actors playing Cleopatra. Always attendant on this reality-effect is, of course, the fact that those characters dismissing theatricality as a suspect form of representation are themselves "mere" actors. And that leads to the second way metatheater works, which is as the mode of operation we are most concerned with here. It requires what Abel calls "self-consciousness" and "commitment," and it involves what the actors described as something like the cultivation of an ethically and emotionally charged relationship between themselves and audience members characterized by "confirmation," "help and support," "complicity," "aggression," and "risk."

A performance-focused account of character that emphasizes the playing out of dynamic relationships that include the audience adds a necessary aspect to a formalist description of character, even one, for example, as sophisticated as Bert O. States' model of character as an unfolding gestalt:

> Traits belong to character in somewhat the way that geographical features belong to the earth. When a character demonstrates a trait it is perceived as we perceive a continental mass on the revolving earth as seen from space. The trait bellies forth as a certain face, or behavioral configuration, that does not exhaust the character, even for that moment in which the trait is perceived.[14]

Form trumps process here. The traits come into view one by one but in such a way as always to point to an underlying coherence. The task of the performers is to play the character gestalt, to find the through-line that connects the various speeches and actions of particular characters; and the business of the spectators is to witness the unfolding, already achieved unity of the characters. To quote William Worthen, such a view collapses the complex specificity of performance into a practice that merely "recaptures or restates the authority of a text."[15] However theatrical an account of character States might be developing, it is clear that it minimizes the "processual" nature of character, that is, character as something actively being made by actors and audience-members, which is what the student-actors discovered about the formation of the characters they played. To be sure, the actors and spectators do not make the characters up whole cloth. Shakespeare has set certain verbal, behavioral, social, generic, and relational parameters, just as he has created very many opportunities for constitutive interactions among the actors, and between the actors and the audience. Modern performance practices, and theatrical training and tradition, also exert considerable influence over the process of characterization. But what we discovered was that none of these framing factors changed the basic processual, collaborative nature of character. It could hardly have been otherwise, especially given how the prominence of metatheater in this performance solicited, challenged, coaxed, even shamed the audience into lending their understanding to the creation of character. Simply put, the Clown is a different character if Sarah fails to connect with the audience. If she fails to win the spectators' support (and we can also note how the character's anti-court humor, at 4.4.742, 801–3, can contribute to her contest against Autolycus), the Clown will remain no more than an unknowing bumpkin; if she can effectively stand astride the actor-character divide, the Clown will emerge as savvy as well as silly, and his self-conscious view of the action will have purchase on the audience's attention alongside Autolycus' influential way of seeing.

There is another, equally important consequence to the dynamic and collaborative nature of character creation. If playing and playgoing involve, respectively, realizing and witnessing the unfolding of an existing, unified character, which is how States sees it, then theatrical performance can be little more than an adjunct to the characterological creativity of dramatic literature. However brilliant the actors and however responsive the spectators, the play and its characters are always already there. Theatrical performance makes nothing new; and therefore actors and audience members have no great responsibility for what transpires in performance. If, however, metatheater anchors the dynamic collaboration of actors and audience in the creation of character as something new, then they do have responsibility for what they make. On this account, metatheater transforms character, not only by making its formation the work of many hands, but also by making it into a focal activity of what could be called ethical spectatorship.

We want, finally, to suggest that Shakespearean metatheatrical characterization and the ethical spectatorship it cultivates (since playgoers must choose and respond in order for the play to work) is an operational response to the powerful objections against theater that were certainly one of the central ideological features of Shakespeare's professional life. Antitheatricalism has a long history and, not surprisingly, it enjoyed an efflorescence in Shakespeare's time, partly due to the growth of a commercial, public theater, and partly because of the expansion of the book trade and the literary public itself, which made attractive and profitable the writing and printing of works of theatrical and social critique, from Stephen Gosson's *The School of Abuse* (1579) to William Prynne's *Histriomastix* (1633). One of the most compelling and influential arguments against playing and playgoing was written long before the rise of a commercial theater in England. This passage, from Augustine's *Confessions*, represents what is most persuasive and troubling in the long-standing case against playing and playgoing:

> The theater enraptured me, for its shows were filled with pictures of my own miseries and with tinder for my fires. Why is it that a man likes to grieve over doleful and tragic events which he would not want to happen to himself? The spectator likes to experience grief at such scenes, and this very sorrow is a pleasure to him. What is this but a pitiable folly? For the more a man is moved by these things, the less free is he from such passions. However, when he himself

experiences it, it is usually called misery; when he experiences it with regard to others, it is called mercy. But what sort of mercy is to be shown to these unreal things upon the stage? The auditor is not aroused to go to the aid of the others; he is only asked to grieve over them. Moreover, he will show greater approval of the author of such representations, the greater the grief he feels. But if men's misfortunes, whether fictitious or of ancient times, are put on in such manner that the spectator does not feel sorrow, then he leaves in disgust and with disapproval. If grief is aroused in him, he remains in the theater, full of attention and enjoying himself.

. . . in my wretchedness at that time I loved to feel sorrow, and I sought out opportunities for sorrow. In the false misery of another man as it was mimicked on the stage, that actor's playing pleased me most and had the strongest attraction for me which struck tears from my eyes. What wonder was it that I, an unhappy sheep straying from your flock and impatient of your protection, should be infected with loathsome sores? Hence came my love for such sorrows, by which I was not pierced deep down—for I did not like to suffer such things, but only to look at them—and by which, when they were heard and performed, I was scratched lightly, as it were. As a result, as though from scratches made from fingernails, there followed a burning tumor and horrid pus and wasting away. Such was my life, but was it truly life, my God?[16]

Augustine poses a hard question, since however true-to-life are the representations on the stage, however much Shakespearean characterization models personhood as dialogic and performative, theater will remain an essentially trivial (not to mention immoral) artform and playgoing will remain a trivial (and immoral) activity because unreal things, which do not pierce deep down, arouse empty, mimic feelings of sorrow and sympathy that mask a guilty, pleasurable passivity.

A first response to this view is that Augustine is being unfair to himself. He was not a ghoulish looker-on who sought crash scenes wherever he could find them. The spectacles of suffering that he loved so dearly were representations of misery rather than instances of real misery. Of course he knows this, and that awareness forms an important part of his guilty recollection: he spent his tears on unreal things to the detriment of his spirit. But the fact that theater features playful representations of life rather than life itself surely calls for a more sustained consideration than he seems prepared to make, especially since what he seeks to understand is the morality of spectatorly pleasure. There must be a difference, which needs to be taken into account, between taking pleasure in other people's suffering and taking pleasure in other people's playful performances of suffering.

The McGill experiment suggested that Shakespearean theater is persistently metatheatrical. The actors moved in and out of the fictional world easily and fluidly: they were one moment in Sicilia or Bohemia and the next in West 25 of the McGill Arts Building. The permeable relationship between the fictional world of the play and the theatrical representation of that world was highlighted in this performance, but it is, as we hope we have begun to show, an integral feature of Shakespeare's drama. What kind of answer, then, would this high level of anti-illusionist metatheatrical performance make to Augustine's accusation of theatrical triviality and viciousness?

Our claim in the face of Augustine's antitheatricalism is that Shakespearean characterization, founded in the awareness of actorly artifice aroused by metatheatricality, prompts real investments on the part of the spectators in the characters of the play and prompts also the real action of spectatorly participation in the actorly making of character. Where Augustine says "the auditor is not aroused to go to the aid of the others," we suggest that the auditors are indeed aroused to go to the aid of the actors, not of course in the sense of providing rescue, but rather in the sense of contributing their attention, responsiveness, and specific responses to the production of artifice.

The statue scene is an enactment and a self-reflexive representation of the intersubjective make-believe that is founded in metatheater and that is at the root of theatrical magic. The statue is a mere statue, an actor doing something that is strenuously artificial, and also a spectacle of Hermione isolated in her own death-like body—beyond the call of any voice, even the prayers of her daughter. Or, rather, it is a spectacle of the actor sealed up in the deathly figure of Hermione, the character being made to show her hand, as it were, to reveal the material reality of performance practice underlying the represented person. The effect that the statue has on both the on-stage and theatrical audience is transparently and simply artificial. Nothing could be clearer. It is artifice when the actor stands still (how long, we ask ourselves, can she hold that pose?), and transparent when "it" floods with physical warmth and inner, individual life (including Hermione's particular personal history). Instead of putting on a new costume on stage, as we have seen Autolycus do, the actor puts on the body and the person of Hermione. The character Hermione revivifies the stone and the actor enters, as it were, and arouses her own body to feeling and movement on the strength of multiple performances (acting, playing music, making magic). The actor finally is allowed to move, to act, to speak, and to become the character. Katie Spurgeon described the moment as "a brimming over of nervous energy of both the character and the actor." But this moment of theatrical magic cannot take place unless and until the on-stage audience "awake [its] faith" and show its readiness to "participat[e] the actor, exchanging its hold on ordinary reality for an embodied, but also of course impersonated, passion."[17]

Katie's reflections on playing the statue of Hermione suggest one further effect of metatheatrical characterization. It is not only the characters who come to life by dint of the faithful exchanges between the actors and audience; the members of the audience themselves enjoy a heightening of vitality and community from the process of watching the play. That becomes evident when we ask, where was the actor when she was the statue? Katie says that she became a member of the audience, looking at herself as the statue from the outside, but also held in the grip of her statuesque stillness and aloneness: "I almost took on an audience point-of-view of the goings-on myself". Since she "bridged the 'metatheatrical gap' between the audience and actor," it should not have been surprising—and it is an entirely typical effect of theatrical performance—that the return of Hermione's personhood, warm life, and experience of community, which the two audiences had helped make happen, was reflected and re-enacted by the spectators, who found themselves released from their suspenseful stillness and solitude into the pleasures of strong emotional response and communal ovation.

Notes

1. James L. Calderwood, *Shakespearean Metadrama: The Argument of the Play in Titus Andronicus, Love's Labour's Lost, Romeo and Juliet, A Midsummer Night's Dream, and* Richard II (Minneapolis: University of Minnesota Press, 1971), 5.
2. All Shakespeare quotes are from *The Riverside Shakespeare*, 2nd ed., textual editor G. Blakemore Evans (Boston: Houghton Mifflin, 1997).
3. Anne Righter (Barton), *Shakespeare and the Idea of the Play* (rpt. Harmondsworth: Penguin 1967), 167, 169.
4. Sigurd Burckhardt, *Shakespearean Meanings* (Princeton: Princeton University Press, 1968); Louis Adrian Montrose, "The Purpose of Playing: Reflections on a Shakespearean Anthropology," *Helios* ns 7 (1979–80): 53–74; Stephen J. Greenblatt, "Shakespeare and the Exorcists," in *Shakespearean Negotiations: The Circulation of Social Energy in Early Modern England* (Berkeley: University of California Press, 1988), 94–128. See also Paul Yachnin, *Stage-Wrights: Shakespeare, Jonson, Middleton, and the Making of Theatrical Value*

(Philadelphia: University of Pennsylvania Press, 1997), where Jonson and Middleton join Shakespeare as inventive and competitive thinkers about and defenders of their own art. Of course, reading the plays as if they recounted a Shakespearean autobiography goes back earlier than Burckhardt, at least as early as Edward Dowden's *Shakespere, His Life and Art*, in 1875.

5. Burckhardt, "Shakespearean Meanings," 227.
6. For a persuasive account of Greenblatt's substantive debts to Kernan's critical approach, see Paul Stevens, "Pretending to Be Real: Stephen Greenblatt and the Legacy of Popular Existentialism," *New Literary History* 33 (2002): 491–519.
7. Greenblatt, "*Pretending to Be Real*," 127.
8. Abel coined the term "metatheater" in *Partisan Review* in 1960.
9. Lionel Abel, *Metatheatre: A New View of Dramatic Form* (New York: Hill and Wang, 1963), 51.
10. Abel, "Metatheatre," 57–58.
11. The questionnaire that the students answered included the following:

    - When did you feel most in character?
    - What was the moment like as you moved into or out of direct eye contact with the audience?
    - In what way did you bring the actual metatheatrical elements in the text alive?
    - Did you feel that the text in general allowed for this contact or were there other compelling reasons that contact with the audience worked or didn't work for you?
    - How did the particular setting affect audience connection (regular class with no theatrical lighting)?
    - Did you think the audience helped you in some way to create the character?

12. Anthony B. Dawson and Paul Yachnin, *The Culture of Playgoing in Early Modern England: A Collaborative Debate* (Cambridge: Cambridge University Press, 2001), 27.
13. See OED "take," 59c, "to take (a thing) with one: to bear in mind, keep in remembrance, take note of"; and "manner," 1, "a distinct type or kind (of person, thing, etc)."
14. Bert O. States, *Hamlet and the Concept of Character* (Baltimore and London: Johns Hopkins University Press, 1992), 12.
15. William B. Worthen, *Shakespeare and the Authority of Performance* (Cambridge: Cambridge University Press, 1997), 27.
16. *The Confessions of St. Augustine*, trans. John K. Ryan (Garden City, NY: Image Books, 1960), 78–79.
17. Dawson, "*The Culture of Playgoing in Early Modern England*," 27.

8
Character, Agency and the Familiar Actor

Andrew James Hartley

Dramatic characters as written, even when they are being read and not staged, imply the bodies of the actors who personate them. Indeed, we cannot discuss the characters in plays without conceding that the words are only one constituent part of the character, and that those words do not (indeed *cannot*) determine what the non-verbal elements of the character are. The theatrical absence in the book (the bodies of actors and audiences in particular) must therefore be acknowledged in even the most textual of character studies. Character itself must be considered most completely manifested in performance, when the scripted role is embodied—*participated* in Anthony Dawson's resonant phrase—by the actor's moving presence before an audience of his or her peers, regardless of how unsettling such infinite variety may seem for the textual critic who wants to constrain the limits of characterization.[1] Character is a nexus, an intersection of various, even dissonant, perspectives and generic technologies (the reflective processing of the book on the one hand, the kinetic semiotics of the theatrical space on the other), something whose full meaning is generated only when all the constitutive parts are present and engaged in a dynamic symbiosis. The character that takes shape in the minds of the audience members is thus particularly marked by the actor playing the role, by his style, competence, physical bearing, "presence," gait, voice, charisma and so forth, regardless of whether such things are in any way prescribed by the text which is being played. Little of such physical conditions that dominate casting and even blocking can be clearly inferred from a Shakespearean text, and when they are suggested—as in the height and coloration of Celia and Rosalind in *As You Like It* (1.2.239; 1.3.109),[2] for instance—they are often inconsistent.

Textual agency

Let me begin by saying that for the purposes of this study I will use the term "character" to mean something quite different from what the term means in the context of the novel. Even on the page, "character" in Shakespeare is dramatic, which is to say that it is partial and always demands at the very least the imagining of a theatrical presence. Character for me, therefore, is the hybrid production of actor and scripted role, something that cannot inhere merely in the material document (the play in the book) and requires the equally material conditions of the stage in order to come into being. Without the actor's body, character only exists *in potentia*, an infinite "hypothetical" requiring the actuality of performance for specificity, immediacy and limit. Character is an embodied phenomenon.

One of the elements that an actor's body brings to the stage is its degree of familiarity. Particularly in the case of "stars," a known or famous actor adds a particular *frisson* to a role, not simply because of celebrity fetishism, but because the performance must necessarily be under(over?)written by the audience's memory of the actor's previous performances. As Paul Yachnin has pointed out, memory and the appearance of memory in a character on stage is crucial to a sense of inwardness, the speaker's sense of his or her own past or lineage countering the spontaneous activity of plot with a reflectivity which confirms dimension in terms of character.[3] The mature actor brings to a role his or her own memories—from life and from performance—which enrich a sense of the performed character's interiority, particularly in the minds of audiences who know their previous work. This is true regardless of the extent to which the current performance is "new" or "different" in that virtuosic tradition which applauds actors for constantly reinventing themselves, partly because that celebration of difference is premised on recollection of what has gone before; the audience is constantly measuring the current performance against those past, even if the verdict marks this one as "original," "unrecognizable" and so forth. What supposedly subordinates the actor to the role does not, in fact, render the actor invisible; on the contrary, it reinscribes the importance of the actor's virtuosic presence as a crucial element in an audience's processing of the resultant character.

Even in the case of such difference from one performance to another (and I think the theatrical medium makes genuine transformation a good deal less common than does film, close-ups notwithstanding), an actor who performs in the same company over time must necessarily invoke those prior performances even as he attempts to move away from them. This continuity is maintained, moreover, not just in the sheer appearance of the actor, but in his gestural vocabulary, his demeanor, his training and other elements of what I am here calling his *performative habitus* in negotiation with his conscious memories of prior performances.

Pierre Bourdieu uses the term *habitus* to suggest the deep structures of human attitude and behavior manifested through certain assumptions, propensities and physical characteristics such as posture, gait, ways of gesturing, and so forth, which the individual absorbs from his or her social environment. Tellingly, this habitus is neither something the individual actively chooses nor a subject-position he is forced into. Instead, and in ways suggesting a middle ground between existential subjectivism and structuralist objectivism, he "falls into" his habitus, something that manifests what Bourdieu calls field specific symbolic or cultural capital. In Renaissance terms, the idea is in some ways analogous to that of *sprezzatura*, and though habitus is less consciously studied and embraced, both suggest that the individual in his or her element projects a certain ease or belonging which claims (and manifests) status within the field. Out of that element, of course, one's habitus can easily betray the extent to which one does *not* belong, though a habitus may include a certain flexibility, an ability to recognize the dynamics of different social situations, permitting adjustment of the habitual demeanor. In choosing the term habitus, Bourdieu says, he "wanted to insist on the *generative capacities* of dispositions, it being understood that these are acquired, socially constituted dispositions . . . [He] wanted to emphasize that this 'creative,' active, inventive capacity was not that of a transcendental subject in the idealist tradition, but that of an *active agent*."[4]

Part of what makes this idea so appealing as a way of thinking about performance is its specifically intermediate position between subject and agent, so that the individual is at once active and self-aware even as he or she is shaped by cultural forces largely outside immediate perception. Of course, an actor's performative habitus must generally and necessarily be more conscious, deliberative and creative than that of ordinary people, because his or her performance is rehearsed and not simply reliant on the habitual skills, attitude and disposition the rest of us use to negotiate daily life. While we may be aware of how we sit or pour a cup of coffee, we rarely scrutinize or choreograph our actions—be they public or private—as would an actor who was preparing to sit and drink coffee *in character* on stage. For us, such actions are largely matters of habit and comfort, but for an actor they are *choices* and thus, to an extent, conscious. What informs such choices (how do I sit? how carefully do I pour the coffee?) depends on the actor's personality, background and experience, and particularly on his or her training. An actor trained in the Alexander technique might approach the act of sitting and pouring in strictly physical terms of balance and equilibrium, while one grounded in Michael Chekhov may view the choices as matters of what the character wants—which may or may not have anything to do with the coffee. One may want the sitting and pouring to mirror the tone of what is being said in the scene, while another may seek the opposite. Yet another may believe that the character's status should determine such actions regardless of the scene's verbal content. In short, the conscious decisions (to sit with straight back or to lounge, to pour the coffee with meticulous care to splash it into the cup) grow out of actorly principles and habits which are rather less than fully conscious because they are rooted in the assumptions the performer falls back on when negotiating such choices.

One way of thinking about the applicability of such a notion to what actors do is through a consideration of how actors relate to the text itself in ways shaping character. Actors are frequently taught to seek a special kind of agency in Shakespeare, an active, energized presence in which thought and utterance occur simultaneously, and in which the actor seeks to embody what Patsy Rodenburg calls "the state of readiness."[5] This place of "poise and alertness" is "a condition that is applicable to any character in Shakespeare." It is "a physical state of vivid alertness and presence that matches the heightened awareness and imagination of the Shakespearean character at this moment." In exploring this concept through examples from the plays, Rodenburg discusses Hal's soliloquy at the end of the second scene of *Henry IV, Part I*, in which the Prince lays out his plan for his "reformation:"

> Something has clicked in Hal's earlier exchanges with Falstaff, a physical and emotional knowledge that gives him a form of epiphany. Now he understands that he has been mixing with villains and will have to change. He is growing up. We will nearly all have a moment like that. We can drink, behave badly and rebel but one day some sense of survival will save us, make us pull ourselves out of that destructive company. Today is Hal's epiphany.[6]

What is telling about this, of course, is that the reading it embodies is dictated by the actorly method, not the other way around. There is nothing to suggest that Hal has had any such epiphany, as opposed to merely articulating his strategy for the first time in our hearing.

In this speech he may just as well be clarifying for himself and the audience something he had in mind throughout—and prior to—the previous scene with Falstaff, in which, it should be said, there seems to be nothing to motivate so grand a realization or shift in his attitude to his tavern friends. Subsequent scenes with Falstaff reinforce the sense that what precedes Hal's soliloquy—and what he returns to thereafter—is mere dissembling. Rodenburg treats the moment as epiphanic because it raises the stakes for Hal, makes him more immediate and honest in his presence and utterance. Above all, it puts him in the state of readiness that foregrounds and enacts the character's agency. Though a dissembling Hal confessing his methods to the audience would still be in control, a Hal coming to a discovery and using that energy to drive him forward into a new course of action (however much it looks suspiciously like the old one) is more vivid, more active. For Rodenburg and many actors of Shakespeare, Shakespearean characters are self-possessed subjects who speak their minds and direct their own course, and it is not mere coincidence that for Rodenburg the word "character" can be used of the scripted role alone. The actor brings into being a character that, for her, has ontological presence in the text, the actor's agency asserted and contained by the script in ways that lend urgency and authority to the performance. The resulting personation is seen to "work" because the creative agency of the performer is subsumed within the cues perceived to be inherent in the text.

A similar dynamic is found in the structure of the verse itself. In discussing the actor's use of the iambic, Rodenburg says "everything in Shakespeare conspires to move and launch you forwards," so that "as you climb on and stay with the iambic, you are moving on a living energy that engages not only your voice and speech but your head and heart."[7] As a psychological sense of character produces agency (the state of readiness), so the verse itself propels the character like waves, creating an analogous forward movement.[8] What is interesting about this analysis is that while the character (the scripted role) is an active agent, the actor him or her self is less so, reduced instead to giving voice to what already exists in the text in a suitable manner, climbing onto the rhythmic waves of the verse and holding on. In Rodenburg's analysis, the actor might not be merely a conduit, but he is certainly being energized and directed by the text in ways that may seem contrary to that sense of actors making an infinite variety of choices as wholly autonomous agents. The resulting habitus feels—or is supposed to feel—like an energetic forward movement akin to agency, but it's also a bit like a ride in which true agency is illusory.

Rodenburg is, of course, only one—albeit powerful and respected—voice on the subject, and her sense of Shakespearean characters as *textually present* comes from a British tradition less central to actor training in the United States. Yet for all the lip-service paid to Method acting and its derivatives in the United States, text looms large, and the familiar issues of "motivation"—(those directorial "what do you want?" questions)—invariably have textual answers. This leads to the frequently articulated assumption by actors and directors that there is no sub-text in Shakespeare, so that the much touted character agency, even in US Shakespeare, is driven by some version of Rodenburg's scripted "state of readiness."

Coming out of that American tradition, Wesley Van Tassel's significantly titled *Clues to Acting Shakespeare* defines itself as "primarily aimed for actors who intend to play Shakespeare but whose training is based on realism."[9] What is striking, however, is how quickly Van Tassel's advice becomes grounded in the text in ways reminiscent of Rodenburg or even Peter Hall. "There are ten basic skills required to play Shakespeare," he says. The first ("Play your action and achieve your objective") comes out of that realist acting tradition, but the other nine are primarily textual, often directly and overtly so:

3. Use scansion, phrasing and caesura.
7. Understand the speech structure and rhythm.
8. Play the antithetical words, phrases and thoughts. Use the caesura to help you. These skills will clarify your phrasing and prevent you from rushing.[10]

Others are more indirect; but, like Rodenburg, they anchor agency in utterance which is in turn anchored in text:

2. Stay in the moment, listening, not thinking ahead.
4. Support the thought all the way through the line. The end of the line is often as important, or more important, than the beginning.
9. Use analysis to understand all words and thought patterns.

The core issue—of trusting the text to carry issues of motivation—Van Tassel explains in a distant echo of Hamlet's advice to the players:

6. Let the words be the expression of your thoughts. Do not think, then speak. Speak what you think when you think it.

The remaining "skills" are really about an embracing an attitude to the text:

> 5. Breathe at the correct places.
> 10. Love the imagery.[11]

Van Tassel's task, of course, is to break down a fear of the Shakespearean script for actors unused to working with it, so it makes sense that his emphasis is on the words and their arrangement, but the extent to which the tenets of realism are so quickly trumped by matters textual is remarkable, particularly the way that such matters are presented in faintly Orwellian terms: breathe at the *correct* places; *love* the imagery. For all its grounding in American, realist acting, *Clues to Acting Shakespeare* (the clues, of course, being in the text) is different from Rodenburg primarily in its supportive tone, not in the meat of its content.

True agency for an actor is difficult to see in actual performance, if only because the actor's choices are hemmed in by matters textual, both in the sense that their words and actions are at least partly scripted, and because the rhetoric of acting Shakespeare presses the actor to find their choices already extant in the script. Whether it is through the coercion of the iambic or the hard-wiring to seek out the state of readiness, the actor doesn't so much make choices as—in Bourdieu's terms—fall into them. Performative habitus thus includes the way actors are trained to see their relationship to the text, and despite the rhetoric about energy, agency, directness and so forth, how the text itself is privileged in ways that actually restrict actorly autonomy. In *A Shakespearean Actor Prepares*, Adrian Brine and Michael York introduce the subject like this: "Interpretation can be taken to mean what the actor brings to the written material, while we are concerned with what the written material brings to the actor."[12] The actor's role in such a formulation is, at most, interpretive rather than constructive, and the good actor seems less even an interpreter than a vessel, a mouthpiece for what lies in the text. Much television and film writing, say the authors, gives little to the actor to work with, forcing him to invest the role with everything his talent and imagination can muster. With Shakespeare, they say, the situation is reversed:

> It is the actor who is the glove, and Shakespeare the hand that gives him body and strength and movement. So complete a playwright is he that, if listened to, he will do three-quarters of the actor's work for him. Of course, this demands a greater dose of humility than some

actors are capable of producing, but paradoxically, *the more the actor relies on Shakespeare the better he acts.*[13]

The actor's body is reduced to the level of puppet, doing the will of the playwright as manifested by the text. Clearly, such rhetorical strategies are invariably the stalking horse from which actors justify choices, their performances reified by claims of merely fulfilling the demands of the play, but the restrictive insistence of such teaching further supports the idea that a Shakespearean actor, unlike other kinds of actor, is coerced into choices by things outside him or herself. Where text is concerned, the extreme form of such a view is embodied by those who see clues to authentic performance in, say, the punctuation of the First Folio, a strategy bizarrely at odds with the acting of almost any other playwright.[14] Despite all actorly claims about Shakespeare living on the stage rather than in the library or the classroom, Shakespeare's cultural weight looms large over theatrical practice, demanding different goals and methods to performance that strive—at least in their defensive rhetoric—to efface utterly the agency of the actor.

The body insistent

When the poets dreamed of angels, what did they see?
History lined up in a flash at their backs.[15]

Text is not the only restraint on an actor's agency. The actor draws on a specifically *performative habitus* which informs the body of the actor, shaping attitude, gesture, vocal inflection and the other aspects of character-building. It goes beyond the merely physical and includes such less easily measurable factors such as "instincts" and "stage presence" which are the result of the actor's prior training, of which Shakespeare-specific work such as Rodenburg's is only a subset. As well as those larger, sweeping influences such as Meisner, Stanislavski, Michael Chekhov, Lee Strasberg, F. Matthias Alexander and others, actors are exposed to various refinements and hybrids that play a significant part in their own physical and mental preparation.[16] These techniques and philosophies become part of who they are as performers and necessarily shape the outcome of a performance as well as the actor's approach to it. We assume that an actor's performative habitus is driven more by conscious choice than is his social habitus, but in fact playing (like living) is driven by the past, especially by the social world of the theater and by the symbolic capital at stake in performance—the audience approval that is itself coded within the actor short-hand of what "works." The hours in the rehearsal room, the years of training, coalesce in the actor's body, shaping a particular performative presence that is manifested not just by the physical mechanism of, say, how an actor stands, but also informs the motivational component, which is less obviously habitual and which more consciously shapes the resultant character: why the character should stand in this particular moment and in this particular way. As mind and body inform each other, so the actor's accumulated past inevitably shapes his or her sense of character motivation and what "feels right" in rehearsal and performance.

Performative habitus thus reveals the actor's choice to be less origin than consequence, the result of previous experience in the theatrical field.[17] In this, even a novice actor makes performative choices which are impelled by her daily habitus as shaped by a performative corollary built from her previous experience as both a performer and a spectator of other performers. As actors sometimes refer to the process of learning lines and blocking on stage as something akin to muscle memory, so the very choices themselves are, broadly speaking, hard-wired into actors through their previous experience.

A simple principle follows from this observation on an actor's performative habitus, one that limits the range of "choices" open to an actor by suggesting that such choices are constructed historically and are "fallen into." In the case of an actor seen regularly over a long period by the audience of a specific company, for example, the audience comes to recognize not just his or her face, but also the performative habitus associated with that face, the stance, the gestural vocabulary, the vocal range, and—most importantly—the use to which the actor puts these attributes. When audiences get to watch an actor over the course of his career, they get to know—for better or worse—what Chris Kayser calls his "bag of tricks." Part of the reason that actors get type-cast is that audiences (including directors) come to know that performative habitus and its limitations, sometimes better than the actor him or herself, because they see only the consequence of the actor's "choices" and are thus not (mis)led by the actor's psychological motivations or other kinds of thinking leading to that choice. The fact that actorly motivation is trumped by audience reception also suggests that in the performative habitus of a familiar actor, an audience sees not just the body they have seen before but also the characters they have seen before, including the temporal and physical locales in which they grew accustomed to that habitus. So Olivier's Lear—to borrow an example from film—necessarily brings his Richard III to mind, or his Hamlet, his Henry V, or his Othello, and one's sense of seeing that Lear is thus layered not just with the sense of the actor but with the intimations of roles that actor has already played. Olivier's age and frailty as Lear, for instance, cannot but remind us of his youth and vigor since we know that vigor well, having seen it in Olivier's other Shakespearean kings, so that we may imagine Lear in his prime. The pathos that gathers around this performance is intrinsically bound to that sense of that actor that we have watched for many years, now near the end of his career.

An audience's sense of a character may thus be informed by an associative richness derived from previous performances, so that even a character who has little time to unfold and develop may seem more complex because of parts the personating actor has played before. This collage effect is especially acute in rotating repertory and must have been so in Shakespeare's day, when familiar actors played different roles on consecutive days. The result is a less conscious version of Alan Dessen's "conceptual casting" (in which doubled roles are linked through the actor personating them), with roles in different plays being strung loosely together by the presence of the actor.[18] On the contemporary stage, this awareness of the actor's past roles serves a notion of character evolution over a long period, an idea derived from nineteenth-century realist fiction and manifested, for instance, by the development of characters in television soaps and long-running drama series.[19] Tim McInnerny's Iago at the Globe (2007) was a coarse, physical and soldierly villain, but the role was marked by flashes of self-deprecating humor in his dealings with Roderigo, which called to mind his Andrew Aguecheek (RSC 1991), the character showing an intelligence in his ironic wit that played against his driving and forceful soliloquies. Those audience members who were familiar with such prior performances as his dry, witty Max in *Notting Hill* got more than a frisson of celebrity; they got a richer sense of Iago's performative disingenuity, the idea that he was not what he played. Rather than undermining the tragic and vicious character, the presence of an actor with such a long comic pedigree made the character more unsettling, more indeterminate. This Iago was defined in part by his protean shifting and indeterminate self so that his Iago's motivation was, finally, even less transparent than is usual.

Staged Shakespeare oscillates between the familiar (known lines, favorite characters, the sheer cultural baggage brought to bear on any production) and the unfamiliar (the increasingly strange language of a more and more alien cultural and historical moment). It is an oscillation that varies tremendously for each individual audience member from moment to moment, and from play to play. The familiar actor grounds the alien words and ethos of the play in what is known (the actor's body and performative habitus). Of course, it can also work the other way: the familiar actor may be able to reconstruct the plays that audience members have known well since grade-school, challenging the readings with which the audience is familiar through embodiment. Few elements of the theatrical apparatus are thus more central to how character is constructed and understood by the audience than the actor's physical presence, and that importance is further complicated and nuanced when the actor is known to the audience community.

Doubling *the comedy of errors*

In the summer of 2005, Chris Kayser, dubbed "Atlanta's favorite actor," played both Antipholi in Georgia Shakespeare's *The Comedy of Errors*, this only six years since playing Dromio of Syracuse in 1999, and Angelo in 1989, both for the same company. In the interim, Kayser has played Richard II, Cassius, Andrew Aguecheek, Belarius in *Cymbeline*, Banquo, Ford in *Merry Wives*, Aufidius in *Coriolanus*, Claudius, Benedict, Autolycus, and a host of others. Kayser, who has been with Georgia Shakespeare for seventeen years, is the most recognizable active member of the company, and has received various best actor awards from the *Atlanta Journal Constitution* and *Creative Loafing*.

Kayser is physically distinctive, a slender, sinewy man with craggy features and a broad, boyish smile that belies his fifty-six years. He has a decent singing voice, an easy facility with Shakespeare's language and a distinctive habit of deep breathing through his mouth. Due to node surgery early in his career, he relies on a diaphragmatic projection which is more than capable of filling the Conant Performing Arts Center theater (Georgia Shakespeare's home on the Oglethorpe University campus), but which he controls so as not to strain his voice. He has a bobbing gait, a tendency to stand with his knees slightly bent, and an idiosyncratically fluid movement, all of which can be traced indirectly to his training in ballet and other forms of dance. In short, his performative habitus renders him a unique presence on stage, one which is instantly recognizable to any regular theatergoer in the region, regardless of the role or how he manipulates his individual characteristics and abilities.[20]

As is often the case in regional theater, the decision to cast Kayser as both Antipholi came out of pragmatic rather than conceptual pressures, though the result clearly has conceptual implications for a thematic sense of character as individual, durable personality. The company had staged *Errors* relatively recently (six years earlier) and thus felt some imperative to differentiate the show from the 1989 incarnation which had been conventionally cast. Budget constraints had also led to the elimination of one Equity contract. The casting of the company's most famous and media-friendly actor as both Antipholi killed two birds with one stone.

Initially, the director's conception of the show was (as is often the case when the roles are doubled) to differentiate the two Antipholi through changes in costume, vocal and gestural habits, and in differences in demeanor and (for want of a better term) *personality*—ideas about which were derived from perceived differences in the text between the twins. Over the course of the rehearsal period, however, this approach was jettisoned, partly because of the difficulty of keeping the characters clearly distinct for the audience and partly because the director became increasingly interested in the idea that the show would be more resonant if the audience experienced some of the bewilderment visited upon the characters in the play. Instead of being clued in to the truth the characters on stage could not see, the audience shared their vertigo, never sure which Antipholus or Dromio was speaking until they heard what was being said, even then (I suspect) following less the precise source of the confusion than experiencing it with a more general sense of *why* such confusion existed.

As well as taking the audience out of what can be a fairly comfortable experience of the play, the undifferentiated doubling also served to contradict the familiar argument that the two Antipholi are measurably different people in the text, that Antipholus of Ephesus is more quick-tempered and violent—in fact with his servant, in intent with his wife—than his Syracusan brother, who is both lenient and easy-going. The problem with such a view, of course, is that it stretches the text's evidence willfully, seeking difference where there is little, relying over much on snapshots of two men in very different circumstances, reading their responses to their predicaments as indicative of their general temperament. Despite the reluctance of literary critics to create unwritten backstory for fictional figures, the brothers are in very different situations, one (Syracuse) venturing into a world he knows by repute as alien, strange and probably magical, and the other (Ephesus) seeing the world he knows and its attitude to him turned upside down for no apparent reason. For Syracuse, the problem concerns the strangeness of the place, for Ephesus it is about the people. For both, the external strangenesses precipitate an anxiety about their own internal constancy and sanity.

The doubling assisted such a view, suggesting that differences between the brothers were reactive, not temperamental. The two men were, after all, the same person. Such a choice makes a virtue of what we ought to know already: that theatrical character is not defined solely by the text, since the text contains only what we hear as it happens (unlike, for instance, the kind of long view we might get from the omniscient narrator of much realist fiction).

The result of these decisions and evolutions was a foregrounding of Kayser as a presence on stage. In not clearly differentiating the two parts, the actor was not pressed to create a role (or, conceivably, two) that was somehow Other to the other or even to himself: both Antipholus of Ephesus and Antipholus of Syracuse shared the actor's distinctive performative habitus, and neither were in any way disguised. While the doubling could be perceived as heightening a realist sense of the play's confusions in all but the final scene (it being perfectly credible that the one character was taken for the other), it was also clearly metatheatrical. The audience—particularly those who were long-time subscribers—rather than being invited to believe in the fiction of the "errors," were brought in on a different joke derived from the notion that Kayser ("Atlanta's favorite actor") could be mistaken for *anyone*, particularly in this venue.

Kayser's Antipholi were both local and foreign, not simply because they were both Ephesian and Syracusan, but because the actor himself was local (a native son) and exotic in the way that all actors are foreign to their audiences: objects of distant admiration known largely through the characters they play. Being a minor celebrity furthers that sense of being both familiar and foreign, each newspaper feature or radio interview furthering the actor's paradoxical status as ordinary (local) and elevated (exotic). On stage, Kayser's familiarly likeable, generous and humble presence seems so genuine that it collapses the actor's public and private self, something which seems confirmed when audience members encounter that same likeable generosity in him off stage. The result is a sense of knowing him, which is largely an illusion, and he says that people often remark to others that he is a close friend of theirs, but pronounce his name *Kaiser*, a shibboleth which exposes them simply as fans.

But the play is similarly shot through with a concern for the discrepancy between inner and outer self, between the notion of identity one constructs for oneself privately and the surprising discovery that such a notion might be at odds with one's social image. Antipholus is "Known unto these and to myself disguised" (2.2.214). He is "to the world . . . like a drop of water" who, in searching for his twin—"another drop"—necessarily "confounds himself" by entering the ocean (1.2.35–38):

> So I to find a mother and a brother
> In quest of them, unhappy, lose myself.
>
> (39–40)

The loss of identity is conditional here not on the strangeness of the mistaken identity plot which has not yet begun, but is the necessary correlative of venturing into a community where, of necessity, identities collapse, intermingle and dissipate. From such a view, identity is only sustainable in isolation, becoming unstable as soon as one encounters the "other drops" which make up the social world.

Two scenes later, Antipholus of Syracuse tries to contain the semiotic entropy he has already experienced in dealing with the Ephesian Dromio by asserting his interior self as the regulator of how others should respond to him:

> If you will jest with me, know my aspect,
> And fashion your demeanor to my looks,
> Or I will beat this method in your sconce.
>
> (2.2.32–34)

Antipholus insists on a private notion of self by cautioning against misreading his demeanor, but the play's steady unraveling of such a "method" demonstrates the fallibility of that other "Method" in which the *actor* tries to regulate audience response through the projection of his own interiority. Even the willing audience member who wants to know the actor's "aspect," his emotional journey or his motivation, is confronted primarily by the actor's external dimension and the attendant performative habitus. The body, expression, gesture and so forth evoke the familiar actor, codify him as a known quantity and circumscribe his meaning externally and with reference to performances the actor has done his best to shed for this production. Actor and role fuse in the character's inability to stabilize audience response in accord with his private intent. As the Antipholi (and Dromios) mirrored each other, then, the on and off stage audiences were similarly reflective, both asserting control of what the body of the individual Kayser/Antipholus stood for, what it *meant*.

Any production that doubles the brothers is always at its most vulnerable in the final scene because the reunification demands that those who had been indistinguishable before now have to be separated. Though various non-realist strategies were toyed with (including the use of a mirror), the director finally opted for body doubles for both the Antipholus and Dromio of Ephesus, and wove them into non-speaking moments of transition at other times in the show. While some audience members were noted flicking through their programs to see if the body doubles had actually played these roles throughout the show (better, somehow, than in the final scene when their separateness was more obvious), the majority of the audience naturally saw through the device. What was interesting, however, was that Kayser's double, Joe Knezevich, was particularly well received because while he does not look like Kayser at all (even in the matching clothes and outlandish wig), and is twenty years his junior, he has worked often enough with him to know his performative habitus and to be able to mimic it in both voice and body. Knezevich's performance thus mirrored not so much Antipholus as it mirrored Kayser, and it did so not in a way circumscribed by this production, the impersonation evoking the other actor's entire career with the company. Again, the actor's private, internal sense of the role he was playing was trumped by a public, external sense of roles he had played before.

A particular kind of humor seems generated by the juxtaposition of known tragic actors in comic roles, but the converse (a comic actor attempting a serious role) provides other challenges. Kayser's Claudius was criticized by some as too sleight for the part, too foppish, a response which had as much to do with what the actor had performed before as what he did as the Danish king. But while actors constantly bewail their being typecast by critics, audiences and directors, it is hard to imagine an alternative unless one performs only once in any given market. Theater, of course, is very much about memory, and memory—combined with the inevitably evocative nature of the performative habitus—must render all performances by an actor—even performances of different characters in different plays—iterative. Whatever the actor's intent, whatever his aspect, audiences see what they already know of him as a kind of memorial shadow which colors the current performance.

For the Syracusan Antipholus, as for Kayser and other successful actors on the local circuit, the solution is to embrace—or "fall into"—what is expected of you, however much it runs contrary to your own desires. So when confronted by the woman who calls herself his wife, Antipholus, despite acknowledging that something is badly amiss, opts to roll with whatever the audience/social world says he is, however much it goes against his self-knowledge or his wishes:

> Until I know this sure uncertainty,
> I'll entertain the offered fallacy.
>
> (2.2.181–86)

And later:

> I'll say as they say, and persever so,
> And in this mist at all adventures go.
>
> (2.2.215–16)

It's a fallacy, this version of himself that is being insisted upon, but not one he sees any point in fighting, however painful or exasperating it is to have to listen to Adriana's berating.

In rehearsal, this moment raised questions, and several people, Kayser included, remarked on the oddity of why Antipholus agrees to go along with the "fallacy." One possibility was that Antipholus has already noticed Luciana and rolls with the situation to get closer to her, but there was also a powerful sense that the actors were being coerced by plot: Antipholus and Dromio have to get inside Adriana's house in order to set up the next scene's confrontation with Antipholus of Ephesus. Actorly agency was shelved in favor of the larger machine which makes the play work. In performance, then, Kayser eyed Luciana, but the key to his embracing of the fallacy was in a knowing shrug to the audience: "easy come, easy go," said the gesture; "I do as I'm told," even, "I only work here." In Kayser's distinctive body, of course, the shrug was a trademark, an underscoring of the actor's presence. The laugh it got each night grew out of the slippage between actor and role confessing that they were on a kind of ride, all control of their predicament abandoned.

Put in the terms of my argument, the discrepancy Antipholus seems to recognize here is between subjectivity and a more limited agency, between an autonomous self and the habitus one "falls into," which restricts as much as it enables. It subordinates the private to the public, invoking the audience as the arbiter of meaning over the performing individual (actor and role). Antipholus the public man is a kind of star in his own city, but stardom strips him of the capacity to control his own meaning; the salutations by strangers, offered gifts and other unwarranted familiarities (4.3.1–11), produce only a need to get away, to retreat into privacy and an asocial identity. His is the desire to regain agency, to define himself according to his own terms and not, like Kayser, be defined and "known" only by those who cannot correctly pronounce his name.

In the final scene, as Egeon attempts to reconnect with Antipholus and Dromio of Ephesus, not realizing that they have never seen him before, he says he is sure they must remember him. Dromio's response, "Ourselves we do remember, sir, by you," is telling (5.1.293). He means that seeing Egeon bound calls to mind his own recent bondage, but the line resonates more generally, suggesting the extent to which our memory of others is inevitably bound to our memory of ourselves. When one sees someone one has not seen for some time, the person evokes a memorial context in which oneself looms especially large: where one was then; what was going on in one's life; what one was feeling or believing; finally, who one was. For the audience seeing Kayser, Burbage, Garrick, Olivier or other familiar actors on stage, the experience is inevitably memorial, even nostalgic, and that nostalgia is finally tied to the audience's own sense of self and the way that self encompasses past experiences which include and are now evoked by a particular actor.

Character, then, is a nexus of the theater's semiotics of participation in which (as Dawson says) the body of the actor participates the character in the liturgical sense, presencing the fictional (role) in the form of the actual (actor) in ways that produce theatrical product (character); but that participation also incorporates the audience, staging a version of community that is defined temporally as well as spatially. The terms Philip Larkin uses in reference to a church building ("Marriage, and birth, and death, and thoughts of these / For which was built this special shell") might equally apply to the theatrical structure, a space in which the rites of mortality are celebrated.[21] Such concerns bind the community not merely through the content of the fictions presented on stage but through the shared experience of weeks, months, years, even decades of embodied character personated by actors we recognize, who have become part of our lives and by whom, in their presencing of the fictive other, "ourselves we do remember." Character inheres not in text but in the performative body, but it is not the actor's manipulation of that body that determines how character is read because the performative habitus grants only a limited agency to the actor. It is that limitation, finally, that opens the generation of meaning to the audience's participation in concert with the performance practices of the actors.

Notes

1. Dawson's term is drawn from Eucharistic theology concerning the "real presence" of the body of Christ in the communion bread. The character is both really present in the body of the actor and simply a representation.

See Anthony Dawson and Paul Yachnin, *The Culture of Playgoing in Early Modern England: A Collaborative Debate* (Cambridge: Cambridge University Press, 2000), 11–37; and Anthony Dawson, "Performance and Participation: Desdemona, Foucault and the Actor's Body," in *Shakespeare, Theory and Performance*, ed. James C. Bulman (London: Routledge, 1996), 29–46.
2. Shakespeare quotes are taken from *Norton Shakespeare*, ed. Stephen Greenblatt, et al. (New York: Norton, 1997).
3. Paul Yachnin, "Reversal of Fortune: Shakespeare, Middleton, and the Puritans," *ELH* 70, no. 3 (2003): 757–86. Yachnin argues that the interiority of Shakespeare's characters is in part a consequence of the adult actors who played them, as opposed to the more plot-driven plays dramatists writing for the boys' companies for whom immediacy is more compelling and playable than memory.
4. Pierre Bourdieu, *In Other Words: Essays Toward a Reflexive Sociology*, trans., Matthew Adamson (Stanford: Stanford University Press, 1990; emphasis mine), 12–13.
5. Patsy Rodenburg, *Speaking Shakespeare* (London: Palgrave Macmillan, 2004), 23.
6. Rodenburg, *Speaking Shakespeare*, 25–26.
7. Rodenburg, *Speaking Shakespeare*, 89, 90.
8. Rodenburg, *Speaking Shakespeare*, 85.
9. Wesley Van Tassel, *Clues to Acting Shakespeare* (New York: Allworth Press, 2000), xvi.
10. Van Tassel, *Clues to Acting Shakespeare*, 13.
11. Van Tassel, *Clues to Acting Shakespeare*, 13.
12. Adrian Brine and Michael York, *A Shakespeare Actor Prepares* (Lyme: Smith and Kraus Inc, 2000), 53.
13. Brine and York, *A Shakespeare Actor Prepares*, 54; italics in the original.
14. The most recent and thorough consideration of this approach—and one which is in many ways supportive of its methods—is Don Weingust's, *Acting from Shakespeare's First Folio: Theory, Text and Performance* (New York: Routledge, 2006).
15. David Sylvian, "When Poets Dreamed of Angels," in *Secrets of the Beehive* (Virgin Records, 1987).
16. Meisner technique, simply put, utilizes exercises (often repetitive) which place the truthfulness of doing something in the given moment over a conventionally rehearsed and memorized approach, so that the final performance is improvisational and fresh. Meisner is a development of Stanislavski, who strove to generate realistic performances from the inside out, particularly by accessing the actor's emotional memory. Michael Chekhov, also a student of Stanislavski, taught the physicalizing of a character's need in an external gesture which the actor then uses to access the internal. Lee Strasberg is the father of what is generally called the Method, and trains actors to express truth within imaginary circumstances by drawing on their physical, emotional and intellectual talents and experience. The Alexander technique involves the use of kinesthetic evidence to overcome habitual misuse of the body and to understand the relationship between thought and movement.
17. Performance is, of course, a negotiated, dialogic practice, particularly in terms of how it is perceived by an audience, so in absolute terms it can never

176 *Character, Agency, and the Familiar Actor*

   be truly origin or outcome. I am considering the performative choice here in more limited terms in order to foreground its mechanism, rather than making claims to its absolute temporal nature.
18. Alan Dessen, "Conceptual Casting in the Age of Shakespeare: Evidence From *Mucedorus,*" *Shakespeare Quarterly* 43 (1992): 67–70.
19. For a discussion on Shakespeare's history plays played as a sequence to suggest a similar on-going character development over a long period, see Nicholas Grene, *Shakespeare's Serial History Plays* (Cambridge: Cambridge University Press, 2002).
20. It is, of course, impossible to track how an individual's personal habitus develops and I am loath to speculate on what has made him the person he is unduly. I can say that Kayser was born and bred in Atlanta, the son of white, lower-middle-class parents, his father a postal worker, his mother a government secretary. Neither parent was college educated. Though his father was not Catholic, the house was dominated by the Catholicism of his Irish grandmother, and Chris spent his high school years in a seminary attached to a Benedictine monastery. He left after his senior year, though Catholicism remained central to his identity, and then had what he calls a "disastrous" experience as an undergraduate, taking eleven years to complete a B.A. in French. He was clearly bright and intellectually curious but was also ruled by his passions, and only became truly interested in his field of study after a trip to France. The French language and culture—particularly its theater—remains an abiding interest of his and he regularly performs French-speaking roles at Atlanta's Théâtre du Rêve. Throughout his college days, he played a lot of sports and pursued an interest in dance. He had no formal actor training until landing his first job as an actor, so he learned by doing, absorbing from those around him. Such a brief sketch is an inadequate means of explaining his current habitus, but several of the details are suggestive.
21. Philip Larkin, "Church Poems," in *Collected Poems*, ed. Anthony Thwaite (London: Farrar, Strauss and Giroux, 2004).

9
The Actor-Character in "Secretly Open" Action: Doubly Encoded Personation on Shakespeare's Stage

Robert Weimann

Talk about "performance" in connection with Shakespeare more often than not tends to convey an interest in the performance *of* his plays; the play is viewed or even edited as a "play in performance" or, as the recent Cambridge University Press series has it, as the "play in production," with particular emphasis on its "theatrical fortunes." These no doubt are laudable projects, and I am the first to applaud the emphasis on the play's text as a text written for and brought to life in the theater. And yet, this emphasis has its limitations, and these especially hinder a new departure in the approach to Shakespeare's characters. Without in the least wishing to reduce an awareness of their literary quality (such as the huge debt they owe to Plutarch's *Lives*), I propose to confront the text-related concept of character with a histrionic practice for which performance is so much more than the scripted performance of a text. In other words, let us push back the frontiers of characterization in search of an actor-character whose performativity exceeds the interpretation or the mediation *of* something. What in a new character criticism is at issue is the *gestus* and the language in which, to paraphrase the chorus to *Troilus and Cressida*, author's pen is in (and beyond) actor's voice while, simultaneously, actor's voice is in (and beyond) author's pen.[1]

As soon as such (qualified) mutuality in relations of texts and bodies is granted, we can, as a first step, acknowledge writing and performing as two different media constituting divergent sources, values, and impulses in the figuration of Shakespeare's artificial persons. Since the suggested interpenetration of script and show can reveal differing degrees of strength and prominence for each of its constituent media respectively, the figuration of imaginary agents is always a *con*figuration. Since this configuration is marked by contingent and often enough impromptu ways of confederation and dissension, there results an immeasurably complex scale of interrelations between the two media. Here we have a largely underestimated clue to the multiple functions and meanings associated with personation in Shakespeare's theater.[2]

In my use of the term "personation" the suggestion is that early modern role-playing cannot be grasped as either a purely formal or an entirely imaginary play of dramatic identities. Rather, the difference between script and show was so pervasive and affected the growth of Shakespearean character so deeply because the two modes of cultural production in the Elizabethan theater were marked by diverse types of socio-cultural provenance. In its roughest outline, there was, on the one hand, the neoclassical tradition, including the literary drama of the schools, dominated by the arts of rhetoric and composition; on the other hand, the partially oral, partially corporeal displays and disguises performed on festive occasions or in the market-place. Between the two traditions—one indebted to Renaissance humanism, the other largely adapted from a native cultural heritage—there had in the past been a certain amount of rapprochement, as for instance in the scripted repertoire of itinerant troupes with their allegorical figurations. Against the background of such previously achieved interactions, the two channels of dramatic production—writing and performance, language and show—continued to vie with one another in seeking prominence. Ultimately, it was this dual inheritance that inspired what bifold authority was embodied by the actor-character.

Here this drastically foreshortened perspective on the interaction between texts and bodies must be sufficient to suggest that in the Elizabethan theater the socio-cultural difference in question was especially marked. In fact, this difference not only expanded the space for the "inherent duality of theatrical activity,"[3] but it also went into the staging and shaping of that strange hybrid, the actor-character. For instance, as long as the Elizabethan performer was sufficiently untamed by the regime of literacy and the more self-contained Renaissance play, his person could shine through the persona. More consequential still, the image of histrionic practice itself could be inscribed as a dramatic device or a characterizing trait, as in the double-dealing artifice of Shakespeare's Richard Gloucester. In any case, early modern role-playing owed a lot to the resilience of premodern or extradramatic patterns of performance which defied neoclassical poetics.[4] Here was a lingering matrix for such vital, even visceral energies as suffused the change and growth of characters in their "swelling scene" (*Henry V*, Prologue, 4).[5] In other words, the early dramatic figuration of an actor-character thrived on a doubleness in (im)personation. Again, this doubleness with its two components possessed a specific impetus, an impelling force which remarkably vitalized and impinged on the contract between the two poles of any dramatic performance. As Julian Hilton phrased it, "performance is simultaneously representation and being."[6] The performance of character is "representation" or, we might say, an imaginary practice in so far as it seeks to re-present what speech, thought, and action a given dramatic figuration suggests about the world in the form of a fiction. At the same time, this performance is "being"; as such, it is an actually practised presentation, a presentational practice constituting a material, visible, and audible display of live bodies and voices. It is of course true that "the actor's self is not a grounding presence that precedes performance";[7] but performance, and especially the early modern performance of character, does exceed textuality (just as, vice versa, textualized meaning in figuration exceeds its own delivery).

Dis-closure in personation

In the readings of Andrew Gurr, Anthony Dawson, Paul Yachnin and others, "personation" just as "person" is envisioned on a broad spectrum of histrionic practices embracing all sorts of role-playing. As against such comprehensive definition, I here propose to examine one particular strategy of personation, one which is specifically revealing about the bifold gestus in the actor-character involving both the personator and the personated. The idea is to focus on a peculiar, often enough "secretly open," delivery of duality in role-playing. Such delivery culminates in an act of disclosure—"disclosure" in a twofold meaning. There is first of all in these specific versions of personation a strategy to disrupt the poetics of closure. What we have is a performance practice that ruptures the self-contained and self-enclosed order of the Renaissance play world as a world apart. Next to such dis-closure on the level of dramaturgy there is the second, ordinary sense of players "disclosing" something partially or entirely hidden, as when they confide to spectators their determination "to prove a villain" and betray their scheming "secret close intent" (*Richard III*, 1.30; 158). In that sense, actor-characters uncover what in the play world can be a concealed motivation so as to share with onlookers a privileged awareness close to a sense of complicity.

Both these different but also overlapping strategies help constitute the "secretly open" manner of the actor-character. The phrase in question occurs in a closely involved, spatially complex scene in *Troilus and Cressida* (5.2.). This scene reveals a fascinating number of ties between actor-characters in personation and what "Bi-fold authority" (5.2.144) informs the doubly encoded mode of staging. To begin with, the tripartite spatial structuring in this *mise-en-scène* provides important cues for different types of performance. On a three-tiered level of action and awareness, we have the angle of, first, Cressida and Diomedes in a strictly localized, self-enclosed amorous dalliance in front of Calchas' tent; second, Troilus and Ulysses as hiding and watching in what was probably a position behind the pillars; and, third, Thersites as sarcastic commentator on both those who watch and those who are being watched.

The speaker of the commentary clearly is privileged almost in the manner of a chorus. While Thersites can overhear and respond to the utterances of both parties, his own speech—inaudible to all characters—is not heard within the play world proper. Remaining aloof, spatially as well as acoustically, Thersites' angle on the play world is close to though not identical with that of the audience. His position is at best that of a scornfully inclined presenter. As such he betrays an unmistakable awareness of the needs and qualities of performed action, as when he spurs, even cheers histrionic delivery ("Now the pledge, now, now, now!" [65]). In Thomas Heywood's terms, to which we shall return, Thersites addresses the personator of Cressida at least as much as the personated role. As elsewhere I have phrased it, this presentational stance allows him to coax performance out of the players, accompany and praise their delivery ("Now she sharpens. Well said, whetstone!" [75]).

At this point, we can perceive the first revealing gap in the compound of the actor-character. The gap is that between the (young male) actor and the (imaginary) character named Cressida. But while Thersites continues to address the personated character with a feminine personal pronoun, Troilus is the one to exclaim, "This is, and is not, Cressid" (146). Again, the phrase serves two different codes: it serves to represent bewilderment in the image of the speaker and yet offers a "secretly open" insight into the material theatrical underside. The imaginary person in the performed figuration (beautiful young Cressida) "is, and is not" continuous with the actual medium of her own personation (involving the work and the body of the boy actor who plays the part). Troilus in his intermediate position is at one remove both from the *platea*-like space inhabited by Thersites and from the *locus* marked by tent and torch. If anything, it is this twofold spatial detachment which allows for a concurrence of his personally passionate and his theatrically distinctive discourses.

There is good reason to recapitulate the double-encoded personation in the entire scene when it prepares us for a comparable doubleness in Thersites' interjection, "A juggling trick—to be secretly open" (24). Not unlike Troilus' phrase, the image inflects the ways the personated "is, and is not" continuous with the work of a personator. On the one hand, the personated (here, Cressida and Diomedes) appear from within a thoroughly representational framework. Their representation aims to render the ambiguities, the tricky back and forth by which Cressida seeks to cope with a hostile male-dominated Grecian camp. But then the heroine is also a coquettish woman, and not without a certain sexual appeal. Thersites, whose main targets are war and lechery, jumps at what he crudely perceives (and distorts) on a totally obscene note. Hence, the double-entendre of "juggling" and "open" in his repeated quibbling.[8] For all its blatant coarseness, the wordplay in question pursues a characterizing purpose.

As distinct from this representational tenor, the same quibbling, on the other hand, contains an altogether different theatrical vehicle. Juggling, like dancing, singing, tumbling, is primarily an act of presentation; it is highly significant that Thersites invokes this practice that was often enough performed on some poor scaffolding in the contemporary market place. The phrase recalls presentational practices in which the performer's show of skill displaces the purely imaginary rendering of an absent self. On this level, "juggling" does not point to the representation of any personated identity; rather, it self-reflexively relates to what type of bodily performance the personator stands for. In other words, Thersites is torn between representational and presentational modes of *mise-en-scène*. As himself an actor-character, there is a composite in his verbal practice: as an *actor*, he speaks for and addresses the world of the theater and the task of a personator; as a *character*, he refers to and helps represent the fashioning of an imaginary personated, including his own.

While these clumsy coordinates can here be sketched only in their barest and most schematic terms, the distinction made between personator and personated appears indispensable in any post-romantic reconsideration of Shakespeare's characters. This distinction is crucial not only for an awareness of the player's material body in its presence that helps impersonate an absent fiction. Even more important, the confluence of live actor and imaginary character constitutes a site of translation, a change of key, so to speak, from written language into oral utterance. Once the *énoncé* in the text of the dramatist is intercepted by the actor's voice and its histrionic *énonciation*, new and often keener shades of dramatic meaning are set afloat. There is not sufficient space here to elaborate on the early modern theater's context, using either

Émile Benveniste's distinction or Bakhtin's notion of heteroglossia. It is enough to acknowledge the actor-character's utterance on stage as, in Bakhtin's phrase, as "a special type of double-voiced discourse." The latter of course refers to more than the conjuncture of written text and oral enunciation. What their sixteenth-century confluence involves is the clash and concurrence of two different ways of perception and experience, two different types of culture and habitus. The "double-voiced discourse," with its burden of socio-cultural discord, can amount in the drama, even more than in narrative, to "another's speech in another's language."[9]

That is why in Shakespeare's theater the discursive compound in the speech of an actor-character must not be conceived as a purely linguistic composite. As I have suggested elsewhere, there was an indisputable difference in Elizabethan England between the largely oral plebeian culture of popular shows and performances and the dominant style and subject-matter in stories, histories, and classical lore. The social and educational background of common players was such that "So great an object" (*Henry V*, Prologue, 11) as royalty and nobility was not easily compatible with what used to be presented on an "unworthy scaffold" (10). In these circumstances, the performer's background and upbringing would indeed constitute "another's speech" resulting in the speaking of an alien text, in "double-voiced" utterances. Over and beyond this sociological gulf, the difference between the world of the play text and its voiced utterance raises questions on another, no less important plane. It certainly provides us with one more reason why, in William Worthen's phrase, performance should not critically be reduced to a "merely interpretive mode of production." The purpose and the power of performance cannot be reduced to a histrionic practice which "recaptures or restates the authority of a text."[10] Here, important issues are at stake which require elaboration in a comprehensive study of personation which seeks to establish what "Bi-fold authority" (again, Troilus' term) inhabits the crucial interplay between the person speaking and the person spoken.

These two terms provide us with an especially revealing clue in our understanding of the actor-character. In Thomas Heywood's *Apology for Actors*, he makes the distinction between "the personator" and "the personated." What seems particularly significant in this text is that the personator's agency is allocated unquestioned space even within a context pleading for "sober" and "temperate carriages" such as "curbe and limit this presumed liberty within the bonds of discretion and government."[11] Thus, although Heywood to a certain extent joins the ranks of the reformers, and although his "limited" picture cancels out "much greater diversity"[12] in playhouse practice, the personator's mediation of character continues to be taken for granted. Even while the "presumed liberty" of extemporal playing is rejected, the personator's function is being affirmed "within the bonds of discretion."

Falstaff's show: personated turns personator

My argument underlying these reconsiderations of a "secretly open" double-voiced personation can be illustrated by its more specific treatment in Shakespeare's plays. Here I look at two or three scenes in which personation is comically exposed, even paraded, so that its artful doubleness itself is put on display and, in the process, comes close to a travesty of figuration.

In Heywood's *Apology*, just as in the portrait "Of an Excellent Actor," contained in Sir Thomas Overbury's collection of characters (1615), the comic register of personation is conspicuous by its absence. And yet there is evidence that contemporary observers appear to have been acquainted with comic forms of personation. For example, one of Heywood's polemical contemporaries describes a "jesting player" who "so truly counterfeited every thing, that it seemed to bee the very persons whom he acted."[13] If that "player" was a clown or fool it seems unlikely that he embodied "persons" seriously. Rather, he may well have been associated with those self-revealing uses of personation that I here propose to look at. In Shakespeare's plays alone, there are several scenes in which a jesting player is made playfully to display mimetic skills in personating other personages.

Among the most conspicuous there is of course Falstaff, who, as in a jest, personates King Henry, Hal's father. There the scene (*Henry IV*, Part One, 2.4.373–480) is set for a hilarious presentation of histrionic game and sport, in which dramatically charged imaginary relations of personator and personated are projected in comic figuration of the play's main agents. Hence, the prelude to the playlet begins when Falstaff, upon the painful disclosure of his cowardice, blandly invokes "all the titles of good fellowship" and proceeds to suggest "shall we have a play extempore" (229–31). But then, unexpectedly, threatening news from the north arrives, summoning Prince Henry to court and the field of battle. Now Falstaff seeks to turn the tables on the heir, apparent by envisioning *his* fear of the enemy and *his* plight when having to confront his father.

184   *The Actor-Character in "Secretly Open" Action*

> *Falstaff:* Well, thou wilt be horribly chid to-morrow when thou comest to thy father. If thou love me, practise an answer.
>
> *Prince:* Do thou stand for my father and examine me upon the particulars of my life.
>
> *Falstaff:* Shall I? Content. This chair shall be my state, this dagger my sceptre, and this cushion my crown.
>
> *Prince:* The state is taken for a join'd-stool, thy golden sceptre for a leaden dagger, and thy precious rich crown for a pitiful bald crown!
>
> *Falstaff:* Well, and the fire of grace be not quite out of thee, now shalt thou be mov'd. Give me a cup of sack to make my eyes look red, that it may be thought I have wept, for I must speak in passion, and I will do it in King Cambyses' vein.
>
> *Prince:* Well, here is my leg.
>
> *Falstaff:* And here is my speech. Stand aside, nobility.
>
> *Hostess:* O Jesu, this is excellent sport, i'faith!
>
> *Falstaff:* Weep not, sweet queen, for trickling tears are vain.
>
> *Hostess:* O, the father, how he holds his countenance!
>
> *Falstaff:* For God's sake, lords, convey my tristful queen.
>
> For tears do stop the flood-gates of her eyes.
>
> *Hostess:* O Jesu, he doth it as like one of these harlotry players as ever I see!
>
> (2.4.373–480)

Here the secret conventions of role-playing are openly exhibited in a context that teems with all those imperfections that representation is heir to. Note the playfully spontaneous, would-be extemporal quality of staging with the help of totally improvised props. Without quite surrendering the play's larger representational design, the entire scene comes close to the parody of a play within a play; or, to be more exact, a play with playing. Emphatically, a presentational element is foregrounded and acknowledged by the onstage audience, as when the Hostess exclaims, "O Jesu, this is excellent sport, i'faith!" (379). The cue is for "sport;" what throughout is greeted by the Hostess and her enthusiasm are the doings of the presenter, not any message that is represented. This emphasis is enhanced by Falstaff's display of a histrionic craftsmanship that foregrounds the more material means and media of playing. To use "a cup of sack to make my eyes look red" invokes (and unashamedly publishes) a stratagem that laughably displaces rhetorical artifice (the orator's tears and passions) in favor of the presentational act of counterfeiting in action. What is "secretly" practiced in conventional personation here comes out into the open.

These theatrically self-conscious uses of personation point beyond the traditional type of duality in the relationship between personator and personated; instead, they envision elements of a tripartite structure. One reason why the personator as compared to the personated looms so large is the former's own duplicity. Here we have not only the corpulent vessel of wit named Falstaff but also, behind this artificial and purely imaginary person, a great and well-known comedian, most likely Will Kemp. The actual, initial performer and the imaginary performed (Falstaff) go together to render the image and the speech of yet another personated figuration. In their unsecret, open role-playing they deliver not simply the presumed speech of King Henry but a burlesque image of the act of impersonation itself. In this tripartite projection the actor together with the character named Falstaff foreground histrionic practice through a show of its mimicry. What is displayed on stage is the most basic, ordinary task in the profession of the actor. As the task of the latter here dominates the personation, it is still the actor in the actor-character who "doth it" in this scene.

For these reasons, the performed character (Falstaff) personating another personated figure (King Henry) is so much more than just metatheatrical artifice. Rather, it is to turn the lowly craft, the common player's skill, into a high Renaissance agency mediating "So great an object" (*Henry V*, Prologue, 11). In its historicity, the achievement is based on accommodating, without blurring, the socio-cultural difference itself between common player and the alien (for him) image of royal authority. Not unlike the young male player who, playing a woman, also personates a young page, the player behind the disguise is pre-eminent. Performance here clearly exceeds what Michael Bristol has called a ministerial function vis-à-vis the text. Instead, the personating player would foreground what comes close to a self-generative delivery of his own work, body and gender.

While the performing actor comes to the fore, the character in the actor-character and its representation are not lost sight of. In Falstaff's case, this mode of personation is in support of the play's larger issues, such as rule versus misrule. Far from blurring the actor-character's configuration, these issues enlarge the unparalleled complexity in character, which is the more impressive in that it is subjected to neither finish nor closure. Not unlike the multi-layered figuration of Autolycus, Faulconbridge, Duke Vincentio, Edgar, and others, this personation opens up multiple perspectives and connections. The actor-character appears to thrive on the friction derived from the gaps and discontinuities among them. In other words, the actor-character moves between the poles of unabashed sport and game and what in the language of Hamlet's advice to the actors is called the "necessary question of the play" (3.2.42–43). In Falstaff's case, these two poles, one presentational, the other representational, are complementary; the guise and *gestus* of common playing meaningfully counterpoint the larger design of *Henry IV, Part One*.

In more than one respect, the balance can also be disturbed. In projecting entirely unconcealed and unashamed use of the props and practices of personation, Falstaff comes close to delivering a "self-resembled show"[14] of the histrionic apparatus of role-playing. But as the scene continues, the apologetic pleading for a "goodly portly man, i'faith, and a corpulent" (422) is *in character*. And yet the scene betrays (in both senses of the word) the effect of representation[15] even as it discloses the vulgar labor of its delivery. Hence, the logic of representation, culminating in the comic image of high "passion," is reduced to the logistics of the bottle, the ingredients of "a cup of sack." This logic is more deeply in question when, in the reversal of roles between Falstaff and Hal, the *quid pro quo* momentarily ceases to function. Even before the change of roles, we are presented with certain strangely unreliable articles of signifying property. These are reminiscent of Launce's clownish tokens of resistance to symbolization as when the latter presents a shoe to serve as icon for his father, or was it his mother? Falstaff, setting the scene, in his own turn spells out a symbolic order of representation in which the achieved degree of similitude leaves much to be desired. For a "chair" to stand for "my state," a royal throne; for a "dagger" to serve as "sceptre"; for a "cushion" to denote a "crown" is poor enough. It is worse still when the Prince sets out to reverse the order of imaginary connotation ("Thy state is taken for a join'd-stool," and so forth). The precarious quality of similitude is such that relations between what performs and what is performed can be read forwards as well as backwards. Whatever order is being chosen, the sign system onstage, unlike Falstaff's own comic act of personation, refuses to be doubly encoded, at least in the uncomic vision of the Prince. True enough, iconic relations between the stool (property of the Boar's Head Tavern) and the throne at court are so weak that the act of symbolization can easily be punctured. This vulnerability in the order of *quid pro quo* is here deliberately foregrounded because it almost totally blots out any standards of verisimilitude in the circumstantial world of personation.

In our scene, the iconic efficacy of props and their symbolic purpose is repeatedly jeopardized; the *raison d'être* is further "to disfigure" relations between personator and personated. Thus, "to present the person" can culminate in the comedy of a grand and grotesque fiasco when the "double-voiced" conversation between the *quid* and the *quo* falters entirely over its own incongruity. To say this is not in the least to claim that any verisimilitude is required in the act of personation or that its practice is premised on any stringent mode of representation in the first place. It is only that the props of amateurish role-playing have their problems when, as we know from *A Midsummer Night's Dream*, relations between staged signs and dramatic meanings are outrageously "disfigured." We only need to recall the case when "one must come in with a bush of thorns and a lantern, and say he comes to disfigure, or to present, the person of Moonshine" (3.1.59–61).

As distinct from Moonshine's signifying practice, Falstaff's handling of props is as buoyant as it is eloquent, and Hal's objections can hardly take hold. Even so, in his act of personation he comes "to disfigure" relations between the *quid* and the *quo* on a more sensitive, vital plane where "So great an object" is accommodated in a shabby tavern. This is in truth what can happen to royalty on an "unworthy scaffold," even when the Prince understandably must register his reservations. From his point of view, to reemploy an ordinary stage property (already predetermined in its signified) results in the inability of this property to stand for anything more substantial than itself. Certainly, this is no vulgar version of politics in verisimilitude, even when Falstaff carries the day by having the pluck to show up the sheer inertia of matter prior to its (re)representation.

What the entire scene, including these uses of stage property, finally exemplifies is an exceptional dynamic in personation. This dynamic largely derives from what difference inhabits the composite of the actor-character. There is an astonishing range and reach in proportioning the latter's constituents; that is, the range between (the image of) material practice and imaginary figuration proper. On its most accessible level we have, on the one side, Falstaff representing a unique character in a fiction; on the other side, there is the same Falstaff and his real-life actor presenting materially acknowledged skill as a player delivering another's speech and role. The difference built into this composite figuration serves as the major energizing impulse in personation, whether in its dramatic image or its theatrical practice. In either case the difference informing the composite of the actor-character is anything but static. As part of a highly volatile dramaturgy, the actor-character is projected onto a broad and changeful spectrum on which the representational can be slanted toward skill-ful presentation and the presentational toward meaning-ful representation.

Ultimately, the difference in personation is integral to what (dis)continuity we have between the rule of kings and the sway of misrule. By any standards, it is a bold gesture to furnish the personated misrule with sufficient authority to serve as personator of royalty in a tavern. No better way to make greatness familiar. This is "double-voiced" discourse in action: to appropriate the highest language of royalty as engaged by and engaging the lowest purpose in Eastcheap. Momentarily to bridge the distance between them is not of course to cancel out the difference in social status and cultural purpose. On the contrary, to stage the precarious ends and means of rendering, through personation, the plight of the Prince and the call from the Court is to *use* cultural difference dramatically.

Peddling Autolycus: double-voiced counterfeiting

Compared with Falstaff's deliberately unsecret performance, Autolycus in *The Winter's Tale* stands for a related, yet very different mode of comic personation. In his case, the "double-voiced" performance of the actor-character is not greeted by an onstage audience but is more directly motivated by the tricky cast of the peddler, as prompted by requirements of theme, atmosphere, and plot. Together, these make for radically unstable parameters of his (virtually nonexistent) "identity." Again, the practice of personation unfolds on a tripartite plane. There is, first of all, the singing voice and supple limbs of the actor, almost certainly Robert Armin. On a second level, there is the cheating, pinching, and happy-go-lucky peddler. As a profoundly histrionic person, this Autolycus shows more than one persona, on what is a third level. In the change from one persona to another, the donning of his guise is a *secret* to his victims but *open* to spectators. The actor-character beguiles other figures but betrays to spectators the "secretly open" artifice of counterfeiting. In the language of personation, the personated person is transformed into the playful image of a devious, wily personator. Here comedy results from pushing the "secret" pursuit of imposture into a game that openly invites comic inspection from a public audience. Hence, we have a personating practice with a difference. This practice does not expect spectators to identify with what is represented in the imaginary world of the play; rather, it is for them to enjoy the ways an open and abusive counterfeiting can, in Sly's word, produce a "comonty" or "gambold" of identities (*The Taming of the Shrew*, Ind. II, 138).

As distinct from *Henry IV, Part One*, 2.4, the comedy of this personation is predicated on a privileged awareness of spectators. The latter are free to enjoy a sense of superiority over all persons in the play deceived by those devious tricks and purposes as are practiced in the protean charade of Autolycus. Hence, the boundary between the comedy in the play and the audience in the playhouse is fortified by social distance. Not unlike the clowns in *The Tempest*, on-stage comic characters (including the innocent rustics) do not laugh *with* the audience. There is no equivalence of what the Hostess calls "excellent sport" shared and enjoyed by all. Even so, and all the more remarkably, the presence of the actor in the triangle of personation retains an extraordinary resilience.

Autolycas: [*Aside*] Though I am not naturally honest, I am so sometimes by chance. Let me pocket up my pedlar's excrement. [*Takes off his false beard.*] How now, rustics, whither are you bound?

Shepherd: To th'palace, and it like your worship.

Autolycas: Your affairs there? What? with whom? The condition of that farthel? the place of your dwelling? your names? your ages? of what having? breeding? and any thing that is fitting to be known—discover.

Clo. We are but plain fellows, sir. [. . .]

Shep. Are you a courtier, and't like you, sir?

Aut. Whether it like me or no, I am a courtier. Seest thou not the air of the court in these enfoldings? Hath not my gait in it the measure of the court? Receives not thy nose court-odor from me? Reflect I not on thy baseness court-contempt? Think'st thou, for that I insinuate, that toze from thee thy business, I am therefore no courtier? I am courtier cap-a-pe and one that will either push on or pluck back thy business there; whereupon I command thee to open thy affair.
(4.4.712–38)

Note how the two heaps of questions beginning, respectively, with "Your affairs there?" and with "Seest thou not the air of the court in these enfoldings?" do not at all serve a dialogic type of question and answer. Rather, they provide a welcome pretext for exuberant histrionics in gesture and language use. Any reconstruction of the scene as performed event would, I suspect, envision a brazen show of gloating arrogance and impertinence in the mouthing of words like "court-odor," "insinuate," "toze," and others. Here the performing person with and through his persona indulges in a self-congratulatory air advertising the skill in teasing out the rustics' resistance. Note the overbearing *gestus* in the lordly tenor of his questionings, even while worming himself into their awesome trust and their open pockets by furtive contrivance. Here, again, we have a performance practice of a third kind, one that is neither formal nor naturalistic but which scandalously betrays, in the act of performance, the disenchanting zest, the potential for travesty, in the uses of mimesis itself.

Even so, the function of disclosure is marked by a remarkable shift. It is true, the role-changing *gestus* in Autolycus' mode of personation is visibly published in his initial aside, with an already "false beard" taken off. The swift and expeditious alternation of disguise has indeed elements of "a juggling trick"—even when it is not quite "*secretly* open." However, as Stephen Orgel notes in his Oxford edition of *The Winter's Tale*, "[A]ll [Autolycus'] representations are taken for truth." Yet, the assumed guise of a courtier (like that of a peddler, shepherd, robbed victim) are so revealed to the audience that "we are placed in collusion with Autolycus."[16] While it is incontestable that, more or less unknowingly, he ultimately furthers a good course in the play, the artful series of his counterfeitings serves an end in itself; as far as they are "representations," they appear truthful only to figures simple in mind. But if the dividing line between artful counterfeiting and professional cheating is unduly thinned out, Stuart audiences would watch these games of skill pleasurably, albeit from a distance.

In other words, collusion with any version of juggling is difficult, especially when these games in personation serve and celebrate performance art in its own right and for its own sake. In the present scene, the dramatic design is to exhibit an imposing type of showmanship tied to a poignantly presentational mode of comic-burlesque personation. There is plenty of mimicry which serves to burlesque a social type, the character of an arrogant, condescending courtier. But the representation of the latter is balanced by a staggering, swaggering display of histrionic prowess. In other words, the artificial identity of a person called Autolycus is not rendered through the image of an overbearing "courtier" and "soldier."

If anything, the balance in question marks the bifold authority of the actor-character, with a performative surplus on the side of the actor. Autolycus is a perfect vessel to exemplify this duality. He has the craft and the craftiness of a personator, but one whose skill is not exhausted in the process of delivering a personated. Over and beyond his personating disposition, there is a strictly performative overcharge, as conveyed not only by an astonishing rate of role-changings but also, and even more so, by the melodious voice of a talented singer. There beautiful songs are *presented*; they can hardly be said to *represent* their performer. But in the end the performing voice and body do not ultimately contradict the representational design in the play. On the contrary, they provide us with a rare image of broadside peddling.

This is not the space for further exploring the linkage between an intense mode of performativity and the world-picturing mirror reflecting the declining culture of popular ballad-mongering. As the salesmanship of these ballads goes hand in hand with both the recital of songs and those dazzling forms of masquerade, another dividing line between representation and presentation is blurred. In Benveniste's terms, it is the line dividing the subject uttering from the subject in the utterance. On the imaginative level of their concurrence, the peddling, the juggling, and the singing are too good to be lost in just another personated figuration. In this performance practice there is a trace of purpose and identity larger than personal talent. Whatever the statement in the text of the character says, the act of uttering qua performance retains an indelible authority in its staging. Shakespeare critics can ill afford to ignore that this source of authority, after centuries obsessed with mongering meanings, shows signs of a wide-spread resurgence on twenty-first century stages. Here again, the actor in the actor-character agency wants attention as never before.

Notes

1. While the bulk of this paper was written for and originally submitted at the SAA Convention in Miami, 2001, the present version has been revised considerably. Some of these revisions are indebted to a study co-authored with Douglas Bruster, *Shakespeare and the Power of Performance* (forthcoming). I am also indebted to Bruster for sharing with me an unpublished paper on late Elizabethan and early Stuart uses of "personate," "personation" and related terms. My special thanks go to Paul Yachnin, whose generous critical and editorial response to the present essay I deeply appreciate.
2. In the use of "personation" I follow Andrew Gurr in his *Playgoing in Shakespeare's London* (Cambridge: Cambridge University Press, 1987), 136–37. More recently, Anthony Dawson and Paul Yachnin, *The Culture of Playgoing in Shakespeare's England: A Collaborative Debate* (Cambridge: Cambridge University Press, 2000) have underlined the concept of "person" as "the key category in theatrical performance" (7–8). Embracing "playgoer" and "actor" or even "in its triple sense—role, body, self" (Dawson's phrase), the reference is to something

"present and palpable." The concept of "person" can qualify any exclusive concern with a "bodily-spiritual connection" in the character (14–15).
3. Jean Alter, *A Sociosemiotic Theory of Theatre* (Philadelphia: University of Pennsylvania Press, 1990), 29.
4. The vigor and expansion of such premodern performance practices in Elizabethan England has again been amply confirmed in Philip Butterworth's *Magic on the Early English Stage* (Cambridge: Cambridge University Press, 2005). See also François Laroque, *Shakespeare's Festive World: Elizabethan Seasonal Entertainment and the Professional Stage*, trans., Janet Lloyd (Cambridge: Cambridge University Press, 1991). Laroque's emphasis on what he calls "the archaic survivals in Shakespeare's work (including 'songs, dances, disguises or spectacles') "provides a new perspective on the whole theatrical process" (187). See this in connection with my own *Shakespeare and the Popular Tradition in the Theatre*, trans., Robert Schwartz (Baltimore and London: Johns Hopkins University Press, 1978), with its strong emphasis on late ritual and medieval sources of performance.
5. My text throughout is *The Riverside Shakespeare*, 2nd edition, ed. G. Blakemore Evans, et al. (Boston: Houghton Mifflin, 1997).
6. Julian Hilton, *Performance* (London: Macmillan, 1987), 152.
7. Philip Auslander, *From Acting to Performance: Essays in Modernism and Postmodernism* (London and New York: Routledge, 1997), 36.
8. As against Wells-Taylor's strangely innocent insistence, there is for this reading "abundant support," as in Gordon Williams, *A Glossary of Shakespeare's Sexual Language* (London: Athlone Press, 1997), 175. The same may be claimed for "secretly open" as, in Eric Partridge's wording, "open, in a secret part and in private, to [. . .] phallic ingression." See *Shakespeare's Bawdy* (London and New York: Routledge, 1990), 179.
9. M. M. Bakhtin, *The Dialogic Imagination: Four Essays*, ed. M. Holquist (Austin: University of Texas Press, 1981), 324. The reference to Émile Benveniste is to his path-breaking *Problems in General Linguistics*, trans., Mary Elizabeth Meek (Coral Gables: University of Miami Press, 1971). Even more relevant is Part II of the *Problems*, for which I was unable to trace an English translation.
10. William B. Worthen, *Shakespeare and the Authority of Performance* (Cambridge: Cambridge University Press, 1997), 27.
11. Thomas Heywood, *An Apology for Actors*, facsimile edn (New York: Garland Publishing, 1973), G 4. For a close study of the socio-cultural positioning in the *Apology* see my *Author's Pen and Actor's Voice: Playing and Writing in Shakespeare's Theatre* (Cambridge: Cambridge University Press, 2000).
12. Charles Whitney, *Early Responses to Renaissance Drama* (Cambridge: Cambridge University Press, 2006), 147, 159.
13. I. G., *A Refutation of the Apology of Actors* (London, 1615), E 3v. For a more detailed study of the difference between I. Cocke's sketch of a "Common Player" and the "Excellent Actor" in Overbury's collection, see my *Author's Pen and Actor's Voice*, 132–36.
14. Joseph Hall's phrase, from his satirical glimpse of the stage clown; see his *Virgidemiarum* (1597), in Joseph Hall, *The Works*, vol. 9, ed. Philip Wynter (Oxford, 1863; repr., AMS Press, 1969), 1.1.31–44, 9.58.

15. A critical reconsideration of "representation" is overdue. See the collection of recent essays, with an Afterword by John Drakakis, *Refiguring Mimesis: Representation in Early Modern Literature*, ed. Jonathan Holmes and Adrian Streete (Hatfield: University of Hertfordshire Press, 2005), 208–16. See also my debate "Representation and Mimesis: Toward a New Theory," *Symbolism* 6 (2006): 3–36; with promising perspectives in recent critical approaches to mimesis and representation such as those by Jacques Derrida, George Hartley, Wolfgang Iser, Louis Marin, Gayatri Chakravorty Spivak, and others.
16. *The Winter's Tale*, ed. Stephen Orgel (Oxford: Oxford University Press, 1996), 53.

Part IV Theatrical Persons

10
Is Timon a Character?

Anthony Dawson

> *Certes, thanne is Envye the worste synne that is. For soothly, alle othere synnes been somtyme oonly agayns o special vertu; / but certes, Envye is agayns alle vertues and agayns alle goodnesses.*[1]
> —Chaucer, *The Parson's Tale*

My title poses a question that might seem superfluous, even pointless. But I think it worth pursuing. Is Timon a "character"? It's easy enough to identify Hamlet or Macbeth as characters, but figures such as Timon are harder to place. On one level, of course, Timon is a "character" in a play, an "actor's name" as the list appended at the end of the 1623 folio text has it. But if we mean a *person*, one who projects a feeling of depth and inscrutability (and that will be my working definition in this paper), does Timon fit? I'm interested in him as a kind of test case, since it's clear that, in comparison with Shakespeare's other tragic heroes, he does not quite qualify. We're used to the idea that Shakespearean character is something large and personal, that it is distinct from allegorical personage or satirical caricature, that it entails psychology, some sense of a match between our own inner experience and our perception of the fictional being constructed by words and stage action. Timon seems to fail these tests, and this has led to a generic confusion and a conviction that the play is somehow incomplete, abandoned by its author, left unfinished, never performed.

Still, I find myself drawn to Timon—he's an attractive figure in his vehemence, in his demand for recognition, in his perhaps fond hope to live in a world of generous impulses. My attraction might suggest that for me he is already a character, which threatens to end my investigation before it begins. But I want precisely to pursue this matter of

198 *Is Timon a Character?*

audience engagement: is it necessary for us to have a sense of "character" in order to feel engaged? And what in particular makes for the appeal, the draw, of Timon? My approach to these questions is multi-sided and I will devote the rest of this paper to ruminating on ways to answer them. Timon, to begin, has valuable ideals—it is clearly desirable to promote a society where one can depend on one's fellows, and where a community of support based on need and the ability to give prevails. And a failure to uphold such ideals makes for a nastier, more brutish (and shorter) life. That Timon is initially blind to human selfishness and greed is not entirely a bad thing; it suggests a potentially dangerous naiveté, perhaps, but his inclination to give derives from something large and expansive. Not only that, he can talk! In Shakespeare, that always counts for something, and in this play it counts for a lot. Both in his eagerness to please and in his laceration of human venality, his speech wins us over. In an obvious sense, of course, literary character is a thing made out of words and words alone, so the ability to talk is always a plus. On stage, the words are all the more present, embodied by breath and voice. So when a charismatic actor masters Timon's way with language the result is matched by only a few other tragic figures:

>   Plagues incident to men,
> Your potent and infectious fevers heap
> On Athens, ripe for stroke. Thou cold sciatica,
> Cripple our senators that their limbs may halt
> As lamely as their manners; lust and liberty,
> Creep in the minds and marrows of our youth
> That 'gainst the stream of virtue they may strive
> And drown themselves in riot.[2]

Here he calls on plagues and sciatica directly, commanding them to strike and cripple. He goes one step further than Lear, who begs an abstract "nature" to "convey sterility" to the inner organs of his potentially fecund daughters. Timon animates the diseases themselves. The whole speech, delivered as he exiles himself from Athens, is a series of imperatives aimed at persons, qualities ("lust and liberty") or illnesses, which, he demands, should do their worst. It inverts Ulysses' famous speech on degree in *Troilus and Cressida*, reversing its terms, calling for the very confusion that Ulysses, in his wily way, seeks to divert: "Instruction, manners, mysteries and trades, / Degrees, observances, customs and laws, / Decline to your confounding contraries— / And let confusion live!" (4.1.18–21). In the hands of a fine actor, such language can have a buoyancy and vital power that cuts against the misanthropic message, a kind of creative nihilism that has sustained the best of recent performances, from John Colicos and Paul Scofield in the '60s to Michael Pennington in the '90s.

The question is what such language has to do with character, with our perception of a certain roundedness, with a delight in human vagary and diversity. It's odd, though it strikes me as true, that such a poetry of surface can create an illusion of depth; perhaps it's a matter of commitment, of the totality of Timon's investment in what he is saying, that creates that impression. We sense a real, if also narrowly obsessive, person behind the words. The verbal attack expands, in fact, into a vision of life as a "forest of beasts" in Apemantus' memorable phrase (4.3.347). But even this may be seen as not exactly an expression of character. We look for something more, hoping for a relenting glimpse at another dimension. As the action continues, Timon's cave becomes the center of a wasteland, falsely brightened by the discovery of glittering gold, which of course only makes things worse. He rails against the gold as he has against mankind. There is no doubt something weirdly admirable in Timon's single-mindedness, his refusal to back away from the dark, though I am not sure this gives him the kind of dimension I am on the look-out for.

Indeed, this is precisely where Timon is unique among Shakespeare's tragic figures. I want to argue, in what follows, for a certain power inherent in the very narrowness of scope that Timon manifests. It might be most helpful to think of him as embodying in concentrated form a particular characteristic, what I, following Melanie Klein, will call *envy*. While fundamental to human emotion, envy in Shakespearean characterization is typically mixed with a wider range of feeling—the sort of thing we associate with Hamlet or Macbeth. Timon's relative narrowness brings him closer to allegory than is usual in Shakespeare. But, at the same time, he avoids the purely allegorical and the rather flat affect associated with it. Part of this, as I have already indicated, is an effect of language. What is fundamental here, both beneath the language (as it were), and as an effect of it, is the intensity (and consequent power to attract) with which a singular, elemental emotion is pursued and opened up. The power of the language is directly linked to that of the emotion. Timon is partial but intensely present in his singularity, just because of the way he appeals to, and articulates, a fundamental human attribute, one that is typically only a part of the more complex mix that distinguishes Shakespeare's richer heroes.

This is not to say that there is no hint of extra dimensions in Timon, though such hints are subordinate to the dominant key. Something extra is to be found, for example, in his final scene, which shifts adroitly between comedy and pathos. Timon's comic mastery both leavens and confirms his heartlessness. When the senators arrive, with Athens under the threat of invasion from Alcibiades, he toys with them, humoring their hopes only to dash them for good: "But yet I love my country [he says to the senators after just having spit plagues at them] and am not / One that rejoices in the common wrack, / As common bruit doth put it." This jolts them from despair to expectation: "That's well spoke." To "ease them of their griefs," he promises his "loving countrymen" a "kindness:" how to "prevent wild Alcibiades' wrath" (5.2.76–78, 83–88). The senators drool with anticipation; they seem to have succeeded and are already imagining their triumphal entry back into the city. Timon stretches out their hopes to the limit before snapping them:

> I have a tree which grows here in my close
> That mine own use invites me to cut down,
> And shortly must I fell it. Tell my friends,
> Tell Athens, in the sequence of degree
> From high to low throughout, that whoso please
> To stop affliction, let him take his haste,
> Come hither ere my tree hath felt the axe
> And hang himself. I pray you do my greeting.
>
> (5.2.90–97)

Immediately after this, the tone shifts to the elegiac and Timon becomes another sort of figure altogether; no longer sardonic, he turns away, muting the aggressive impulse, while the language signals a lyric turn:

> say to Athens
> Timon hath made his everlasting mansion
> Upon the beachèd verge of the salt flood,
> Who once a day with his embossèd froth
> The turbulent surge shall cover; thither come,
> And let my gravestone be your oracle.
>
> (5.2.99–104)

Earlier he has told the senators that he has been "writing of my epitaph;" he is aware, even eager, that his "long sickness / Of health and living now begins to mend / And nothing brings me all things" (71–72). The paradox of a wished-for death, a "nothing" that (as with Richard II, Macbeth and King Lear) will bring him "all things," links him to many of Shakespeare's tragic figures, but his persistence in cursing is his alone. As he bids his final farewell before disappearing from the stage (presumably) to die (he is unique among Shakespearean heroes in that his death remains uncertain and mysterious), he offers that epitaph as his enigmatic, oracular legacy.

That this seemingly singular epitaph multiplies mysteriously as the play winds toward its end is one of its textual puzzles, a sign of its prickliness as well as its seemingly unfinished state. I won't pause long over the textual problems, but it is worth noting that the three epitaphs that ensue are to some degree contradictory. The first is what is usually interpreted as an inscription read aloud by an anonymous soldier who, as the stage direction stipulates, arrives in the penultimate scene "*seeking Timon;*"[3] the other two are contained on a tablet that the same soldier says he cannot read (because they are in a language he doesn't know?) and therefore copies in wax to bring to his captain Alcibiades, who declaims them in the final moments of the play. Here is what the soldier finds: "*Timon is dead, who hath outstretched his span, / Some beast read this, there does not live a man*" (5.4.3–4) And here is what he brings to Alcibiades, quoted here directly from the 1623 Folio:

> *Heere lies a wretched Coarse, of wretched Soule bereft,*
> *Seek not my name: A Plague consume you, wicked Caitifs left:*
> *Heere lye I Timon, who aliue, all liuing men did hate,*
> *Passe by, and curse thy fill, but passe and stay not here thy gate.*[4]

What is striking is that the latter two couplets contradict each other, the second providing the name forbidden by the first. And the second accords with the soldier's couplet from the previous scene.

However we interpret the textual puzzles and seeming contradictions, what appears clear is that this is Timon speaking from beyond the grave, and the mixture of elegiac and minatory language seems an attempt to give more weight to his voice, to round out this person who has been for the most part remote. Like the soldier, we may very well be seeking for Timon, but we have a hard time finding him. The last part of the play has unquestionably a tragic tenor, but its single mindedness remains, and our sense of Timon's character, despite our engagement with him, seems more attenuated than we are used to in Shakespearean tragedy. Timon remains primarily a voice, though a powerful one, a partly allegorical figure who articulates a dark vision and thus appeals to our own tendencies to misanthropy, pronounced or diluted as they may be, who confirms our fears about the extent of nastiness and ingratitude to which human beings are prone. We are not likely to think of him as a companion, as we might with Hamlet; as someone we *know*. So even at the end he curses, and the play closes on a stiffly ironic note, with the aggressive and characterless Alcibiades taking over Athens while the remaining senators scurry to hold on to their lives and positions of influence. Nevertheless, the lone soldier's attempt to find Timon offers a kind of bridge to sympathy, if a frustrating and unfulfilled one. The last part of the epitaph does not abandon the harshness or the dark vision, but it adds to the invective a fleeting though not entirely insubstantial concern with those who remain; if we want, we are free to curse, but, more compellingly, we are invited simply (like Yeats's "Horseman") to *pass by*,[5] to forget what in fact refuses to be put entirely to rest. The epitaph undermines itself, since in telling us to forget, it inevitably reminds us of what has taken place. In doing so, it speaks of Timon's own impossible project of forgetting mankind.

Thus the presence of the unknown soldier figures both a desire to do more than pass by and a baffling of that very hope. Another way of saying this would be to suggest that, as the play reflects on Timon's fate, it begins to shift away from his headlong misanthropy into a subtler configuration: Timon's hatred of mankind is put into dialogue with the audience's feelings of displacement, our inability directly to speak to or hear from the dead—a dilemma that was especially pronounced in the later sixteenth and early seventeenth centuries.[6] We are left with our sense of loss; cursing is painful and useless, passing by our only alternative.

But passing by is not the best avenue to an understanding of character. Better, no doubt, to be invited *in* rather than *by*. So I am still struggling to define what sort of being Timon is, whether he should be accorded the dignity of personhood or no. Of course, it's not as if Timon has *no* character. We can, for example, legitimately wonder what lies behind his need to give, to be the most generous and bountiful man in Athens. There is clearly an element of competitiveness in this, a desire to be the top dog on Fortune's hill (to invoke a couple of the play's most dominant images). He's a lonely man who surrounds himself with friends in order, it seems, to keep from facing his loneliness. He gives obsessively throughout the play; in his rich phase he gives money and goods and in his vituperative phase he offers curses with the same reckless abandon. He has been read as a kind of perverse maternal figure in a play, and apparently a society, with no women in it except the tawdry whores and entertainers who appear from time to time to amuse the assembled gentlemen. His "bounty" defines him, as to some degree it did James I, to whom Timon has been compared.[7] But these characteristics fold easily into allegory, and, together with the skeletal morality-play structure that seems to underlie the narrative, lead in the direction of abstraction. There is less surprise than one encounters in Shakespeare's richer tragedies, little of that sudden and illuminating deviation from a set path. I think of Antony bidding farewell to his followers or sending Enobarbus' goods after him, or Macbeth's "She should have died hereafter," or Lear's sudden withdrawal of his hand: "Let me wipe it first, it smells of mortality"—(4.6.133). Such touches are mostly absent from Timon; his is a trajectory that hardly wavers from its course. Only at the end, as we have seen, is an unexpected direction briefly hinted at, the tragic temperature raised as he retires to bury himself on the "beachèd verge" of the sea. But even then there is something abstract in the zone of cosmic negation he has entered, whether one interprets it positively as G. W. Knight famously did,[8] or regards it as a kind of empty retreat, the low point of the spiritual desiccation that his misanthropic stance has led to.

What sort of a play is this, then? It's important to remember that Shakespeare and his co-author (Thomas Middleton) inherited the story of Timon as a satire, not a tragedy, that Timon, from the ancient world and down to the Renaissance, was primarily a figure of ridicule, a one-note caviler who could be relied on to discharge a certain amount of amusing bile, more like a barking dog than a rational man. As Plutarch tells his story (it is a mere digression in the *Life of Antony*), there is a hint that Timon, like Antony, was betrayed by his friends; but otherwise there is very little to explain how or why he became a misanthrope. Nowhere is Timon treated as a tragic figure. What then were our authors doing when they decided to flout the tradition?[9] The play was written during the same two or three year span that produced *King Lear*, *Macbeth*, *Antony and Cleopatra*, and *Coriolanus*, one of Shakespeare's most productive periods certainly, and one in which he was exploring the extremities of character. The major figures in these plays all tend to be possessed and at the same time deeply susceptible—even Coriolanus, for all his fanatical devotion to self-authoring, is defeated when he holds his mother by the hand, silent. Timon lacks this susceptibility, though he shares the obsessiveness. And this oddity in the way he is represented, this simplicity that is, I think, part of the inheritance of satire, makes me wonder about his relation to conceptions of tragic character.

What I have said so far about Timon's language and appeal does, I believe, give him some claim to tragic status. What I am working towards is a conception that allows not only for his richness and the appeal that involves, but also for his relative narrowness and the intensity that engenders. What I would propose is that Timon is somehow pre- or post-character, a figure on the outer edge of representation, what Shakespeare's richer tragic characters must both include and get past. Timon remains somehow unintegrated, partly because of his social position—he is both central and peripheral, but always alien. As his world's only giver, its patron, he occupies a spot at the top, and then later, as its main critic, a spot at the bottom—or, more precisely, on the extreme margins. Near the end of the play, when the Senators arrive to implore him to return and lead the Athenian defense against the onslaught of Alcibiades' army, he is suddenly regarded as once again central; but, as we have already seen, he refuses the proffered integration and turns to the writing of his epitaph, meanwhile inviting his fellow citizens to use his tree to hang themselves. He is defined mostly by his invective against his fellow citizens and, indeed, all of mankind; he is a fount of magnificent, if ultimately fruitless, verbal abuse. More even than Lear on the heath or at Dover, more than Coriolanus in Rome or in exile, he is forever apart.

In a brief but telling essay on the play,[10] Kenneth Burke suggests that invective "is rooted extralinguistically in the helpless rage of an infant" and that Timon's diatribes can have a wide appeal just because they give "full expression to a desire that is intrinsic to language."[11] It is precisely the "unbridled" nature of infant utterances that gives diatribe its power as well as the need in practical life to control it. We enjoy the poetry of imprecation because it revisits early experience and allows for a free expression of desires normally harnessed. In drama, says Burke, "unresolved tensions" of this kind can be given full expression and thereby transformed to aesthetic pleasure. At the level of adult social life, this plays out as a struggle between gratitude and rage, one that is focused on *goods*. *Timon* is a play all about goods. Burke argues that it is an unrelenting account of the "predicament of substance" whereby one, in seeking communion with others through bounty, establishes only a suspect bond. And the suspicion attached to such bonds is allied to the double valuation of money in the play, which Burke memorably characterizes as "fecal gold."[12] Invective, he says, is early in life associated "with the excrementiously tabooed,"[13] and hence its "perverse" appeal when it is rendered into drama. This element adds a dimension to the pleasure of self-contempt that William Empson identifies as a key to the play, which is linked to the common Elizabethan motif of the Malcontent figure and derives from the paradox that contempt for all mankind necessarily includes contempt for oneself.[14] Empson regards the play as consistently probing the puzzle of this, but locates the issue most especially in the encounter in 4.3 between Timon and Apemantus as they excoriate each other; each, he says, "has strong grounds for priding himself on his own version of self-contempt and despising the other's."[15] Burke and Empson, taken together, suggest a correlation between aggressive self-assertion and ironic self-contempt, both linked in this play to gold and expressed in extravagant language of fellowship or abuse. The play's fullest development of this double mode, and thus the point at which these complex and even uncomfortable pleasures intersect most vigorously, is in the exchange between Apemantus and Timon in the forest, a scene to which I will turn in a moment.

But before doing so I want to think about the claims made by Empson and Burke in terms of the unique perspective on psychoanalysis developed by Melanie Klein in her analysis of *envy*. Klein's theory that envy is an intrinsic and inescapable component of infant development is both controversial and ambiguous. Some have seen her as claiming that envy—what she defines as the desire to destroy what is good just because it is good—arises spontaneously and inevitably; others argue that she sees envy as a response to deprivation; still others have suggested that she at different points adopts both these views.[16] For my purposes, since I am not engaged in developing a Kleinian reading, nor making specific claims about her theory, but only developing an analogy, it is enough to note that she builds the theory around the bounty and the withholding of mother's milk, an idea that is fundamental to *Timon*.[17] Klein is trying to figure out the early source of envy as a way of explaining its manifestations in later life. For her, the infant responds powerfully to the breast as a good, but at the same time reacts with rage at its withdrawal or non-appearance. At such times, the infant perceives the mother as withholding what it desires and this generates envy, the urge to destroy what it at the same time perceives as good. This double valuation produces conflict between gratification and gratitude on the one side, and fury at the withholding on the other: "The infant's feeling of failed gratification is experienced as the breast *withholding*, or keeping for itself, the object of desire . . . there is an aim to possess the good object, but when this is felt to be impossible, the aim becomes a need to spoil the goodness of the object, in order to remove the source of envious feelings."[18]

I am struck first by the lines of connection between her ideas about the source of gratitude and fury at ingratitude, and Burke's (perhaps Freudian) account of fecal gold (which is characterized by a similarly double valuation). More than that, as I indicated above, the insistence on maternal bounty and its relation to withholding, rage, envy and invective also has suggestive links to the play. Coppelia Kahn, in an influential essay, has shown how the language of giving and bounty in *Timon* could be interpreted in terms of a "core fantasy" focused on the "appeal and peril of largesse." Appeal is linked to the image of "maternal bounty" while peril is linked to "fraternal betrayal."[19] This is smart and valuable, but doesn't quite explain the attraction of misanthropy and its expression in curses and abuse. If, with Klein, we adopt the view that envy is somehow at the root of the ego, that it is inescapable, an "unresolved tension" in Burke's terminology, then we can see the two halves of the play as complementary: love and hate; gratification and imprecatory rage. Indeed, from this point of view, the split structure of the play, far from being a flaw, can be seen to express the crucial idea that the bounty of the first half is as much bound up with the thematics of envy as the cursing of the second. The appeal of this is radical in that it goes to the root (as Klein and Burke see it) of both character and language.

Another way of approaching the idea here might be to regard Timon as both nurturing breast and furious infant. His appeal is simultaneously to our desire for gratification and our delight in invective (i.e. to our own engagement with the anxious doubleness of envy). But all this still remains rather schematic. Timon as a *character* continues to be elusive, even though—perhaps *because*—he comes to be defined in terms of radical envy. In the first part of the play he is jealous of his own pre-eminence. He says to Ventidius, who has offered to pay back the money Timon gave to bail him out of debtor's prison, "Honest Ventidius, you mistake my love: / I gave it freely ever, and there's none / Can truly say he gives if he receives" (1.2.9–11). "What need we have any friends," he asks a little later, "if we should ne'er have need of 'em?" (1.2.94–95) While this has the sound of reciprocity, it is really a way of saying that he is the friend of whom others do and must have need. He is the chief recipient of his own bounty, insofar as it feeds his gratification. This is easily transformed to its opposite—implacable hate—just as the evaluation of gold switches from high to low. Klein thinks of envy as the desire to destroy what is good just because it is good, and Timon's attack on human community in both parts of the play expresses something of that desire, though in the benevolent half it is occluded.

So in what way can we say that Timon, who in the foregoing has begun to sound like quite a complex figure, is a non-character, or, more precisely, a pre-character? I am proposing that other Shakespearean tragic figures given life around the time when this play was written assimilate Timon's brand of envy into a wider network. Timon is like an element which, in figures like Lear, Macbeth or Antony, combines with other elements to make characters; he is a sort of extremity, an experiment in character-making if you will. Hence the allegorical construction. If, by contrast, we were to explain Macbeth as motivated by the sort of envy that seeks to destroy what is good just because it is good (the bounteous Duncan), we would see immediately the poverty of such a formulation. It fits but it isn't enough. In Lear, the character closest in many ways to Timon, the fury and invective associated with envy, are combined with a kind of love that is undeniable even as we witness its corrosive consequences. So again it looks like Lear's character depends on an inclusion but also a transcendence of envy. Even Coriolanus, like Timon in his absolute disdain and his refusal to compromise, is softened by his love for his mother and, more intimately and surprisingly, for his wife.[20] Such figures assimilate envy in the sense that they experience it in tension with other warring elements; they do not overcome it—such is the nature of tragedy. But what gives us the sense of depth, of a person struggling with the inner occasions and consequences of rage and betrayal, is the self-alienated split between love and hate. So I lean toward the view that Timon is a partial character, a distilled element—pure and unmixed, powerful but incomplete.

Another way of coming at the character of Timon is through the insistent probing of the boundary between humans and animals in the play. A lowering and blurring of the threshold of humanity characterizes the latter half and dogs the speaking hero even as he tries to dodge the implications of his misanthropy. It's generally assumed that Shakespeare was not a dog lover, and the word and its cognates frequently feature as insults throughout his works (although the one actual dog to appear in his plays is Launce's rather loveable mongrel, Crab). In *Timon*, dogs are allied with the accumulation of money, and, more specifically, with the system of credit and patronage relations between men; the mechanism for this linkage is the cannibalism motif. This recalls a similar association in *Merchant of Venice* where Shylock is repeatedly connected to dogs and by extension to a cannibalistic desire for human flesh. Dogs on such a reading are barking embodiments of envy, the desire to feed and destroy simultaneously. In the opening scene of *Timon*, Alcibiades, invited to the feast, greets his patron with ominous affability: "Sir . . . I feed / Most hungrily on your sight" (1.1.258–59). Timon's response ignores the darker implications of this: "Ere we depart, we'll share a bounteous time / In different pleasures" (260–61). But we are led to infer that the limitless feasting of the first part of the play is a mark not only of Timon's bounty but of the threat to him that accompanies that bounty—the focus is not, to adopt Hamlet's witty phrase, on "where he eats, but where he is eaten." There is a reciprocity between feeding and being eaten; as in *Merchant of Venice*, the cannibalism images register a threat to the ease and smooth functioning of patronage relations. In the latter play, the threat is lodged primarily in Shylock's desire to "feed fat the ancient grudge" he bears Antonio, whereas the language of cannibalism in *Timon* is more widespread—it expresses the disposition of most of the characters toward their bountiful patron, who feed on his goods and end up consuming him wholly. Only one person recognizes this fact from the outset, and that is Apemantus, who is persistently linked to dogs throughout the text: when Timon invites him to dine, his answer is, "No, I eat not lords" (207). Apemantus' association with dogs is thus paradoxical, since he is the only one who refuses to feast on Timon's flesh; through him, dogs get surprisingly good press.

Just before Apemantus makes his vegetarian declaration, he is insulted by the painter:

"you're a dog!"

Apemantus: Thy mother's of my generation—what's she, if I be a dog?

Timon: Wilt dine with me, Apemantus?

Apemantus: No, I eat not lords.

(1.1.203–7)

He may be a dog in some ways, but it's his very humanity, as against the "dogginess" of the more voracious and predatory characters, that distinguishes him. And this exchange is typical; again and again it is Apemantus' *humanity* that is marked by the repeated references to him as a dog.

What I am suggesting is that the eating motifs are an expression of envy in the sense that I have been discussing it. Apemantus escapes the worst implications of this, but the other characters, notably Timon and his sycophantic friends, do not. If in the first half of the play Timon is the nurturing figure, a prey to the cannibalistic inclinations of the others, in the second half he becomes his opposite, he who would devour the rest of humanity. But there is also an inescapable element of self-loathing here, an unbridled envy that turns destructively inward. All this emerges in the brilliant confrontation between Apemantus and

Timon in the forest, where the matter of man and beast is most fully explored. "What wouldst thou do with the world, Apemantus," [asks Timon] "if it lay in thy power?"

> *Apemantus:* Give it the beasts, to be rid of the men.
>
> *Timon:* Wouldst thou have thyself fall in the confusion of men and remain a beast with the beasts?
>
> *Apemantus:* Ay, Timon.
>
> *Timon:* A beastly ambition, which the gods grant thee t'attain to.
> (4.3.320–27)

Here's the nub of the question: Timon is perfectly aware of the implications of his inversion of man and beast; it requires that one include oneself in the general curse. He must fall with the other men. But it is not something he can sustain. He launches into an extended bestiary, as a way of showing how inescapable domination and aggression are bound to be, even among beasts, all of whom are subject to other beasts, and almost all of whom are at the same time self subversive; but he leaves himself out of the equation:

> If thou wert the lion, the fox would beguile thee . . . if thou wert the ass, thy dullness would torment thee . . . if thou wert the wolf, thy greediness would afflict thee and oft thou shouldst hazard thy life for thy dinner. Wert thou the unicorn, pride and wrath would confound thee and make thine own self the conquest of thy fury . . . What beast couldst thou be that were not subject to a beast? And what a beast art thou already that seest not thy loss in transformation!
> (4.3.327–44)

The passage underscores two failures: one inevitable—being dominated by another beast; and one quasi-moral—being unaware of one's diminishment in having crossed the indeterminate border between man and beast. We never learn whether he sees himself as exemplifying that transformation, though the image of the unicorn hints at a stubborn blindness. The reference is to the legend of the unicorn, told, for example, by Edward Topsell: "[the Unicorn] and the Lion being enemies by nature, as soon as the Lion sees the Unicorn he betakes himself to a tree: The Unicorn in his fury and with all the swiftness of his course running at him sticks his horn fast in the tree, and then the Lion falls upon him and kills him."[21] The "pride and wrath" that Timon identifies as the unicorn's ruin reflect back on him, but he seems not to recognize that fact. He cannot include himself in the general curse, nor is there a Cordelia around to redeem nature. Apemantus adds the summary phrase, but it too fails to take the full measure of what is at stake here: "The commonwealth of Athens is become a forest of beasts" (346–47).

What is at stake is not a polarized opposition between man and beast, nor even a moral attack on humanity's inhumanity. The sequence suggests that the interplay between being an animal and being a man is part of the business of being human. At the same time, it highlights the labor of self-alienation which seems a substratum of character as Shakespeare sees it. Timon never quite achieves the awareness implied by the debate between himself and Apemantus; he hints at an understanding that his misanthropy must include himself—that if all men are mere beasts he too must be in that number. Apemantus's summary judgement doesn't quite cut it either, though the hint of possible community and reciprocity contained in "commonwealth" hovers above the declaration. (We might note as well that for all his cynicism Apemantus never actually leaves Athens—he remains within the beast/human community.) But Timon does not really take such implications in. For him to do so would threaten to derail the movement of the plot, but at the same time his failure keeps him at the level of primitive envy. Instead of inner doubt or conflict, the sort of thing that gives vitality and a sense of reality to figures like Macbeth or Antony, we get a character whose failure to see himself from the outside is represented by his failure to see himself as an animal.

My assumption in this paper has been that Shakespearean character is always interiorized and complex, that our sense that we know such people, that they are our *semblables*, derives from just this capacity to confound simplicity. Another, more paradoxical way of making this claim would be to say that our conviction that we know them depends on a sense that we do not know them, that we never can know them fully. By these kinds of criteria Timon remains a little apart; he lacks the self-alienation that is an essential part of the mix.[22] But at the same time he has an undeniable power, one that is felt compellingly in the theater when a strong actor takes the role. I think that power is related to his connection with envy, a characteristic I am willing, for the purposes of this argument, to accept as fundamental, but which is also partial. Insofar as it dominates Timon, defining him almost wholly, I take him to be less complete than characters that we typically regard as richer (such as Macbeth or Lear), for whom envy is only an element in their interior make-up, one that, in combination with other elements, generates conflict and uncertainty. From this vantage point, Timon is a "pre-character," as I have called him, but one that flames with a brilliant, black light.

Notes

1. I am indebted to D. R. Hiles for reminding me of this passage from Chaucer's pious but also psychologically acute cleric. I have benefitted from Hiles' essay on Melanie Klein, "Envy, Jealousy, Greed: A Kleinian Approach," delivered at CCPE in London, November 2006, which is available at www.psy.dmu.ac.uk/drhiles/ENVYpaper.htm. I also want to thank Adam Frank for suggesting the relevance of Klein's work and stimulating my thinking about its relation to *Timon of Athens*. This paper develops ideas broached in parts of the Introduction I wrote for the Arden edition of the play (Third Series), edited by myself and Gretchen E. Minton (London, Cenage, 2008).
2. 4.1.21–28. In quoting the play, I follow the text of the Arden edition, cited in note 1. Other Shakespeare texts are quoted from *The Riverside Shakespeare*, 2nd edition, ed. G. Blakemore Evans, et al. (Boston: Houghton Mifflin, 1997).
3. There is some doubt about the exact status of this "inscription" since the couplet is not marked as a quotation in F, and the precise stage action is quite uncertain. See *Timon of Athens*, ed. John Jowett (Oxford: Oxford University Press, 2004), 317–18, and note to 5.4.3–4 in *Timon of Athens*, eds Anthony B. Dawson and Gretchen E. Minton (Arden Shakespeare, 2008).
4. I quote from F here since in our edition of the play, which is the one I am quoting from in this essay, Gretchen Minton and I have omitted the first of the two couplets of the epitaph. Our view of the textual problem is as follows: uncertain as to which epitaph to use in the final version, Shakespeare copied out both versions (making only minimal changes) from Plutarch's *Life of Antonius*, where both appear almost exactly as here but are clearly distinguished from each other rather than run together. He thus postponed the final decision about which one to include, though at some point (perhaps before, perhaps after) he drafted the last scene, he inserted the immediately preceding scene with the soldier, which suggests that he planned to cut the first of the Plutarchan versions in a final draft.
5. In Yeats' poem "Under Ben Bulben," he composes his own epitaph, later etched on his gravestone:

> Under bare Ben Bulben's head
> In Drumcliff churchyard Yeats is laid.
> An ancestor was rector there
> Long years ago, a church stands near,
> By the road an ancient cross.
> No marble, no conventional phrase;
> On limestone quarried near the spot
> By his command these words are cut:
>   *Cast a cold eye*
>   *On life, on death.*
>   *Horseman, pass by!*

6. The whole issue of the relation between the living and the dead was painfully contentious during the sixteenth century in the wake of the Reformation and various attempts on the part of reformers to curtail ceremonies for the dead and the assumptions they gave shape to. The voices of those who had died were choked but not quite silenced by the many attempts to separate the community of the living from those who had passed beyond it. I have dealt with this issue at more length in "The Arithmetic of Memory," *Shakespeare Survey* 52 (1999): 54–67; see also Eamon Duffy, *The Stripping of the Altars: Traditional Religion in England, 1400–1580* (New Haven: Yale University Press, 1992), and Michael Neill, *Issues of Death: Mortality and Identity in English Renaissance Tragedy* (Oxford: Oxford University Press: 1997), among others.
7. Coppelia Kahn, "Magic of bounty: *Timon of Athens*, Jacobean patronage, and maternal power," *Shakespeare Quarterly* 38 (1987), 34–57, and David Bevington and David L. Smith, "James 1 and *Timon of Athens*," *Comparative Drama* 33, no.1 (1999) 56–87.
8. *The Wheel of Fire* (London: Methuen and Co, 1965).
9. I am bypassing the question of authorship in this paper, but it is by now fairly clear that the play is collaborative and that Middleton co-wrote the play, contributing about 35% of it. (See Brian Vickers, *Shakespeare Co-Author* (Oxford: Oxford University Press, 2002); M. P. Jackson, *Studies in Attribution* (Salzburg: Jacobean Drama Studies, 1979); and Jowett. Shakespeare probably took the lead, not only contributing the other 65% but producing the overall plan. By 1606-7, when the play was most likely written, he was the foremost playwright of the time, while Middleton was just coming into prominence, with a series of biting urban comedies as well as the irreverent and parodic *The Revenger's Tragedy* (1606). Shakespeare no doubt recognized his younger colleague's satirical skills and seems to have suggested his partner take on certain elements: the tawdry masque and banquet scene, spiced up with witty commentary on the part of the cynic Apemantus (1.2.), the scenes of attempted borrowing (3.1 to 3.3), the debt-collecting sequences (parts of 2.2, 3.4), and at least some of the sections involving the faithful steward, Flavius. The long opening sequence, with its brilliant interweaving of ambiguous magnanimity in the characterization of Timon and satirical portraiture in the representation of the friends who flock to his house, is certainly Shakespeare's, as are the great speeches of imprecation that dominate the fourth act and the elegiac, muted ending. For the purposes of the present paper, what counts most is that Shakespeare is almost certainly responsible for the play's overall shape and mixed tone, as well as for the conception of the central figure.
10. Kenneth Burke, "*Timon of Athens* and Misanthropic Gold," in *Language as Symbolic Action* (Berkeley: University of California Press, 1966), 115–24.
11. Burke, "*Timon of Athens* and Misanthropic Gold," 120, 121.
12. Burke, "*Timon of Athens* and Misanthropic Gold," 120.
13. Burke, "*Timon of Athens* and Misanthropic Gold," 122.
14. William Empson, *The Structure of Complex Words* (London: Chatto and Windus, 1977), 179–80.
15. Empson, *The Structure of Complex Words*, 180.

16. See D. R. Hiles (cited in n. 1) and R. D. Hinshelwood, *A Dictionary of Kleinian Thought* (London: Free Association Books, 1989), 171–74.
17. *Bounty*, as Coppelia Kahn has shown in "Magic of Bounty," is a key word for both the character and the play. Timon is associated with an almost limitless bounty; generosity flows from him like mother's milk—but of course he cannot sustain it. See below.
18. Hiles, his emphasis; the quotation is from section 6 of the online version of his paper.
19. Kahn, "Magic of Bounty," 35–41 (quotations taken from 35 and 40).
20. Volumnia's notorious comment that "the breasts of Hecuba, / When she did suckle Hector, look'd not lovelier / Than Hector's forehead when it spit forth blood / At Grecian sword contemning" is obviously germane here. It has attracted extensive psychoanalytic comment (see especially Janet Adelman, "'Anger's my Meat': Feeding, Dependency and Aggression in *Coriolanus*," in *Representing Shakespeare: New Psychoanalytic Essays*, ed. Murray M. Schwartz and Coppelia Kahn (Baltimore: Johns Hopkins Press 1980), 75–91; but what it might imply about Martius's later envy in Klein's sense has not, to my knowledge, been explored.
21. *The History of Foure-footed Beasts* (1607), 557.
22. What I am calling self-alienation seems linked to Aristotle's notion of *anagnorisis*, though I am thinking of it less as a point in the plot, as he does, and more as a condition, reached in some cases only at certain stages of the action, though in others (as with Hamlet or Falstaff) an intrinsic part of the person that we claim to know.

11
When Is a Bastard Not a Bastard? Character and Conscience in *King John*

Camille Slights

Although the characters in Shakespeare's plays continue to fascinate playgoers, actors, and general readers, to talk about fictional characters in academic circles has been for considerable time now to risk dismissal as hopelessly old-fashioned and naive, and probably politically reactionary. After L. C. Knights' famous attack on Bradleian character, criticism warned that Falstaff "is not a man, but a choric commentary,"[1] the danger of confusing fictional figures with real people became critical orthodoxy. Indeed, the "presumption of twentieth-century criticism," as A. D. Nuttall observed some thirty years ago, is that "choric exegesis precludes characterization."[2] More recently, poststructuralist critics have rejected character as an analytic concept not because it conflates the fictional with the real but because it misrepresents historical reality. By assuming a universal human nature, they argue, character criticism imposes on early modern texts a liberal humanist self that had not yet fully emerged and thus becomes complicit in naturalizing and perpetuating an oppressive ideology. According to Catherine Belsey, for example, the illusionary liberal humanist self is "the author and origin of meaning and choice."[3] It is defined by interiority and is unified and stable, whereas the fictional figures in early modern plays are fragmentary and discontinuous. And so, when Alan Sinfield poses the question "When Is a Character Not a Character?" he focuses not on the distinction between the real and the imaginative but on degrees and kinds of change and inconsistency. A character is a character, he argues, only when it gives "an impression of subjectivity, interiority, or consciousness, and a sense that these maintain a sufficient continuity or development through the scenes of the play." Desdemona, for example, is not a character but "a disjointed sequence of positions that women are conventionally supposed to occupy. . . . A character is not a character when she or he is needed to shore up a patriarchal representation."[4]

Since critics as well as theater audiences persist in responding strongly to Shakespeare's characters, scholars should, I think, continue to study those characters while taking into account the twentieth-century critiques of character criticism. We should acknowledge difference between the imaginative and the real, recognizing that expecting fictional characters to conform to our understandings of the values and motivations of people we know leads to misunderstanding and blocks our access to the imaginative worlds of the plays. Nevertheless, participating in the make-believe of Shakespeare's commercial secular theater is, as William Dodd has argued, "very different from the ritual involvement in a single transcendent reality of earlier religious drama."[5] The dramatis personae of Shakespeare's plays are not allegorical figures but mimetic representations of people with interiority (Hamlet's "that within which passes show") as well as identifiable positions in the social order, and we can understand them only by drawing on our knowledge of actual human beings. But we also know that people are shaped by their historical environments. While extreme versions of new historicist and cultural materialist approaches have been effectively challenged for a denial of human agency that impoverishes understanding of history and of plays, poststructuralist critiques of criticism that assumes an unchanging human nature prior to the shaping of identity by language and by familial, economic, and political structures have demonstrated compellingly that self-understandings of men and women in early modern England were significantly different from ours. I believe, then, that the most fruitful approaches to Shakespeare's characters now are those that ground analysis in early modern understandings of subjectivity.[6] In this paper I propose to contribute to that effort by suggesting that conscience was a concept basic to early modern self-understanding and that it provides historical grounding for analyzing characters on the early modern stage. I test this hypothesis by looking at characters in Shakespeare's *King John*.

As Anne Ferry points out, the words we use to talk about self-awareness were not current in early modern England. Terms such as *superego* and *unconscious* were unavailable, and ones such as *identity* and *subject* were used in different senses. The closest term available for continuous internal awareness, she suggests, was *conscience*.[7] Anyone in early modern England exhorted to *know thyself* understood they were being instructed to examine their conscience. William Fenner, for example, observes that conscience "sticketh so close that a man may as soon shake off himself as his conscience. And indeed his conscience is himself. Let a man examine himself, that is, his conscience."[8] As Fenner's warning of the inescapability of conscience implies, the sense of guilt that afflicts the wicked is the work of conscience, but conscience is a more capacious concept than the emotional turmoil of the guilty. Its primary sense was cognitive rather than affective. According to William Perkins, who lectured on conscience at Cambridge in the 1590s, conscience "signifieth a knowledge, ioyned with a knowledge, . . . First, because when a man knowes or thinkes any thing, by meanes of Conscience, hee knowes what he knowes and thinkes. Secondly, because by it, man knowes that thing of himselfe, which God also knows of him."[9] The understanding, Perkins explains, performs two functions: "the one is simple, which barely conceiueth or thinketh this or that . . . ." The other, the work of conscience, is "a *reflecting* or doubting of the former, whereby a man conceiues or thinks with himselfe what he thinks." Through conscience "I conceiue and know what I know." The first act of conscience is to bear "witnesse of our thoughts, of our affections, of our outward actions."[10] The second is to give judgment, "in euery action either to accuse for sinne, or to excuse for well doing: or to say, this may bee done, or it may not be done."[11] The concept of conscience, then, included both self-reflection and knowledge of moral principles, the voice of God speaking within each person. Internal and private, open directly only to God, the conscience directed and judged external action.

The explicit references to conscience in *King John* are informed by the common understanding as articulated by Perkins. For example, when King John bases his claim to England and the French territories on "Our strong possession and our right" (I.i.39),[12] his mother Elinor whispers:

Your strong possession much more than your right,
Or else it must go wrong with you and me,
So much my conscience whispers in your ear,
Which none but heaven and you and I shall hear.

(I.i.40–43)

Her response not only directs audience interpretation of a crucial political issue,[13] it also informs us of her internal state. Her reference to her conscience lets us know that in pursuing John's political goals, she and, perhaps, John deliberately act against their own moral judgments. Similarly, Lord Salisbury, fearing John's murderous intentions toward his nephew

Arthur, who has a strong claim to the throne, interprets the king's outward appearance as evidence of a struggle with his conscience:

> The color of the King doth come and go
> Between his purpose and his conscience,
> Like heralds 'twixt two dreadful battles set.
>
> (IV.ii.76–78)

And John validates Salisbury's judgment. Convinced that Hubert has killed Arthur at his urging and fearing the nobles' suspicious indignation, John initially repents Arthur's reported murder as much because it is proving politically damaging as because it is morally repugnant: "There is no sure foundation set on blood; / No certain life achiev'd by others' death" (IV.ii.103–5). But he betrays his own sense of guilt even as he struggles to shift responsibility to Hubert, who "made it no conscience to destroy a prince" (IV.ii.229). Threatened by both foreign invasion and loss of support from the English nobles outraged by Arthur's death, John confesses suffering spiritually as well as politically:

> ... in the body of this fleshly land,
> This kingdom, this confine of blood and breath,
> Hostility and civil tumult reigns
> Between my conscience and my cousin's death.
>
> (IV.ii.245–48)

Although the audience does not have direct access to Elinor or John's consciousness through soliloquy, these references to conscience establish that their outward actions are significant in terms of their knowledge of themselves in relation to their knowledge of moral law. By deliberately acting contrary to the judgment of their consciences, they also demonstrate that in the violent, ruthless world of *King John* knowledge of traditional moral values and self-awareness fail to control behavior. Admittedly, consciences are not totally powerless. In one of the play's most moving scenes, Hubert struggles with the conflict between his loyalty to his sovereign and compassion for his victim and chooses to spare Arthur's life (IV.i). In the last act, the French lord Melune reveals that Lewis plans, as soon as the fighting is over, to execute the English nobles who have transferred their allegiance to France, and he attributes his decision to expose Lewis's treachery to his awakened conscience (V.iv.43). Melune's change of heart in turn wakens the consciences of the English nobles to renewed obedience to their English king.

But even though characters' consciences occasionally motivate events, they have negligible impact on the political conflicts that constitute the dramatic action. Arthur dies despite Hubert's decision to save him. Melune's intelligence and the English nobles' rediscovered loyalty have no effect on the military situation. The French invasion is not turned back by the strengthened English force but withdrawn in accordance with a political agreement negotiated with Lewis by Pandulph the papal legate. These assertions of conscience, moreover, fail to provide the audience with a satisfying moral perspective on the dramatic action. Hubert spares Arthur not because he thinks through his case of conscience and comes to understand that torturing and killing an innocent child are morally wrong, but because the child's eloquence moves him to pity in spite of his sworn purpose. The dying Melune's conscience is awakened by his affection for Hubert and his remembering that his "grandsire was an Englishman" (V.iv.42). Why Melune's betrayal of his allegiance to French authority should inspire the English nobles to renew their allegiance to English authority is left unclear. What Salisbury in retrospect constructs as sinful disobedience was provoked by outrage at the death of an innocent child and confirmed by a solemn oath. While consciences in *King John* occasionally demand behavior that is not self-serving and punish violations of traditional responsibilities and obligations with feelings of guilt, they are ambiguous and unreliable guides through Shakespeare's vision of the tangled loyalties and treacheries of England under John.

The most interesting figure in terms of character and of conscience is Philip Faulconbridge, a.k.a. Sir Richard Plantagenet, a.k.a. the Bastard. To some critics, he is a great Shakespearean character. L. A. Beaurline, for example, sees him as "a profoundly realized character";[14] and to Herschel Baker he is "one of Shakespeare's grand creations", who "becomes the hero of the play."[15] On the other hand, E. A. J. Honigmann argues that he is not the hero but a commentator and complains that his choric duties "impinge upon his psychological integrity."[16] In an early soliloquy, he dedicates himself to self-interest, yet he is the most attractive character in the play and the only major figure who does not betray a trust. He mocks the moral failures of the society he aspires to and shrewdly demystifies the monarchy he loyally defends. Variously identified by critics as a folk hero, a Vice figure, and a Machiavel,[17] he is, according to Walter Cohen, "less a coherent fictional figure than a series of discontinuous theatrical functions."[18] A better argument, I suggest, is that his very inconsistencies constitute a continuous consciousness, a self-reflective moral awareness that develops in response to the moral confusions of his world and that adumbrates a significant change in the concept of conscience in early modern England.

In the opening scene, Philip Faulconbridge is at the center of an exploration of the basis of identity. Although he first identifies himself as the eldest son of Sir Robert Faulconbridge, his brother Robert challenges his right to inherit Faulconbridge land on the grounds that he is not Sir Robert's son but the issue of his mother's adultery with Richard Cordelion. King John denies young Robert's appeal, ruling that children born in wedlock are legitimate regardless of biological paternity.[19] Initially, then, law and custom trump biology. But, even as King John supports Philip's legitimacy, he accepts Robert's claim about paternity on biological grounds through Philip's physical resemblance to King Richard. Elinor, the Queen Mother, first notices the family resemblance: "He hath a trick of Cordelion's face, / The accent of his tongue affecteth him" (I.i.85–86); and King John agrees: "Mine eye hath well examined his parts / And finds them perfect Richard" (I.i.89–90). Elinor then presents Philip with a choice of identities:

> Whether hadst thou rather be a Faulconbridge,
> And like thy brother, to enjoy thy land;
> Or the reputed son of Cordelion,
> Lord of thy presence and no land beside?
>
> (I.i.134–37)

Philip chooses to reject his Faulconbridge identity, and King John confirms his choice:

> From henceforth bear his name whose form thou bearest:
> Kneel thou down Philip, but rise more great,
> Arise Sir Richard, and Plantagenet.
>
> (I.i.160–62)

Although Elinor and John understand the change as correlating "name" with "form," basing identity on genealogy, Philip chooses to ally himself with his putative biological father's family rather than with his mother's husband not so much to welcome a Plantagenet identity as to reject a Faulconbridge one, subtly mocking the Plantagenet reverence for blood line by flippantly announcing his choice in terms of his physical superiority to his brother:

> Madam, and if my brother had my shape
> And I had his ....
>
> ....

> And to his shape were heir to all this land,
> Would I might never stir from off this place,
> I would give it every foot to have this face;
> It would not be Sir Nob in any case.
>
> (I.i.138–39, 144–47)

Attributing his identity to his personal qualities and preferences, and to the contingencies of fortune, he welcomes the freedom of possibility offered by illegitimacy and takes leave of his Faulconbridge heritage without regret: "Brother, take you my land, I'll take my chance" (I.i.151). When Elinor invites him to enjoy the privileges of his new role in the royal family—"I am thy grandame, Richard, call me so" (I.i.168), he impudently quips about his adulterous conception, dismissing his parentage as irrelevant and claiming individual autonomy: "Madam, by chance, but not by truth; what though? / . . . / Near or far off, well won is still well shot, / And I am I, howe'er I was begot" (I.i.169, 174–75).

Welcoming his new social role, the Bastard enthusiastically sets about the task of self-fashioning, a process that involves self-reflection as well as acquisition of the external manners appropriate to his rise in status.[20] His self-awareness contrasts radically with the consciences of other characters. His conscience neither accuses him for violating moral norms as John's does nor commands obedience as Hubert's does. Instead, it registers his difference and directs his detachment from the ethical standards of society. In his first soliloquy, reflecting on the privileges as well as the affectations and hypocrisies of courtly society, he announces that he intends to succeed *in* courtly society but not to be *of* it, to use the devious manners of the age to his own advantage without being corrupted by them.

Unlike the other characters in *King John* who exhibit conscience by judging themselves on the basis of moral standards articulated in religious and political traditions, the Bastard judges and condemns society on the basis of a personal sense of right and wrong that develops as he self-consciously constructs an identity. Hannah Arendt, writing about the collapse of morality in Nazi Germany, provides, I think, a helpful gloss on Shakespeare's representation in the Bastard of a conscience in which the self is the moral standard. Arendt describes growing up with the assumption that "Whatever the source of moral knowledge might be—divine commandments or human reason—every sane man . . . carried within himself a voice that tells him what is right and wrong," and she tells of the shock when "all this collapsed almost overnight, and then it was as though morality suddenly stood revealed . . . as a set of *mores*, customs and manners, which could be exchanged for another set with hardly more trouble than it would take to change the table manners of an individual or a people."[21] When morality collapsed, she argues, the only people who could be counted on were those whose ultimate moral standard was the self. "We might call them moral personalities, but . . . this is almost a redundancy; the quality of being a person, as distinguished from merely being human, is not among the individual properties, gifts, talents, or shortcomings, with which men are born . . . . An individual's personal quality is precisely his 'moral' quality . . . ."[22] For Arendt, a reliable conscience is not innate, the voice of God speaking identically within all people, but constructed individually through the activity of thinking, which she defines as "a dialogue carried on by the mind with itself . . . .[T]he moral precept rises out of the thinking activity itself." In "this process of thought," she explains, "I explicitly constitute myself a person, and I shall remain one to the extent that I am capable of such constitution ever again and anew."[23]

I do not mean to imply a close analogy between Nazi Germany and the play's version of England during John's reign, only to suggest that Arendt's analysis of the inadequacy of traditional understandings of conscience to explain a twentieth-century collapse of morality can illuminate two conceptions of conscience operating in *King John*. A taxonomy of characterization from the perspective of the traditional concept of conscience as innate, universal knowledge of moral law would include most characters in such categories as those who obey their conscience, those who act against their conscience, those who ignore their conscience, and those who struggle with cases of conscience. But the Bastard would not fit easily into any of these categories; instead, he shows the process of thinking, by which he constitutes an individual conscience that comes into play when traditional values and principles fail. This process, I suggest, can account for both his distinctiveness as a character and his inconsistencies.

The Bastard's changing moral awareness demonstrates continuing self-critical responses to particular sets of circumstances. In the opening scene, he dismisses conventional pieties of sex and family flippantly, but in soliloquy he reveals a self-reflective habit of mind, the "intercourse between me and myself (in which we examine what we say and what we do)" that Arendt calls thinking.[24] The soliloquy begins with exuberant, if ironic, anticipation of his new role as Sir Richard:

Well, now I can make any Joan a lady.
"Good den, Sir Richard!" "God-a-mercy, fellow!"

> And if his name be George, I'll call him Peter;
> For new-made honor doth forget men's names;
> 'Tis too respective and too sociable
> For your conversion. Now your traveller,
> He and his toothpick at my worship's mess,
> And when my knightly stomach is suffic'd,
> Why then I suck my teeth, and catechize
> My picked man of countries. "My dear sir,"
> Thus, leaning on my elbow, I begin,
> "I shall beseech you"
>
> (I.i.184–95)

But, after several lines mocking this "dialogue of compliment," he concludes that the language of "worshipful society" is appropriate for a "mounting spirit like myself" (I.i.201, 205, 206):

> For he is but a bastard to the time
> That doth not smack of observation—
> And so am I, whether I smack or no;
> And not alone in habit or device,
> Exterior form, outward accoutrement,
> But from the inward motion to deliver
> Sweet, sweet, sweet poison for the age's tooth.
>
> (I.i.207–13)

Yet he realizes he is not a true son to courtly society any more than he is a true son to either Sir Robert or King Richard. As "a bastard to the time," he resolves to remain detached from the values of courtly society while he acquires the necessary skills to flourish within it:

> ... [T]hough I will not practice to deceive,
> Yet to avoid deceit, I mean to learn;
> For it shall strew the footsteps of my rising.
>
> (I.i.214–16)

In this dialogue with himself, the Bastard eagerly anticipates the glamour and excitement of the courtly chivalric world suddenly open to him and also admits the political and moral dangers of both that world and his attraction to it. Although the revelation of his mother's adultery does not disturb him unduly, it sharpens his critical perspective on social hypocrisies. When Lady Faulconbridge enters, he ignores her protests that her sons should be defending her honor, demands to know the truth of his parentage, and offers comfort and support only after she confirms King Richard's paternity.

In the first scene, then, the setting aside of Sir Robert's will and the establishment of Faulconbridge's bastardy undercuts the moral authority of the family. Although Elinor's admission that King John's claim to territory in France is invalid and John's comment that "Our abbeys and priories shall pay / This expedition's charge" (I.i.48–49) hints at future problems, social and political authority seem secure. King John authoritatively applies to the Faulconbridge dispute the English law that recognizes Philip's legitimacy and decisively implements the solution by which Philip voluntarily delegitimizes himself, thus satisfying everyone: Robert inherits his father's estate; Philip the Bastard is confident he can use his illegitimacy to his advantage. In the following scenes, issues of legitimacy take more serious and violent forms that undermine the moral authority of political and religious institutions.

In Act 2, when the English forces under King John and the French forces led by King Philip meet before Angiers, charges and countercharges of usurpation, adultery, and bastardy punctuate portentous invocations of right and law. John presents himself to the citizens of Angiers as "your lawful King" and confronts King Philip as "God's wrathful agent" (II.i.222, 87). Philip, claiming authority derived from "that supernal judge that stirs good thoughts / In any breast of strong authority, / To look into the blots and stains of right" (II.i.112–14), champions Arthur's rights and exposes the weakness of John's claim to the English throne. John implicitly acknowledges the weakness of his legal and moral position when he takes Elinor's advice to strengthen his "unsur'd assurance to the crown" (II.i.471) by implementing a proposal to make peace with France through a marriage between his niece Blanch and Philip's son Lewis. Philip and his allies, Lewis and the Duke of Austria, moreover, lose the moral high ground they have claimed as champions of oppressed innocence by sacrificing Arthur's cause to the expediency of this arrangement. The pace of abandoning solemnly undertaken goals and of breaking oaths and promises accelerates when religious authority as represented by Pandulph, the papal legate, intervenes. After excommunicating John, who is defying the authority of Rome, Pandulph persuades Philip and Lewis to renew arms against England in spite of their vows of peace and friendship with John. Then, after an initial French defeat, he convinces Lewis to invade England by chillingly predicting that the invasion will provoke John to kill Arthur and that the child's murder will open a path to the English throne for Lewis. John comforts captive Arthur, "thy uncle will / As dear be to thee as thy father was" (III.iii.3–4), and a few lines later complains to Hubert that his nephew is "a very serpent in my way" (III.iii.61), instigating his death. Melune betrays Lewis's confidence, and the English nobles, Salisbury, Pembroke, and Bigot, switch allegiance from John to Lewis and back to John. John himself not only abandons his project of securing English territory in France in order to protect his crown, but, after proudly proclaiming that "as we, under God, are supreme head, / ... / Where we do reign, we will alone uphold / Without th' assistance of a mortal hand" and refusing to defer to the Pope's "usurped authority" (III.i.155–58, 160), capitulates and humbly receives his crown from Pandulph's hand "as holding of the Pope, / Your sovereign greatness and authority" (V.i.3–4).

John's hypocritical expression of family affection for his young nephew is, of course, deliberate deceit, but the usual pattern in these dizzying spectacles of broken promises and betrayed allegiances is to adapt traditional moral language and conventional standards of conduct to new power relations. For example, the Duke of Austria, in Act 2, swears to fight until young Arthur is recognized as England's king and assures Arthur's mother Constance that "The peace of heaven is theirs that lift their swords / In such a just and charitable war" (II.1.35–36), but he makes no protest when King Philip agrees to sacrifice Arthur's cause for his own advantage. When Pandulph excommunicates John and orders the renewal of hostilities, Austria immediately advises Philip to "listen to the cardinal" (III.i.198). Philip, who in the previous scene accused John of having "done a rape / Upon the maiden virtue of the crown" (II.i.97–98), now describes his new friendship with his recent enemy as "the conjunction of our inward souls / Married in league, coupled, and link'd together / With all religious strength of sacred vows" (III.i.227–28). But, unable to persuade Pandulph that to renounce his pact with John is to "jest with heaven" (III.i.242) and threatened with excommunication, he too defers to the authority of the church. The English nobles also dress changes of allegiance in the language of religion. Disavowing obedience to King John, Salisbury kneels by Arthur's body to breathe "The incense of a vow, a holy vow" to avenge his death, words that Pembroke and Bigot "religiously confirm" (IV.iii.67, 73). Arthur is still not avenged when they learn that Lewis plans to execute them as soon as the fighting is over and Salisbury speaks for them again:

> We will untread the steps of damned flight,
> And like a bated and retired flood,
> Leaving our rankness and irregular course,
> Stoop low within those bounds we have o'erlook'd,

And calmly run on in obedience
Even to our ocean, to our great King John.

(V.iv.52–57)

In short, the betrayals and changes of allegiance in *King John* are not acts of men who have taken evil to be their good and are determined to prove villains, but self-deceptive adaptations to shifts in power conceived in terms of conventional religious piety by characters who do not habitually examine events in an inner dialogue. "Clichés, stock phrases, adherence to conventional, standardized codes of expression and conduct," as Arendt observes, "have the socially recognized function of protecting us from reality."[25]

The Bastard, in contrast, characteristically examines and reflects on events. Although his mockery of pretension and hypocrisy in his first soliloquy is acute, it shows more amusement than outrage. As he observes the failure of traditional values and principles on the larger stage of the state and international politics, his diagnosis becomes more penetrating and scathing. After the meeting where King John and King Philip agree temporarily on a mutually beneficial pact, the Bastard in soliloquy reflects on the hollowness of their earlier claims of noble motives and goals:

Mad world, mad kings, mad composition!
John, to stop Arthur's title in the whole,
Hath willingly departed with a part,
And France, whose armor conscience buckled on,
Whom zeal and charity brought to the field
As God's own soldier..

....
Hath drawn him from his own determin'd aid,
From a resolv'd and honorable war
To a most base and vile-concluded peace.

(II.i.561–66, 584–86)

Examining a specific event and the motives of two particular people leads the Bastard not to self-righteous vilification of the specific offenders but to broader consideration of the formation of codes of conduct.

He is most disgusted that Philip, who was not fighting for himself but for powerless Arthur, has abandoned his cause. Rather than demonizing the French enemy, he assumes that Philip has been a man of conscience who has been corrupted by a general collapse of values. I want to emphasize two points in the Bastard's analysis of the moral bankruptcy of his world. First, Philip has been corrupted by adopting external social norms rather than engaging in an inner dialogue and making himself his ethical standard: this "bias, this commodity, / This bawd, this broker, this all-changing word, / Clapp'd on the outward eye of fickle France / Hath drawn him from his own determin'd aid" (II.i.581–84). Instead of looking with his inward eye into his own conscience, he has looked with his outward eye on the expediency and self-interest of the world around him and abandoned his own decision to help Arthur.[26] Second, the Bastard's primary emphasis is on the pervasiveness of the moral vacuum and the consequent destabilization of society:

> ... that same purpose-changer, that sly devil,
> That broker that still breaks the pate of faith,
> That daily break-vow, he that wins of all,
> Of kings..., of beggars, old men, young men, maids,
> ......
> That smooth-fac'd gentleman, tickling commodity,
> Commodity, the bias of the world—
> The world, who of itself is peized well,
> Made to run even upon even ground,
> Till this advantage, this vile-drawing bias,
> This sway of motion, this commodity,
> Makes it take head from all indifferency,
> From all direction, purpose, course, intent—
> (II.i.567–70, 573–80)

Commodity that motivates John and Philip, the Bastard concludes, is an "all-changing word" (582), corrupting everyone from king to beggar and subverting all social enterprises.

In his silent dialogue with himself, he next examines his own motives. When his mockery of pretension and hypocrisy in his first soliloquy involved self-mockery, he was confident he could master the skills of a duplicitous world without being corrupted by them. Now his self-criticism is more unsparing: "And why rail I on this commodity? / But for because he hath not woo'd me yet" (II.i.587–88). He concludes sardonically: "Since kings break faith upon commodity / Gain, be my lord, for I will worship thee" (II.i.597–98).

As several critics have observed, although the Bastard announces his intention to pursue his own advantage, we do not in fact see him act out of self-interest. We observe him as adept at detecting deceit and hypocrisy, but we do not see him practice deception. Still, we should not, I think, dismiss his claim to cynical self-interest as merely ironic. Arendt points out that cynicism, or what she terms nihilism, is a danger inherent in thinking: "All critical examinations must go through a stage of at least hypothetically negating accepted opinions and "values" by finding out their implications and tacit assumptions, and in this sense nihilism may be seen as an ever-present danger of thinking."[27] The Bastard does not remain in the stage of cynical disillusionment or pursue a program of self-gain, but he is no longer confident that he can remain invulnerable to the temptations of that "smooth-fac'd gentleman" commodity. In a world where commodity is the accepted standard of conduct, where faithlessness and treachery are social norms, the best that he can do is to act within the limits he sets for himself. Acutely aware of the fragmentation and chaos threatening a society without common values or respected authority, he devotes himself to England's need for social stability and political legitimacy by continuing to serve his king in spite of John's limitations. When fighting resumes, he takes an active and responsible role, rescuing Elinor from French attack, revenging Cordelion's death by killing Austria, and returning to England to seize revenues from the monasteries to finance the war. When the war comes to England, he struggles to rally the English forces. Acts 3 and 4 present the Bastard as more fighter than thinker.

Only Arthur's death presents a moral crisis that again incites the Bastard to examine and reflect. And again his response is distinctive. When King John mistakenly thought his warrant had been responsible for Arthur's death, his first thought was for political consequences and his second thought was fear of damnation. When Arthur's body is actually discovered, Salisbury, Pembroke, and Bigot lament ostentatiously, vow revenge, and attack Hubert, wrongly assuming his guilt. The Bastard suspects Hubert but does not rush to judgment or threaten punishment. Instead he predicts the intolerable suffering of a ravaged conscience:

> If thou didst but consent
> To this most cruel act, do but despair,
> And if thou want'st a cord, the smallest thread
> That ever spider twisted from her womb
> Will serve to strangle thee; a rush will be a beam
> To hang thee on; or wouldst thou drown thyself,
> Put but a little water in a spoon,
> And it shall be as all the ocean,
> Enough to stifle such a villain up.
>
> (IV.iii.125–33)

The Bastard's hyperboles, I think, express his assumption that one's standard of conduct is the self and that one refrains from evil not from fear of external punishment but because, in Arendt's words, "I cannot do certain things, because having done them I shall no longer be able to live with myself."[28] The Bastard is shaken by Arthur's death and admits a sense of moral confusion: "I am amaz'd, methinks, and lose my way / Among the thorns and dangers of this world" (IV.iii.140–41). He explicitly acknowledges the truth of Arthur's claim with his death:

> The life, the right, and truth of all this realm
> Is fled to heaven; and England now is left
> To tug and scamble, and to part by th' teeth
> The unowed interest of proud swelling state.
>
> (IV.iii.144–47)

But discovering that political reality offers no morally unambiguous paths does not lead the Bastard to cynical withdrawal from the public sphere. In fact, he increasingly exercises agency in public affairs. As Philip Faulconbridge, he is John's "faithful subject" (I.i.50) submitting a family quarrel to the king's judgment. As Sir Richard Plantagenet, he follows his liege lord to France, striving to avenge his father by winning back from the Duke of Austria the lion skin seized at King Richard's death. As part of King John's forces at Angiers, he is contemptuous of the citizens' passive detachment and angrily proposes that England and France join forces to destroy the city and then fight over its ruins, scornfully congratulating himself on his mastery of the manners of "worshipful society": "How like you this wild counsel, mighty states? / Smacks it not something of the policy?" (II.i.395–96). When the fighting moves to England, he acts as John's spokesman until finally John turns command of the English forces, "the ordering of this present time" (V.i.77), over to him. As John's inadequacies as king become clear and the Bastard takes on more responsibilities, he conceives of his rise to power as soldier, royal spokesman, counselor, and decision-maker not as an achievement of his "mounting spirit" but as an opportunity to serve England. He speaks and acts not for personal gain or personal honor but for the common good. In mourning Arthur's death, he mourns the plight of England, governed by a king of uncertain title and threatened by foreign invasion and internal unrest. Without a king of recognized legitimacy, says the Bastard,

> ...... vast confusion waits,
> As doth a raven on a sick-fall'n beast,
> The imminent decay of wrested pomp.
>
> (IV.iii.152–54)

In the time of crisis, he grieves for Arthur and for England and then he resolves to act, concluding, "Bear away that child / And follow me with speed. I'll to the King" (IV.iii.156–57).

Although he is not confident of success, he attempts to inspire in John the dignity and fortitude needed to act effectively as England's king, to spur the English to greater military effort when resolve wavers, and to act as peace-maker when dissension breaks out among the English. He is loyal to the king in spite of John's faults and failures and, after John's death, presents his "faithful services / And true subjection" (V.vii.104–5) to Henry, John's son. The subjection that the Bastard offers Henry is obviously not the unquestioning, passive submission of the medieval subject or the personal fealty of the chivalric knight. It is rather the voluntary obedience of a citizen who actively participates in the public sphere. The Bastard, not Henry, delivers the play's final lines: "Nought shall make us rue, / If England to itself do rest but true" (V.vii.117–18).

In our own time, we tend to think of our inner selves as individual and unique while recognizing that outwardly we conform to models defined by social norms of gender, family, class, and profession. Conversely, in early modern England, external appearances registered diversity, while inner selves where the voice of God speaks in every person's conscience revealed universality. Today conscience most often refers to moral diversity, to the basis of resistance to social or political norms. For example, we have free votes in parliament so that members can vote their consciences rather than adhere to party policy; we speak of conscientious objectors, not of conscientious followers. In contrast, in the sixteenth century, traditional understanding of conscience as the voice of God within each person implied universal understanding of moral truth. Since divine law was held to be everywhere and always the same, consciences theoretically ensured obedience and uniformity—docile subjects and social cohesion. In practice, of course, consciences disagreed. By the 1640s, the word "conscience" in a pamphlet title indicated politically controversial material rather than widely acceptable Christian piety. During the Civil War, many conscientious Englishmen thought of themselves as responsible citizens rather than as dutiful subjects and killed and died for conscience's sake. I have tried to show here that *King John* explores a strand in the transition from a universal to an individualized conscience and the transformation of subjects into citizens. Most characters in the play judge themselves and others on the basis of a shared traditional moral code. In contrast, the Bastard judges good and evil in a confusing world without relying on external authority. Looking at the Bastard from this perspective shows his inconsistencies to be the material of a continuous consciousness, a self-reflective internal dialogue through which he constitutes a moral self. As he becomes his own moral authority, he simultaneously transforms his social identity from eldest son in a patriarchal family, to feudal retainer, and then to responsible citizen.

As an exemplar of an independent conscience, the Bastard is both attractive and disturbing. He loyally serves England and England's king despite clear-eyed recognition of John's questionable title and personal faithlessness, but his efforts are largely futile. The announcement of his rescue of Elinor in Act 3 is followed shortly by the announcement of her death in Act 4. The rebel lords defect to France despite the Bastard's efforts to command their loyalty. He fights to defend England, but the French invasion is averted by the political maneuvering of the papal legate rather than by the Bastard's courage and patriotism. The play suggests that a single moral voice may have little effect in a time when Commodity is the world's bias. Perhaps more troubling, while the play invites us to admire the Bastard's independent conscience, through the scornful malice of the "wild counsel" he offers at Angiers and the despairing nihilism of his soliloquy on Commodity, it also warns us that the subjectivism of the individual conscience is unstable and potentially dangerous.

Notes

1. L. C. Knights, *How Many Children had Lady Macbeth?* (Cambridge: Cambridge University Press, 1933), 21 n. as quoted in A. D. Nuttall, *A New Mimesis: Shakespeare and the Representation of Reality* (London and New York: Methuen, 1983), 100.
2. Nuttall, *A New Mimesis*, 147.
3. Catherine Belsey, *The Subject of Tragedy: Identity and Difference in Renaissance Drama* (London and New York: Methuen, 1985), 35.
4. Alan Sinfield, *Faultlines: Cultural Materialism and the Politics of Dissident Reading* (Berkeley: University of California Press, 1992), 52, 62, 53, 54.
5. William Dodd, "Destined Livery? Character and Person in Shakespeare," *Shakespeare Survey* 51 (1998), 148.
6. I have in mind such work as Katharine Eisaman Maus, *Inwardness and Theater in the English Renaissance* (Chicago: University of Chicago Press, 1995); Elizabeth Hanson, *Discovering the Subject in Renaissance England* (Cambridge: Cambridge University Press, 1998); Cynthia Marshall, *The Shattering of the Self: Violence, Subjectivity, and Early Modern Texts* (Baltimore: Johns Hopkins Press, 2002).
7. Anne Ferry, *The "Inward" Language: Sonnets of Wyatt, Sidney, Shakespeare, Donne* (Chicago and London: University of Chicago Press, 1983), 45–46.

8. William Fenner, *The Sovles Looking-glasse . . . With a Treatise of Conscience* (Cambridge: R. Daniel for J. Rothwell, 1640), 38.
9. William Perkins, *The Workes of . . . Mr William Perkins*, 3 vols. (London: J. Legatt, 1612–13) 2:11.
10. Perkins, *The Workes*, 1:518.
11. Perkins, *The Workes*, 1:519.
12. I quote throughout from *The Riverside Shakespeare*, 2nd edition, ed. G. Blakemore Evans, et al. (Boston: Houghton Mifflin, 1997).
13. Unlike the chronicle histories, which did not question the legitimacy of John's succession, *King John* assumes throughout that John is king *de facto* but not *de jure*.
14. *King John*, The New Cambridge Shakespeare, ed. L. A. Beaurline (Cambridge: Cambridge University Press, 1990), 41.
15. *The Riverside Shakespeare*, 807.
16. *King John*, The Arden Shakespeare, ed. E. A. J Honigmann (London: Methuen, 1954), lxxi, n1.
17. Emrys Jones, *The Origins of Shakespeare* (Oxford: Clarendon Press, 1977); Robert Weimann, "Mingling Vice and 'Worthiness' in *King John*," *Shakespeare Studies* 27 (1999): 109–33; Michael Manheim, "The Four Voices of the Bastard," in *King John: New Perspectives*, ed. Deborah T. Curren-Aquino (Newark: University of Delaware Press, 1989): 126–35.
18. *The Norton Shakespeare*, ed. Stephen Greenblatt, et al. (New York and London: W. W. Norton, 1997), 1019.
19. Honigmann cites H. Swinburne, *Briefe Treatise of Testaments* (1590): "Ahe which maried the woman, shall bee saide to bee the father of the childe, and not hee which did beget the same . . . for whose the cow is, as it is commonly said, his is the calfe also." See *King John*, Arden, I.i.124 n.
20. Critics who discuss the Bastard's self-fashioning include Virginia Vaughan, "*King John*: A Study in Subversion and Containment," in *King John: New Perspectives*, 62–75; Edward Gieskes, "'He Is But a Bastard to the Time': Status and Service in *The Troublesome Raigne of John* and Shakespeare's *King John*," *ELH* 65 (1998): 779–98; and James P. Saeger, "Illegitimate Subjects: Performing Bastardy in *King John*," *Journal of English and Germanic Philology* 100 (2001): 1–21.
21. Hannah Arendt, "Some Questions of Moral Philosophy" in *Responsibility and Judgment*, ed. Jerome Kohn (New York: Schocken Books, 2003), 61, 50.
22. Arendt, "Some Questions of Moral Philosophy," 79.
23. Arendt, "Some Questions of Moral Philosophy," 92–95.
24. Hannah Arendt, "'Thinking and Moral Considerations,'" in *Responsibility and Judgment*," 187.
25. Arendt, "Thinking and Moral Considerations,"160.
26. L. A. Beaurline cites Digby Mysteries (1485): "with thine inward eye / Seest the deepest place of man's conscience." *King John*, New Cambridge Shakespeare, 174.
27. Arendt, "Thinking and Moral Considerations," 177.
28. Arendt, "Some Questions of Moral Philosophy," 97.

12
Arming Cordelia: Character and Performance

Sarah Werner

In the Folio text of *King Lear,* Cordelia's reemergence onto the stage—and into the action of the play—occurs at the head of the French army: "Enter with drum and colours, Cordelia, Gentleman, and Soldiers" (4.3.0).[1] According to Alan Dessen and Leslie Thomson's *A Dictionary of Stage Directions in English Drama, 1580–1642,* the items "drum and colours" usually indicate "readiness for battle and are part of a show of power."[2] As Cordelia's exchange with the Messenger in this scene suggests, such a military context is fitting: the Messenger arrives with news that "The British powers are marching hitherward" (4.3.21), to which Cordelia replies, "Tis known before. Our preparation stands / In expectation of them" (4.3.22–23), suggesting that the soldiers she has led on stage are an indication of her readiness to battle her sisters' armies. Given this preparation for battle, this show of power, and Cordelia's position at the head of her army, it seems not unlikely that Cordelia herself appears in armor.

I use this odd locution—"not unlikely" rather than "likely"—because it is not a possibility that seems to occur to editors or scholars. It is true that the text does not contain language that refers directly to her costuming—there are no descriptions of her as "a woman clad in armor" (as Talbot describes Joan [*Henry VI, Part I,* 1.7.3]), nor does she state, "I am ready to put armor on" (as Margaret declares [*Henry VI, Part III,* 3.3.230]).[3] But many early modern stage directions (whether internal or explicit) are permissive, allowing the staging to match a company's resources, and it seems clear that the King's Men had access to the armor needed for costuming Cordelia: not only are there armed figures in other plays in their repertoire, in this play, Edgar must appear disguised in armor as part of his challenge to his brother. As equally important as these logistics of "drum and colours" is a rethinking of how Cordelia is characterized and its impact on the play's gender dynamics. Once we look closely, there are signs of a forceful Cordelia from the start, suggesting that her appearance in armor is not anomalous, but part of an ongoing investigation into what constitutes appropriately feminine behavior. As we shall see, not only does the script allow for Cordelia to wear armor, it deliberately invites us to think of her as an armed general.

If part of my analysis lies in rethinking Cordelia, another part calls for exploring not only how early modern stage effects contributed to the shape of a character but whether, and how, such stage effects can be incorporated into our study of early modern drama. Too often, a sensitivity to theatrical effect gets lost in literary criticism. It might not be surprising to learn that although editors and scholars have not noted that Cordelia might wear armor, theater directors and costume designers have certainly been aware of this possibility. John Gielgud's 1950 production with Peggy Ashcroft as Cordelia had her costumed in a dress with an armored breastplate; Richard Eyre's 1997 production for the National Theater (later televised) also dressed Cordelia in armor. It is clear that from a theatrical perspective, the potential of arming Cordelia is readily available. But it is also clear that such moments do not help us better understand Shakespeare's play. Reviewers of Eyre's production likened Cordelia's appearance leading her army to Joan of Arc's; while that resonance might play out positively today, a link between Cordelia and Joan carries different associations in the early modern period. And twentieth-century performances can hardly stand in as proof for seventeenth-century ones. That tension between thinking theatrically and yet restraining from tying current performance practices to early modern practices is the central tension in trying to think about how early modern theater might have shaped Shakespeare's characters. As anyone immersed in theater history knows, concrete evidence of theatrical practice is hard to come by, and even harder for scholars to agree upon. While an earlier generation of performance scholars argued that we could learn about Shakespeare's meaning by studying the plays in performance today, most would agree now that such a line of argument is not tenable. The languages of performance are constantly changing, and what armor signifies today is not what it would have signified to Shakespeare's audiences. Through my exploration of what it might mean for Cordelia to have been dressed in armor on the early modern stage, I hope to model a way of thinking about the relationship between early modern theater and character that is able to draw on theatrical performance without ahistoricizing either performance or character.

Perhaps one thing that has blinded scholars to the possibility of Cordelia as an armored military leader is the long absence of women from military history. As Barton C. Hacker argued in an article that began to rewrite that history, "[W]omen were a normal part of European armies at least from the fourteenth century until well into the nineteenth century." Women were a significant part of the army followers that provided vital support to fighting soldiers in ways akin to the roles they played in civilian life: "finding, cooking, and serving food; making, washing, and mending clothes; tending the sick, the infirm, and the wounded; sporting with men, helping other women when they could, bearing and raising children."[4] Although Hacker assumes that their work "rarely included combat," he also notes that "In the often fluid and ill-defined contexts of warfare before the mid-seventeenth century, women must have fought, or at least helped in the fighting, as a matter of course in the peril of the moment.'[5] But as military institutions began to change—as new weapons came into use and armies began to take direct control of more support functions—women played less and less of a role in military life. The result was not only a departure from the battlefield, but from the history books: "Women's absence from late nineteenth-century armies debarred them from military history in its formative stages, and ever since has obscured the meaning of their presence in other armies at other times."[6]

Hacker's research opens up new ways of thinking about how warfare is depicted in the period and how its depiction interacts with gender ideology. Jean Howard and Phyllis Rackin, for instance, use Hacker to estrange the insistent maleness of the military action in *Henry V*.[7] In the first tetralogy, they argue, women are present as soldiers in the figures of Joan and Margaret; Elinor in *King John* is another formidable woman warrior. But there is only a brief mention of nameless women fighting against the king in *Richard II*, and the Welsh women in *Henry IV, Part I* are stripped not only of their names but of their deeds, the brutality of which the play refuses to identify. By the time we get to *Henry V*, not only are there not any female soldiers, Henry's military success is defined in terms of his sexual conquest over women. The theatrical implications of the playscripts' erasure of women from the battlefield serve to centralize all power into male hands—not only are there fewer women onstage as the plays progress, but those women still present have less and less political power and theatrical appeal.[8] Henry not only eliminates the specter of female power as a challenge to his kingship, he uses the power of performance to consolidate his control over his countrymen and his throne.[9]

If the historical presence of women on the battlefield is removed from the later history plays, the potential danger of those warrior women is central to the early plays and can perhaps account for some of the success of the *Henry VI* plays. As many scholars have noted, women warriors loomed large in the early modern imagination. One need only think of Edmund Spenser's *The Faerie Queene*, and the depictions not only of Britomart but of Radigund, to get some sense of their powerful presence in romances, allegories, and lists of worthies.[10] On stage, the figure of the woman warrior has been most visible through the character of Joan in *Henry VI, Part I*. Gabriele Bernhard Jackson speculates that Shakespeare's Joan was the first presentation of an armed woman on stage, and suggests that her appearance would have been "sensational."[11] But why, precisely, would the spectacle of a female character in armor be sensational? Jackson is not entirely clear on this point, stating only that it had not been done before and that Elizabethans of the period were fascinated by Amazons. One possibility suggested by the play is the *frisson* of imagining a woman usurping such a powerful male position—Joan is not merely a foot soldier, but the leader of her army. Certainly for both Joan and Margaret, their wearing of armor is linked to their sexual availability and to their troubling dominance over the men closest to them. Even before the final act, when Joan is revealed to be a witch and claims to be pregnant with a child fathered by a series of different men, the sexual puns that circulate around her mark her armored body as titillating. As for Margaret, York's description of her as an "Amazonian trull" (*Henry VI, Part III*, 1.4.115) succinctly yokes the two tropes together.

It is easy to pass over the elision that Jackson and the characters in the *Henry VI* plays make in moving from "woman in armor" to "Amazon"—it was a jump made frequently in the period, and both then and today Amazons are generally the first example that comes to mind when discussing women who were warriors. But when we are turning our attention to Cordelia and to female characters dressed in armor on stage, we ought to keep those terms apart, at least initially. For one thing, images of Amazons often depict them not in armor but bare-breasted, dressed in buskins, and carrying weapons—arrows, but also swords and axes. More significant than this costume difference is that Amazons were imagined to exist literally at the margins of society, their lands continually being pushed farther and farther outward as Europe moved into territories farther and farther off. As Kathryn Schwartz argues, Amazons were seen as just outside of society, and although they might be brought back in to be domesticated, they were fundamentally different.[12] In this way, Joan and Margaret are indeed Amazons—they are French, and thus outside of and needing to be interpellated into the English historical project.

But there are also domestic warrior women, some of whom were at the heart of England's history. Foremost among those is Boadicea (or Voadicia or Bonduca, to identify two of her many other names), a British queen who led a revolt against the Romans in the first century and who almost succeeded in sending them packing. Boadicea was not only a queen, she was also the military leader of her army (which consisted of both men and women). But as Jodi Mikalachki argues, early modern historiographers saw her not as a heroic British queen defending her people from foreign invasion, but as a savage and insubordinate woman resisting civilization. The need to recover a native antiquity meant, for these historians, the disavowal of non-Roman traits, including the achievements of unruly women; indeed, as Mikalachki demonstrates, they worked to recast "the national problem of ancient savagery as an issue of female insubordination."[13] And Boadicea's achievement, in the eyes of Holinshed, was particularly unruly for the ways she made horrific the norms of motherhood and femininity. The only specific account Holinshed provides of the behavior of her army on the battlefield is the following:

> They spared neither age nor sex: women of great nobilitie and woorthie fame they tooke and hanged up naked, and cutting off their paps, sowed them to their mouthes, that they might seeme as if they sucked and fed on them, and some of their bodies they stretched out in length, and thrust them on sharpe stakes.[14]

In the focus on women's breasts, there seems to be a similarity here between Amazonian behavior and that of Boadicea's warriors. But there is also a crucial difference: Amazons cut off their own breasts in order to become better warriors; Boadicea cuts off the breasts of her victims in order to desecrate their femininity. What makes Boadicea terrifying is not that she is an Amazon, but that she is *not* an Amazon. The targets of her anger are not only men, but women, and she is not beyond the borders of England, but in its heart: she is a domestic inversion of civilization and motherhood.

As an early British queen, Cordelia bears a closer resemblance to Boadicea than to any Amazon. For Holinshed, however, the rule of Cordeilla (as he names her) did not provoke anxiety. Rather, he saw her as almost completely heroic, an exception to the barbarity that marked early Britain. In Holinshed's history of Cordeilla, she is the first reigning queen of Britain, one who in her five-year "g[y]narchie" ruled "right worthily" until her capture by her rebellious nephews and her decision, as "a woman of manly courage," to kill herself.[15] There is only one sentence-long paragraph devoted to her reign, but as Mikalachki discusses,

Holinshed "single[s] out [Leir [sic] and Cordeilla] as examples of royal integrity and national prosperity" who promise a "recuperation of the civility of the Trojan founding."[16]

But if that's Holinshed's "Cordeilla", Shakespeare's is different: she dies before her father, and instead of heralding a recuperation of civility as Britain's first queen, she leaves the nation in a state of atavistic disarray. Her sisters are, of course, the play's primary examples of barbaric (would-be) queens. Gonerill and Regan are sexually incontinent, cruel, and martial. On the one hand, they are an illustration of everything that Cordelia is not: she wants to restore Lear's rule, they want to destroy Lear's rule; she is chosen by her husband out of his love for her, they seem neither to have love for nor to be loved by their husbands; she, in the usual reading of the play, is the good daughter, they the bad. But Cordelia is not always so clearly opposed to Gonerill and Regan, as is made clear by the quick succession of scenes in the middle of the fourth act that bracket Cordelia's return to the play at the head of her army.

The scene before Cordelia's return focuses on Gonerill's unfeminine behavior: Gonerill enters with Edmond, to whom she complains that she must "change names at home and give the distaff / Into my husband's hands" (4.2.18–19), and Gonerill wishes to herself that she might give Edmond "a woman's services" (28). Her desire for Edmond is followed by an argument with her husband, in which she calls Albany a "milk-livered man" (4.2.33) and he retorts that "Proper deformity shows not in the fiend / So horrid as in woman" (4.2.36–37)—one of many links made in the play between evil and women.[17] The scene following Cordelia's "drum and colours" entrance in 4.3 focuses on her other sister, devoting equal energy to Regan's desire for Edmond and to her wish for Gloucester's murder. Regan's solution to both of these problems—securing Edmond for herself and securing Britain by removing the sympathy-inducing obstacle of the blinded old man—is to win Oswald over to her side. "I'll love thee much" (4.4.23), she tells him in an effort to read the letter he is carrying from his mistress to Edmond, a phrasing that in the context of her discussion of wished-for union with Edmond is hard not to hear sexually.

Bracketed by these explicitly unchaste, unkind sisters is Cordelia's appearance at the head of her army. Cordelia, as opposed to her sisters, says all the right things:

> O dear father
> It is thy business that I go about:
> Therefore great France
> My mourning and importuned tears hath pitied.

> No blown ambition doth our arms incite,
> But love, dear love, and our aged father's right.
>
> (4.3.23–28)

There is no hint of ambition, of inconstancy, of cruelty. Instead, we hear her forswear ambition, declare her daughterly love, and uphold her father's legitimacy, all of which she can do because of her womanly tears. But this is what she says at the end of the scene, what she says once she has displayed her military might. And in many other ways, this scene suggests that Cordelia is as unruly as, or even more unruly than, her sisters. First, Cordelia appears as the leader of the army. There is no other named military leader, Cordelia herself identifies the army as hers ("our preparation" [4.3.22]), and the stage direction for "drum and colours" (4.3.0) emphasizes the martial nature both of the scene and of Cordelia's role in the scene.[18] It is equally shocking that she, unlike her sisters, has no man to whom to answer. Although married to France, she functions as essentially unmarried; France makes no appearance in the play after the first scene, and no explanation is provided for his absence. And while both of her sisters long to exchange their husbands for a new lover, Cordelia appears to be linked in this scene with no man: the Gentleman accompanying her is clearly subservient, and the opening description of Lear's madness makes clear his inability to rule her. At least as troubling as her martial independence is the fact that the army Cordelia leads is clearly identified as French, both in its opposition to the "British powers" (4.3.21) and in its alignment in Cordelia's final speech of the scene with "great France" (4.3.35), and in the presence of the French colors brought onstage with her army.[19]

Rather than being in contrast to the bracketing barbaric sisters, Cordelia's appearance suggests her similarity to them: the opposites of Cordelia and her elder sisters threaten to collapse into each other. Cordelia's speech might mark her off as good, as dutiful, but her presence in armor calls up images of barbaric women warriors and invading Amazonian trulls—images of violence and truant sexuality that are evoked and reinforced by her sisters. In the Folio, we move straight from Gonerill's audacity to Cordelia's to Regan's.

If the bracketing of Cordelia suggests troubling similarities between her and her sisters, the subsequent proliferation of martial entrances makes things worse. It is not *only* Cordelia who appears with "drum and colours" in the play. Although she gets the first such entrance, in Act Five we see Edmond and Regan enter with drum and colors (5.1.0), followed fifteen lines later by Albany and Gonerill's entrance with drum and colors (5.1.14). This face-off between the elder sisters' armies could function as a contrast to Cordelia's earlier entrance with her army (the bad armed sisters versus the good armed sister), but a comparison between the entrances highlights what is particularly startling about Cordelia's: unlike her sisters, who appear in the company of their male companions, Cordelia had no man leading her army.[20]

This is not the first appearance of an unruly Cordelia in *King Lear*. There is, of course, the disobedience that she shows in refusing to participate in her father's scripted love test in the opening scene of the play. There are also other signs of her unruliness, albeit signs that, like her armor, are often obscured by modern senses of how early modern women behaved. When Kent argues against Lear's disowning Cordelia, Lear's fury toward him provokes others on stage to step in and calm him with the words, "Dear sir, forbear" (1.1.156). The Folio speech prefixes for this line—"*Alb.* and *Cor.*"—are emended by most editors to specify Albany and Cornwall. But Beth Goldring argues that it is Cordelia who speaks the line with Albany. Her analysis of the Folio text demonstrates that the speech prefix for Cordelia is, with only one exception, "*Cor.;*" the speech prefix for Cornwall, on the other hand, is overwhelmingly "*Corn.*"[21] But the history of this speech prefix after Goldring's 1983 article shows how firmly editors' notions of gender-appropriate behavior shape their editorial decisions. Only Gary Taylor's edition for the 1986 Oxford Complete Works accepts Goldring and identifies Cordelia as the speaker with Albany of "Dear sir, forbear." Halio's 1992 New Cambridge Shakespeare text makes Cornwall the speaker; although he notes that "F's *Cor.* can indicate either Cordelia or Cornwall," he provides no further explanation for why he prefers Cornwall.[22] René Weis's 1993 parallel-text edition and Stephen Orgel's 2000 Pelican parallel-text edition both assign the line to Cornwall with limited commentary on their choice.[23] R. A. Foakes's 1997 Arden third edition of the play, a conflated text marked to show Q- and F-only variants, makes Cornwall the speaker of the line with the explanation that "the action [of preventing Lear from drawing his sword] is more appropriate to men."[24]

Fewer than twenty lines later, France and Burgundy arrive on stage, and there is again another potentially unruly moment. In the Folio, their arrival is announced by "*Cor.:*" "Here's France and Burgundy, my noble lord" (1.1.182) Although Goldring does not focus on this line, her argument holds the same: *Cor.* almost always refers to Cordelia, rather than to any other character on stage. Taylor's edition identifies Cordelia as the speaker here, as does Halio's, with the comment, "Cordelia seems a more appropriate speaker [than Cornwall], since Burgundy and France

240 *Arming Cordelia: Character and Performance*

are her suitors;"[25] Orgel also chooses Cordelia here. But Foakes believes that Cornwall must be the speaker because, although making Cordelia the speaker "fits modern ideas" it is more logically Cornwall "since Lear told Cordelia to avoid his sight at 125, and it would be inappropriate for her to put herself forward here."[26]

Both of these moments are early indications of Cordelia's unruliness—her moving out of an appropriately silent, obedient, and feminine subject position. The comments made by editors who choose Cornwall as the speaker over Cordelia are revealing in the degree to which the play has been shaped by the desire for Cordelia to be *appropriate*. But what it means to be appropriate is rarely examined. What ought Cordelia be appropriate to? Are editors looking for behavior appropriate to their notions of femininity? To their sense of early modern femininity? To the play's standards of behavior? If we use different notions of what might be appropriate, it is easy to make the argument that a Cordelia who chastises her father for not adhering to a patrilineal traffic in women—"Why have my sisters husbands, if they say / They love you all?" (1.1.94–95)—would also be a Cordelia who restrains her father from attacking Kent and who would refuse to obey his dictate to leave his sight. In this reading, the Cordelia who refuses to play her father's script is consistent with her later actions refusing to play the part of a quiet woman.

I do not want to suggest that Cordelia is as "bad" as her sisters. It is important to recognize that even as Cordelia is being her most unruly, she is also arguing for a return to patriarchal values. She resists her father's totalizing love in order to insist on the importance of her being handed over from her father's household to her husband's. She leads an army into England in order to restore her father to his rightful place on the throne. On the one hand, Cordelia's actions and armor mark her as a disturbance and a threat that is carried out in her sisters' behavior. On the other hand, however, are her words; as Maureen Quilligan phrases it, "she mouths a thoroughly conservative statement of what women should do in her society."[27]

Quilligan's reading of Cordelia illustrates the complications of identifying the character as either "good" or "bad." She looks at Cordelia through the lens of the intersection of incest and agency in early modern culture. As she argues, early modern society depended on women acquiescing to a patrilineal traffic in women; chaste, silent, and obedient daughters needed to be married out of their father's family in order to forge alliances between men. Incest disrupted these alliances by preventing the exogamous marriages that maintained them. A female agency that spoke against this docile traffic in marriageable women also disrupted these alliances, and in so doing, that agency was aligned with the incestuous desire that broke those bonds as well. As Quilligan argues, female agency in the early modern period is repeatedly linked to incest, from Queen Elizabeth herself through fictional narratives such as that of Cordelia and Lear. In defying her father's incestuous desire to have her all to himself, Cordelia is not claiming her own independence, but her adherence to her dutiful transfer from father to husband; in Quilligan's terms, she is speaking in order to insist on her silence. It is her sisters who use the language of incestuous love to create a space for their own agency at the start of the play.

This balance between incestuous agency and chaste obedience becomes more troubling the closer we get to the end of the play. Cordelia's agency as the unhusbanded military leader leads directly to her incestuous reunion with her father, in which they make up a world unto themselves that mirrors the kind nursery Lear had looked for at the beginning of the play. It is here, in the last acts of the play, that Quilligan's analysis of incest and agency helps us to understand the complicated nature of Cordelia's character in this play. Cordelia's return is neither a sign of her dangerous independence nor her dutiful rescue of her father. It is rather the uneasy moment when the two paradigms meet. Quilligan sees here Cordelia's "own desiring agency" and "her own distinctly gendered activity, a woman rescuing her father."[28] Both of these are linked to the incestuous reunion that she identifies as at the heart of Cordelia's mission: "Incest opens the space for female agency because the traffic is halted; Cordelia's presence on stage—finally answering her father's transgressive desire for her—after she has been banished in silence, reveals the paradigm at work."[29] But it is precisely that incestuous desire that leads to Cordelia's death. For, unlike the modern period, where victims of incest are usually seen as blameless, the early modern period blamed both father and daughter for the sin, and it is for that transgression that Cordelia is punished, and for that sin that she dies.[30] In other words, Quilligan highlights exactly what has so often been troubling about this play: Cordelia's death feels like a punishment that we don't understand, but that is exactly deserved in early modern terms.

Quilligan locates the unease at the end of the play in modern readers and audiences, who cannot see incest in the terms that justify Cordelia's death, but it is also visible in early modern terms through the paradoxical figure of a woman in armor. As I have discussed above, other scholars have seen in the woman warriors of Shakespeare's first teratology the fear and fascination behind the depiction of those characters. But there are other, more complicated depictions of armed women on stage if we allow ourselves to see them, depictions that link the woman in armor with a multivalent feminine subjectivity. There is even complexity in the case of Margaret, who is typically invoked as I did earlier in this paper, as a paradigm of the unnatural woman whose bloodthirstiness is linked to her sexual voracity and her usurpation of male political prerogative. But Margaret's greatest bloodiness happens before she puts on armor. Once she declares herself ready to put aside her "mourning weeds" in favor of armor (*Henry VI, Part III*, 3.3.239), she operates primarily as a wife and mother protecting the claims of her husband and son to the English throne. Her first appearance in armor comes late in the play, when she rallies her soldiers at Tewkesbury to resist despair over their recent losses and to let her and her son pilot their course (5.4.1–38). Her son, Oxford, and Somerset both attest to the courage they draw from her example, leading to Margaret's final, weepy speech:

> Lords, knights, and gentlemen—what I should say
> My tears gainsay; for every word I speak
> Ye see I drink the water of my eye.
> Therefore, no more but this: Henry your sovereign
> Is prisoner to the foe, his state usurped,
> His realm a slaughter-house, his subjects slain,
> His statutes cancelled, and his treasure spent—
> And yonder is the wolf that makes this spoil.
> You fight in justice; then in God's name, lords,
> Be valiant, and give signal to the fight.
>
> (5.4.73–82)

Margaret does not seem less feminine for her armor, but more so in her tearful exhortation for justice for her husband. Randall Martin, editor of the Oxford edition of the play, links Margaret's rhetorical strategy to Queen Elizabeth's, "deliberately drawing attention to her 'natural' female weakness or subservience in order to contrast her own exceptional courage and abilities."[31] Randall even suggests that Margaret's call for putting on armor "may have reminded playgoers" of Elizabeth at Tilbury, building on Leah Marcus's reading of Elizabeth's composite body and the unease that circulated around her.[32]

If there is a contrast here between Margaret's armored body and her tearful adherence to her husband, that contrast becomes even stronger in the next scene, when Margaret is immediately led back onstage as a prisoner and then witness to her son's death. In one of the play's rawest and most uncomfortable moments, Margaret laments her son's death, perhaps, as suggested by Arden editors John Cox and Eric Rasmussen, even cradling his body as she struggles to put a name to her grief:

> O Ned, sweet Ned—speak to thy mother, boy.
> Canst thou not speak? O traitors, murderers!
> ....
> What's worse than murderer that I may name it?
> No, no, my heart will burst an if I speak;
> And I will speak that so my heart may burst.
> (5.5.50–51, 57–59)

As Cox and Rasmussen comment, "She is more pitiable in this and the following lines than at any earlier point in the *Henry VI* plays." They link this moment on stage to the *pietà*, and argue that "No one can think of Margaret merely as a domineering female while she laments for her young son."[33] But that tension between Margaret's grief and her earlier violence is exactly what is in play here. At the end of her lament, she lashes out at Edward, Gloucester, and Clarence:

> You have no children, butchers; if you had,
> The thought of them would have stirred up remorse.
> But if you ever chance to have a child,
> Look in his youth to have him so cut off
> As, deathsmen, you have rid this sweet young Prince!
> (5.5.63–66)

It would seem impossible that her audience—onstage and off—would not at this moment remember her taunting York at the beginning of the play with the death of his son, the brother of the men now onstage. The only comment Michael Hattaway's New Cambridge Shakespeare edition provides on the speech is to quote Samuel Johnson: "The condition of this warlike queen would move compassion could it be forgotten that she gave York, to wipe his eyes in his captivity, a handkerchief stained with his young child's blood."[34] If the first part of Margaret's lament speaks volumes about a mother's grief for her murdered son, the second clearly and deliberately recalls her actions as a heartless and bloodthirsty queen.

How does Margaret's armor fit into this tableau? Does it undercut our sympathy toward her, pointing to her violent nature even before her words do? There is certainly a tension between her costume and her speech, but to see her armor as signaling only her violence ignores her appearance in the previous scene and the connection made there between her courageous armored body and her weak and tearful interior. Scholars have too often seen Margaret solely through the York family's eyes as a bloody Amazon who has disastrously "stolen the breech" from her husband (5.5.24). But there is more to her character than that, and her grief and defeat at the end of the play are crucial to that reading. Jean Howard and Phyllis Rackin identify the central problem of the *Henry VI* plays as the paradoxical dependency of patriarchy upon women's obedience, and find that "it is only in *Part III* that the hollowness at the center of the patriarchal edifice is fully exposed" by revealing Henry's inability to act as patriarch and Margaret's assumption of that role both as military leader and as protector of her son's right to the throne.[35] For Howard and Rackin, "in the *Henry VI* plays, there is always the anxiety that women, whether lovingly submissive or aggressively independent, will undo the patriarchal edifice and, with it, an always endangered masculinity." Central to depicting that anxiety is Margaret and "the transformation [in *Richard III*] of her powerful sexuality and her Amazonian strength into the anger of an embittered, desexualized crone."[36] In that arc of transformation, Margaret's donning of armor is the pivotal moment when her character is neither dangerous nor powerless, but both.

If we are still tempted to think of women wearing armor only as dangerous or seditious, we would do well to think also of Philippa in *Edward III*. When news is brought to Edward, in France, of Scotland's attack, their subsequent defeat and David's capture is attributed to "the fruitful service of your peers / And painful travail of the queen herself, / That, big with child, was every day in arms" (4.2.43–45).[37] With the single word "travail" linking together military effort, the labor of childbirth, and the difficulty of crossing the Channel, Philippa is depicted as a powerful defender of England whose laboring body protects her country through warfare and reproduction.[38] The next few lines, however, reveal that David's captor, Copland, refuses to surrender his prisoner to Philippa, insisting that he will give him up only to the king himself. Copland's refusal serves to mitigate any potential danger that Philippa might undermine Edward: she is no threat to Edward's throne, and when Edward declares that the matter of Copland be decided by summoning him, he is told that Philippa is already on her way to him.

When Philippa does arrive, in the last act of the play, it is as if she has just come from the battlefield, and she enters the stage with Edward already in the middle of a conversation about Copland. Given the earlier, vivid description of the pregnant queen as a warrior, Philippa is likely to evoke that image on stage here and is perhaps even still armed as she was for her battle. But, as it was earlier, any threatening associations with an armed woman are quickly curtailed. Before she and Edward can settle the matter of Copland's prisoner, they are presented with the Calais citizens who wish to surrender themselves in order to save the rest of Calais. Edward, after some squabbling about their rank, agrees that he will honor his promise to spare Calais in return for their deaths. But Philippa pleads with Edward to show mercy, arguing against ruling through violence, "For what the sword cuts down or fire hath spoiled / Is held in reputation none of ours" (5.1.45–46). Shortly after Copland has surrendered his prisoner, Edward and Philippa are told of the capture of their son. Philippa weeps at the news, a reaction that contrasts sharply with her husband's urging to replace tears with bloody revenge (5.1.157–75); moments later, Prince Edward enters with the captured French king and prince and is reunited with his parents, and Philippa's last lines in the play are her motherly words to him, along with her kiss: "Be this a token to express my joy, / For inward passions will not let me speak" (5.1.190–91).

Philippa carries with her almost none of the threatening aspects that Margaret does in the *Henry VI* plays; they do, however, share the trait of motherly devotion to their sons. Although Philippa is not necessarily dressed in armor in this scene, nor does Margaret have to be wearing armor in her last appearances in *Henry VI, Part III*, both women do take on the role of military leader and are described as such by their countrymen. I do not want to use the example of Philippa to argue that Margaret is not violent or that her military prowess and armored body is not threatening. But the depiction of Philippa in *Edward III* allows us to see that disorderly violence is not the sole characteristic of armed women, and encourages us to recognize the liminal position of Margaret at the end of the *Henry VI* plays: both violent and maternal, both submissive to and disruptive of patriarchal order, Margaret renders uneasy the audience's complicity in the violence of the plays and her armor is the focal point for that unsettling. In ways similar to the depiction of Margaret in *Henry VI, Part III*, the effect of seeing Cordelia dressed in armor and at the head of the French army in the Folio text of *King Lear* is to mark the disruption of patriarchal order and the troubling restoration of that order through a woman acting as the patriarch of her family.

Throughout this paper, I have been assuming—albeit cautiously—that the characters I discuss appear on stage in armor. I need to acknowledge that there is no direct evidence that this was so. There are no stage directions referring to their armor; except for the description of Joan as "clad in armour" (*Henry VI, Part I*, 1.7.3), which is immediately followed by her entrance onstage, the references to the other characters as armored are indirect. Margaret's assertion that she is "ready to put armour on" (*Henry VI, Part III*, 3.3.230) could be understood as metaphorical rather than a reference to an actual costume change; the description of Philippa as "every day in arms" (*Edward III*, 4.2.45) requires imagining her in armor for her offstage battle, but does not require her to be so dressed on stage; and Cordelia's entrance "with drum and colours" (*Lear*, 4.3.0) does not, strictly speaking, insist that she is wearing armor. But as any theater historian knows, nearly all evidence of what happened on the early modern stage is sketchy and open to interpretation. There is plenty of evidence that early modern theatrical companies had access to armor given the references to specific items of armor in plays of the period.

One of the primary reasons that we fail to recognize the presence of female characters on stage dressed in armor is our own assumptions about early modern gender. As Phyllis Rackin asserts, scholars have clung to the understanding of early modern women as oppressed, silent subjects, even as material histories repeatedly give evidence of women in a wide variety of active, empowered roles.[39] We do not see Cordelia in armor because such a role falls outside how we imagine early modern women. In order to see Cordelia—and Margaret, and the other armed female characters now hidden in early modern playtexts—we need to look for anomalies and to rethink our sense of what is appropriate.

Another reason we fail to take account of this aspect of Cordelia's role is our tendency to value words over other theatrical languages. It's easy to understand why: the only concrete traces we have left of early modern performances are the words spoken by the characters. Even the stage directions found in early modern printings are scarce at best, and are often incomplete or incorrect. If we cannot know concretely about something that might have happened on stage, it could be easiest to overlook its possibility. But just because we are in the habit of experiencing the plays through reading spoken words, we must not assume that early modern audiences would have responded in the same way. On the page, stage directions speak powerfully, but the other actions and visual languages of the theater are harder for us to access. We trust what we see, and what we see are the words written on the page.

But while what we see are words, words are what early modern theatergoers hear. What they see on stage might be just as powerful, or sometimes even more powerful, in shaping their responses to the characters and actions. A character dressed in armor can be saying volumes, even if she is not speaking at all.

Notes

Earlier versions of this paper were presented at Contestation and Renewal in Early modern Studies: A Conference in Honor of Phyllis Rackin and at the third Blackfriars Conference. My thanks go to those audiences for their comments and suggestions. But my greatest thanks are to Phyllis Rackin, whose scholarship lies at the heart of this project and whose wisdom continues to inspire.

1. This entrance is markedly different than in the Quarto text, in which she enters with "Doctor and others" (Sc. 18) and in which Monsieur La Far has earlier been named the head of the French army after the King of France's return home (Sc. 17.1-9). Throughout this paper, I am concerned primarily with the Folio text, although I will be referring to the Quarto at times in order to highlight some of the choices made in the Folio version. Unless otherwise noted, all quotations from *King Lear* are from *The Tragedy of King Lear*, ed. Jay L. Halio (Cambridge: Cambridge University Press, 1992). Quotations from the Quarto are taken from *The First Quarto of King Lear*, ed. Jay L. Halio (Cambridge: Cambridge University Press, 1994). Unless noted quotations from other Shakespeare plays are taken from *The Norton Shakespeare*, ed. Stephen Greenblatt et al. (New York: Norton, 1997).
2. Allan Dessen and Leslie Thomson, *A Dictionary of Stage Directions in English Drama, 1580–1642* (Cambridge: Cambridge University Press, 1999), "colors," 53.
3. *3 Henry 6*, ed. Martin Randall (Oxford: Oxford University Press, 2001).
4. Barton C. Hacker, "Women and Military Institutions in Early modern Europe: A Reconaissance," *Signs* 6 (1981): 643, 653.
5. Hacker, "Women and Military Institutions," 644, 658.
6. Hacker, "Women and Military Institutions," 645.
7. See Jean Howard and Phyllis Rackin, *Engendering a Nation: A Feminist Account of Shakespeare's English Histories* (London: Routledge, 1997), 201–6.
8. See Phyllis Rackin, *Stages of History: Shakespeare's English Cronicles* (Ithaca: Cornell University Press, 1990) for her argument that the early history plays' demonization of theatrical power shifts in the later plays to a harnessing of theatricality to monarchical power.
9. Although Henry is adept at playing different roles within the playscript, the character does not successfully manage to control the early modern audience watching him in the theater. I have argued elsewhere that the presence of the boy actor consistently undermines Henry's position by calling attention to the actor's male body and thus thwarting Henry's attempt to solidify his claim to the English throne by fathering an heir with Katherine. For a discussion of this argument see Sarah Werner, "Firk and Foot: The Boy Actor in *Henry V*," *Shakespeare Bulletin* 21, no. 4 (Winter 2003): 19–27.

10. See Simon Shepherd, *Amazons and Warrior Women: Varieties of Feminism in Seventeenth Century Drama* (Sussex: Harvester Press, 1981) and Leah Marcus, *Puzzling Shakespeare: Local Readings and Its Discontents* (Berkeley: University of California Press, 1988) for two different approaches to considering the early modern fascination with women warriors.
11. Gabriele Bernhard Jackson, "Topical Ideology: Witches, Amazons, and Shakespeare's Joan of Arc," in *Shakespeare and Gender: A History*, eds Deborah E. Barker and Ivo Kamps (London: Verso, 1995), 152. Jackson's speculation depends, of course, on whether one assumes that *1 Henry VI* was written before *2* and *3 Henry VI*. The chronology by Stanley Wells and Gary Taylor, eds, *William Shakespeare: The Complete Works* (Oxford: Clarendon Press, 1986) places it after, presumably making Margaret the first armed woman on stage.
12. Kathryn Schwartz, *Tough Love: Amazon Encounters in the English Renaissance* (Durham: Duke University Press, 2000).
13. Jodi Mikalachki, *The Legacy of Boadicea: Gender and Nation in Early modern England* (London: Routledge, 1998), 13.
14. Raphael Holinshed, "The Historie of England," vol. 1, *Chronicles of England, Scotlande, and Ireland* (London: 1587), 44. STC 13569.
15. Holinshed, "The Historie of England," 13.
16. Mikalachki, *The Legacy of Boadicea*, 76.
17. This argument is significantly shorter than in the Quarto, in which Albany comes across as a stronger character, scolding his wife's treatment of her father, and Gonerill is generally more irrationally violent. Halio characterizes Gonerill as "softer" in the Folio text (73) and notes that Albany seems "less sure of himself" (74); for more on the changes to Albany's character, see Michael Warren, "Quarto and Folio *King Lear* and The Interpretation of Albany and Edgar," in *Shakespeare: Pattern of Excelling Nature*, ed. David Bevington and Jay L. Halio (Delaware: University of Delaware Press, 1978), 95–107.
18. In the Quarto "Monsieur La Far" has earlier been identified as the head of the French army in the King's absence during a conversation between Kent and the Gentleman (Sc. 17.1–9). This information is followed by Kent's description of Cordelia's grief upon learning about the mistreatment of Lear, a grief that moves her "Not to a rage" (17.17) but to such a display of patience and sorrow that "Sorrow would be a rarity most beloved / If all could so become it" (17.23–24). This Quarto-only scene follows the vicious fight between Goneril and Albany, and sets Cordelia up as an emblem of feminine virtue. That emblematic reading is furthered with Cordelia's entrance at the top of Scene 18: "Enter [Queen] Cordelia, Doctor, and others" positions Cordelia as helpmeet and caretaker.
19. The specter of a French army invading England has often troubled critics; see Richard Knowles, "Cordelia's Return," *Shakespeare Quarterly* 50 (1999): 33–50 for a history of how critics have tried to make sense of this problem and for his own argument that Shakespeare has deliberately left vague the reason for Cordelia's invasion. Other versions of the Lear story emphasize that Lear was the head of the army or that both Cordelia and her husband accompanied Lear and the army. In Holinshed, Cordeilla accompanies Lear in order to claim the land that Lear has promised to give her on his

death; the land clearly remains British rather than being incorporated into France. References to France and to the French army occur more frequently in the Quarto text than in the Folio. But while spoken references to France's invasion are clearly purposely cut from the Folio, Ernst Honigmann notes that the insertion of numerous entrances with "drum and colours" highlights visual indications of nationality. See Halio, *The Tragedy of King Lear*, 78.
20. Cordelia is accompanied by Lear in the next "drum and colours" entrance, when they pass over the stage in 5.2, but that happens only after this first link of Cordelia's martial prowess with her sisters'. It is unclear how powerful a leader Lear is here, although Halio notes the difference between the Folio entrance and the Quarto one, which calls for "the powers of France" and "Cordelia with her father in her hand;" he suggests that the Folio emphasizes Lear's "strength and defiance" (243).
21. Beth Goldring, "Cor.'s rescure of Kent" in *The Division of the Kingdoms: Shakespeare's Two Versions of King Lear*, ed. Gary Taylor and Michael Warren (Oxford: Clarendon Press, 1983), 143–51.
22. Halio, *The Tragedy of King Lear*, 104.
23. *King Lear: The 1608 Quarto and 1623 Folio Texts*, ed. Stephen Orgel (New York: Pelican, 2000); *King Lear: A Parallel Text Edition*, ed. Rene Weis (London: Longman, 1993).
24. *King Lear*. The Arden Shakespeare, Third Series, ed. R.A. Foakes (London: Routledge, 1997), 169.
25. Halio, *The Tragedy of King Lear*, 106.
26. Foakes, *King Lear*, 171. Although Foakes chooses in favor of a more appropriately feminine Cordelia here, his edition is elsewhere sensitive to a reading of Cordelia that sees her as "more active and warlike" (140); see his introduction (esp. pp. 139–41) and his commentary at 4.3.0.
27. Maureen Quilligan, *Incest and Agency in Elizabeth's England* (Philadelphia: University of Pennsylvania Press, 2005), 3.
28. Quilligan, *Incest and Agency*, 235.
29. Quilligan, *Incest and Agency*, 234.
30. Quilligan, *Incest and Agency*, 235.
31. Randall, *3 Henry VI*, 95.
32. Randall, *3 Henry VI*, 95; see Marcus, *Puzzling Shakespeare*, esp. 51–66, for her argument about Elizabeth's dual genders.
33. *3 Henry VI*. The Arden Shakespeare, 3rd ser., ed. John D. Cox and Eric Rasmussen (London: Thomson Learning, 2001), 357, 146.
34. *3 Henry VI*, ed. Michael Hattaway (Cambridge: Cambridge University Press, 1993), 193.
35. Howard and Rackin, *Engendering a Nation*, 85.
36. Howard and Rackin, *Engendering a Nation*, 99, 98.
37. All quotes from *Edward III* are taken from *King Edward III*, ed. Giorgio Melchiori (Cambridge: Cambridge University Press, 1998). Questions about the play's authorship are not important for my purposes here. Regardless of who wrote the play, the figure of Philippa is useful for exploring how audiences might react to a female character dressed in armor.
38. Melchiori notes, "Qq's wording is deliberately ambiguous, since 'trauell' was a current alternative spelling of 'travail'" (138).
39. Phyllis Rackin, *Shakespeare and Women* (Oxford: Oxford University Press, 2005).

Index

Note: Shakespearean characters are in **bold**.

Abel, Lionel, 142–4, 151
absent self, 32–3, 158
Les Abusz (Estienne), 88
acting styles, 124–6, 160–1, 163, 165
actio, 119, 125–6
actions as character definition, 148, 160–1
action-supporting functions, 90–1
active/passive constructions, 8
actor-audience communications, 71–2, 130, 140
  specific nature of, 144–8, 150, 156
actor-character distance, 129–30, 140, 180–1
actor-characters, 177–8, 185–6, 188, 191
  and disclosure in personation, 179–83
actors, 62–3, 67–8, 70–3, 91, 94, 123–4
  boys as women, 6, 9, 16, 70, 140–1, 151, 180, 185
  choices of, 160–6
  familiarity of, 159–60, 166–8, 170, 172–4
  habitus of, 160–2, 164–6
  see also acting styles; actor-character distance; actor-characters; actor-text relationships; *individual actors*
actor-text relationships, 161–5, 169–70, 177–8
Aeschylus, 92
affective attachment, 93–4
agency, 91, 160–5, 173–4, 182, 241
agent-concepts, 42, 52–4, 58–60
agents, mental, 26–8
Albany, 102, 105, 109
Alcibiades, 202, 207

Alexander, F. Matthias, 165
Alexander technique, 161
alienation, 204, 210
allegory, 101, 199, 201, 203, 207, 215
Alleyn, Edward, 123
All's Well that Ends Well, 7–8
Amazons, 235–6, 238, 244
American theatrical traditions, 163–4
amnesia of infancy, 26–7
Andrew Aguecheek, 167–8
Andrew, Edward, 25
Angelo, 35–6, 102
animality, 9–12, 207–10
Antipholi, 168–74
antiquity, 88–9
antirealism, 49–50
anti-Semitism, 10–12, 24
antitheatricalism, 153–5
Antonio, 24–5
Antonio and Mellida (Marston), 85, 124, 129
Antony, 203, 207
Antony and Cleopatra, 140–1, 150–1, 203, 207
Antwerp Chamber of Rhetoric, 87
Apemantus, 205, 208–10
Apollinaire, Guillaume, 91
Apothecary, 74
appreciation and realism, 58–60
Arendt, Hannah, 17, 91, 220–1, 225–8
Aristophanes, 90, 92
Aristotelian tragedy, 75, 91
Aristotle, 7, 30, 90, 128
Armin, Robert, 75, 188
armour, 232–3, 235, 244, 246–7
Artaud, Antonin, 3, 90
Arthur, 36, 217–18
artifacts, characters as, 50–1, 53–5, 62, 120–1

250

Ashcroft, Peggy, 233
As You Like It, 28-9, 83, 158
audience engagement, 5-9, 12, 67-70, 73, 75, 93-4, 117, 149, 151
  see also actor-audience communications; participation; spectators' experience
Augustine, 101, 153-5
authors as *personnages*, 92
Autolycus, 145-6, 148, 150-3, 188-91

Bacon, Francis, 85, 128
'bad' quartos, 72-3
Baker, Herschel, 218
Bakhtin, Mikhail, 29, 182
Bale, John, 88
Balthasar, 74
Baptiste, ou La Calomnie (Buchanan), 88
Barker, Howard, 139
Barrault, Jean-Louis, 93
Barton, Anne, 141
Basilicon Doron, 107
beast/man inversion, 9-12, 207-10
Beaurline, L. A., 218
Beckett, Samuel, 3, 91, 94
being-in-the-world, 118-19, 179
Belsey, Catherine, 4, 214
Benveniste, Émile, 182, 191
Berger, Harry, 25
Berg, James, 14-15
Bergson, Henri, 90
Bertram, 8
betrayals, 224-5
blinding motif, 111-12
Boadicea, 236
body-subjects, 118-19, 123-4, 127-8, 130
Boehrer, Bruce, 11
Bolingbrook, 6
Bonjour, là, Bonjour (Tremblay), 139
Booth, Stephen, 110
Bouchard, Michel Marc, 92
Bourassa, André, 8, 14, 119, 122
Bourdieu, Pierre, 63, 160, 164
Bradleian character criticism, 3
Bradley, A. C., 2-3
Brecht, Bertolt, 3

Brine, Adrian, 164-5
Brisset, Roland, 88
Bristol, Michael, 3-5, 13, 144, 185
British theatrical traditions, 163
Brooks, Cleanth, 3
Browne, Thomas, 101
Brutus, 69
Bruyère, Jean de la, 89
Buchanan, George, 88
Büchner, Georg, 89
Bulwer, John, 126-7
Burbage, Richard, 63, 67-74, 123, 174
Burckhardt, Sigurd, 141-2
Burgundy, 104, 107
Burke, Kenneth, 204-6
burlesque, 86-7, 185
Burns, Edward, 117, 130

Caesar, Sid, 26-7
Calderwood, James, 140
caninity, 9-12
cannibalism motif, 207-8
caractère, 83-5
Caractères (Bruyère), 89
Cartesian ego, 26
Casaubon, Issac, 85
Cassio, 64, 75
Cassius, 69
The Castle (Barker), 139
Cavendish, Margaret, 1-2
Celia, 158
Cerasano, Susan, 124
Châteauvieux, Cosme de, 88
Chaucer, Geoffrey, 197
Chaurette, Normand, 92
Chekhov, Michael, 161, 165
choices, actors', 160-6
Chomsky, Noam, 23
chora, 93
choric exegesis, 214
Christian culture, 10-11, 24, 37, 101-3, 229
chronicles/chronical plays, 107
cinematic characters, 41-8, 50, 52-3
classical conventions, 75, 94
Claudel, Paul, 93
Claudius, 8, 131, 168, 172
Cleopatra, 140-1, 150-1

The Clouds (Aristophanes), 92
Clown *(Winter's Tale)*, 146, 150–3
cognition, 216
Cohen, Walter, 218
coherence of self, 27
Coleridge, S. T., 2
Colicos, John, 199
collaborative character, 152–3
The Comedy of Errors, 168–74
comic roles, 68, 87, 150–3
Commedia dell'arte, 87–9
commitment, 151
complicity, sense of, 179–80
concepts, 52–3
conceptual casting, 167–8
conscience, 215–18, 220–1, 227, 229–30
Constance, 36–8
constructivism, 44
contingent psychohistorical relations, 54–5, 58
continuity, 214, 230
contradictions, 200–2, 205–6
convergence/difference, 23
Cordelia, 104–9, 232–3, 235–41, 245
Coriolanus, 203–4, 207
Cornwall, 105, 111–12, 239–40
corporeality, 118, 122–6, 128–9, 131
corruption, 225–6
costume, 232–3, 235, 244, 246–7
Courgenay, Claude Billard de, 88
Cox, John, 243
Cressida, 180–1
cuckoldry motif, 68–9
cue-lines, 73–4

Dawson, Anthony, 16, 139, 149, 158, 174, 179
deceit, 224–6
declamation, 98–9, 102–6, 109, 111–12
dependent entities, 51
Descartes, René, 26, 83–4, 86–7, 95
Desdemona, 4, 6, 8–9, 63, 65–6, 70, 75, 108, 214–15
Dessen, Alan, 167, 232
Diomedes, 180–1
direct address to spectators, 144, 147

disclosure in personation, 179–83, 186–7, 190
discourse biographies, 7–8, 62–6, 68–9, 71–2, 74–5
discursive contexts, 95
disempowerment, 31
disguise, 28, 31–2, 91–2, 170, 190
dispositions, 48–9
distance
  actor-character, 129–30, 152
  social, 182, 185, 188–90
divestment images, 103, 105, 109
Dodd, William, 7, 13–14, 215
dog motif, 9–12, 207–8
Dollimore, Jonathan, 4, 22
Donne, John, 101
double disguise, 91–2
doubleness, 178–80, 183
double valuation, 205–6
double-voiced counterfeiting, 188–91
double-voiced discourse, 182–8
doubling, 168–74
  of *personnages*, 90–1
dowries, 103–4, 109
Dromios, 171–4
duality, inherent, 178–9, 185, 190
dynamic relationships, 145, 148, 150–1, 153

Earle, John, 122
early modern context
  psychological, 3–5, 11–12, 215–16, 229
  theatrical, 62–3, 67–8, 70–1, 74–5, 83, 118–20, 122–7, 132, 167, 178
  see also Christian culture; gender issues; historical inquiry; race issues; rhetorical traditions; staging
Edgar, 99–100, 103, 109–12
Edmond, 109–11, 237
education, 127–8
Edward III, 244–6
Elinor, 216–17, 219–20, 223, 235
Elizabeth I, 241–2
embodied subjectivity, 118–19, 123, 125, 127, 131

embodiment, 118, 121–2, 158–9, 165–8, 174, 179
 of spectators, 130–2
emotion, extravagant, 36–7
empathy, 38, 102
empowerment, 31
Empson, William, 204–5
L'Enchanteur pourrissant (Apollinaire), 91
Endgame (Beckett), 91, 94
Enlightenment, 87
Les Entrailles (Gauvreau), 91
envy, 199, 205–8, 210
essentialism, 22–3, 62–3, 142
Estienne, Charles, 88
ethics, 143–4, 151, 153
 see also moral dimensions
Euripides, 92
Everyman, 87
Every Man In His Humour, 68
exaggeration in love, 36–7
exile, 30
existentialism, 143, 160
extemporal elements, 184, 186
extremities of character, 203, 207
eye contact, 145–6, 149
Eyre, Richard, 233

The Faerie Queene (Spenser), 235
Falstaff, 161–2, 183–8
Faulconbridge/Plantagenet/Bastard, 218–30
Fenner, William, 216
Ferry, Anne, 215
fictional interaction scripts, 70–4
fictive existence paradox, 49–51
Flecknoe, Richard, 71, 73
Foakes, R. A., 239–40
Folio texts, 72–3, 232, 238, 245
Folkerth, Wes, 4
Fool *(King Lear)*, 108, 110–11
forgetting, 34–5
formal dimensions of *personnage*, 85–9
Francastel, Pierre, 86–7
Freinkel, Lisa, 101
French theatrical traditions, 83–4, 88
functional dimensions of *personnages*, 89–92
functionalism, 141

Gagnon, André, 92
Garel, Hélie, 88
Garnier, Robert, 88
Garrick, David, 174
Gauvreau, Claude, 91
gender issues, 8–9, 12, 233–7, 239–46
generosity, 202–3, 205–6
genre, 142–3
gestalts, 152
gesture, 125–7
Ghost *(Hamlet)*, 131
Giddens, Anthony, 63
Gielgud, John, 233
Gilgamesh, 89
Gloucester, 100, 104, 109–12
goals, character, 145–7, 149
Goldberg, Jonathan, 4
Goldring, Beth, 239
Gonerill, 103–4, 106–7, 109, 111–12, 237–8
Gorboduc, 107
Gosson, Stephen, 153
Grazia, Margreta de, 100
Greco-Roman mystery plays, 84
Greek Church, 84
Greek theatre traditions, 75, 86, 90–2, 122
Greenblatt, Stephen, 141–2
Greene, Robert, 88
Greg, W. W., 72
Grévin, Jacques, 88
grief, 37–8
Grote, David, 69
Gurr, Andrew, 126, 179

habitus, 160–2, 164–6, 182
Hacker, Barton C., 234
Halio, Jay L., 239
Hall, Joseph, 120
Hall, Peter, 163
Hal/Prince Henry, 161–2, 183–4, 186
Hamlet, 7–8, 28, 34, 64–8, 73, 131, 143, 148, 150, 199, 202
Hamlet, 72, 92–3, 172
 see also Hamlet
Harding, Sandra, 23
Hartley, Andrew, 15–16
Hattaway, Michael, 243

Hays, Jean de, 88
Hazlitt, William, 2, 113
Healey, John, 85
Hellenic period, 86, 92, 122
Henry IV, Part 1, 7, 161–2, 183–8, 234–5
Henry V, 234
Henry VI, 232–3, 235, 242–6
Hermione, 145–6, 155–6
heroic tradition, 68, 75, 88
heteroglossia, 182
Heywood, Thomas, 100, 117, 121, 123–5, 129–30, 132, 180, 182–3
Hieronimo, 129
Hillel the Elder, 29–30, 33
Hilton, Julian, 179
historical inquiry, 22, 25, 37, 233–7, 240–2, 246
historic characters, 88
histrionic practices, 177–9, 183–6, 188–90
Holinshed, R., 236–7
Honigmann, E. A. J., 218
Horatio, 64, 131
Howard, Jean, 234, 244
Hubert, 217–18, 220
humanism, 22–3, 62, 74–5, 143, 178, 214
human nature, 22–6, 38, 126, 144, 214
hypocrite, 84, 91

Iago, 64, 66–70, 72, 75, 167
iambic pentameter, 162
idealism, 198
identification, 64–5, 123, 127–8
 individuation and, 54–8
identity, 219–20, 230
 loss of, 170–1
ideological differences, 6, 8, 11–12
illegitimacy, 219–20, 223
illocutionary language, 141
illusionism, 44, 48
image-making functions, 90–1
imagination, 128
impersonation, 99–101, 185
incest, 240–1
inconsistencies, 218, 221, 224–5, 229–30

individuation, 43–5, 47–8
 and identification, 54–8
inner dialogue, 225–6
innovation, 95
interactions with audiences *see* actor-audience communications; audience engagement; direct address to spectators; eye contact; spectators' experience
interiority, 27, 29, 210, 214–15
 see also inwardness
interpretation, 70, 90, 93, 120, 164
intersubjectivity, 118–19, 123, 125, 127, 129, 155
invective, 202, 204, 206, 225
inwardness, 3, 159, 210, 229
 see also interiority

Jackson, Gabriele Bernhard, 235
Jackson, Henry, 6, 8
Le Jaloux (de Larivey), 88
James I, 107, 203
Jameson, Anna, 2
Le Jeu de l'amour et du hasard (Marivaux), 92
Joan, 232–3, 235, 246
Jodelle, Estienne, 88
John, 216–17, 219–20, 223–4
Johnson, Samuel, 1–2, 5, 21, 243
Jonson, Ben, 64
Joseph, B. L., 123, 127–8
Judaic traditions, 29–30
Julia, 34
Julius Caesar, 69

Kahn, Coppélia, 206
Kayser, Chris, 166, 168, 170, 172–4
Keaton, Buster, 21–2
Kemp, Will, 75, 185
Kent, 98–9, 102, 104–5, 107–8
Kermode, Frank, 109
Kernan, Alvin, 141
King John, 36–8, 215, 218, 221–2, 225–30, 234–5
 see also John
King Lear, 98–100, 102–13, 232–3, 237–41, 245
 see also Lear
Klein, Melanie, 199, 205–6

Klotz, Volker, 85, 93
Knezevich, Joe, 172
Knight, G. W., 203
Knights, L. C., 2, 214
Kurosawa, Akira, 43–4, 47, 50, 52–7

Lady Macbeth, 34–5
Lady Macduff, 38
Langer, Monika M., 119
language, 29, 141, 199
  see also lexical associations; speech
  effects, character as
Larivey, Jean de, 88
Larkin, Philip, 174
larva, 86
latent potentiality, 22–3
Latin Church, 84–5
Launat, Pierre de, 83
Launce, 186
Lear, 23, 99, 102–10, 112–13, 166–7, 198, 203–4, 207, 241
legendary characters, 88
Leinwand, Theodore, 4
Leontes, 146–7, 150
Levinas, Emmanuel, 30
Lévi-Strauss, Claude, 103
lexical associations, 103, 105–6, 108–12
Lieblein, Leanore, 15, 100
lighting, 149
Lilies (Bouchard), 92
literary character, 198
Lives (Lucian of Samosata), 88
Livingston, Paisley, 53
Lowin, Richard, 63, 69
Loyer, Pierre le, 88
Lucian of Samosata, 88–9

Macbeth, 34–5, 56–60, 199, 203, 207
  see also Washizu
Macbeth, 34–5, 38, 50, 56–60, 199, 203, 207
  see also *Throne of Blood* (Kurosawa)
Magnusson, Lynne, 63–4
malcontent motif, 205
Les Mamelles de Tirésias (Apollinaire), 91
Marchessault, Jovette, 92
Marcus, Leah, 242

Margaret, 235, 242–6
Marivaux, Pierre de, 92
Marlowe, Christopher, 10, 88, 101
Marowitz, Charles, 3
Marston, John, 85, 124–5
Martin, C. B., 49
Martin, Randall, 242
mask management, 85–6, 94–5, 122–30
materialism, 4, 62, 100, 102, 142–3, 215
Mathieu, Pierre, 88
Matthews, Eric, 118–19
Maus, Katherine, 4
McInnerny, Tim, 167
meaning, 7–8, 141, 151
Measure for Measure, 7, 25, 35–6, 102
Meisner technique, 165
Melune, 217–18, 224
memorial reconstruction of texts, 72–3
memory, 34–5, 159–60, 166, 172, 174
mental agents, 26–8
The Merchant of Venice, 11, 24–5, 139, 141–2, 207–8
Mercutio, 69
Merleau-Ponty, Maurice, 118–19, 123
The Merry Wives of Windsor, 89
Metamorphoses (Ovid), 36
metatheater, 139–43, 146, 148–51
metatheatricality, 67, 69, 91–2, 144, 146, 153, 155, 185
Method acting, 163
Middle Ages, 87
Middleton, Thomas, 203
A Midsummer Night's Dream, 187
Mifune, Toshiro, 43–4, 46, 50
Mikalachki, Jodi, 236–7
mimetic representations, 2, 62, 74–5, 90, 128, 154, 183, 215
mind, 33–5, 113
mind-independence, 41, 44, 46
Minsky, Marvin, 25–7
Le Miroir de la félicité, 87
misanthropy, 199, 201–3, 206–7
Mistress Quickly, 184
modernism, 90–1
Molière, Jean-Baptiste, 89
Montaigne, Michel de, 125

Montchrestien, Anthoine de, 88
Montreux, Nicholas de, 88
Montrose, Louis, 141
moral dimensions, 31, 38, 88, 130–1, 154, 198, 209, 216–21, 223–30, 237–8
  see also ethics
Le Morfondu (de Larivey), 88
Morgann, Maurice, 2
La Mort de César (Voltaire), 90
motivation, 163
Le Muet insensé (le Loyer), 88
Muret, Marc-Antoine, 88
mystery plays, 84, 86, 91

narrative, 52–3
nature, 125
Nelligan (Gagnon and Tremblay), 92
Nemo, 87
neoclassical traditions, 178
neoMarxism, 143
Neptune Theatre, Halifax, 139
New Criticism, 2–3
New Historicism, 141–2, 215
Nietzsche, Friedrich, 27, 30
nihilism, 226–7, 230
non-characters, 214–15
non-verbal character elements, 158
Nussbaum, Martha, 23
Nuttall, A. D., 214

objecthood, 43, 47–8, 101–2, 110, 113
objectivism, 160
Oedipus, 92
Olivier, Laurence, 166–7, 174
ontologies, 41–5, 49, 51, 55, 58
opening lines, 73
openness of texts, 93
organic social variables, 23
organizing principles, 6–7, 12
Orgel, Stephen, 101, 190, 239–40
Orlando, 28–9
Orsino, 31–2
Oswald, 98–9, 103
Othello, 9, 62–70, 72
Othello, 4, 6, 8–9, 62–70, 72, 75, 108, 167, 214–15
outsider positions, 63–6, 68

Overburian Characters, 120–1, 125, 130, 183
Ovid, 36

painting, 90–1
Pandulph, 37–8, 223
parsing, 98, 100, 102–12
part-based learning, 70–3, 100
participation, 149, 155–6, 174
  see also audience engagement; spectators' experience
particularization, 63
passivity, 154
Paster, Gail Kern, 22
patriarchal values, 240–1, 244–5
patronage relations, 207–8
Pavis, Patrice, 86
Pennington, Michael, 199
perception, 118–19, 123
performance, 151–2, 159–60, 191
performance-focused characterization, 152–3
performances, 62, 67–8, 70–2, 93, 132, 139
performative habitus, 160, 164–6, 168, 170–2, 174
performativity, 29, 67, 69, 141–2, 177, 190–1
personation process, 117–19, 123–5, 127, 178, 183–8
  disclosure in, 179–83
  doubleness, 178–9
  persons personated, 119–23
personnages, 8, 83–4
  formal dimensions of, 85–9
  functional dimensions of, 89–92
  and the mask, 85–6, 94–5
  virtuality, 92–4
perspectives, contest of, 6
phatic signals, 71–2
phenomenology, 118–19, 123, 127
Phillips, Augustine, 63, 69
philological approaches, 94–5
physical conditions, 158
Plato, 93
Plautus, 89
plays within plays, 183–8
plot, 7, 173
plural/single self, 26–9

Plutarch, 203
Polanski, Roman, 56–8
political contexts, 90, 107, 217–18, 223–5, 227–9
Polonius, 34
Ponech, Trevor, 4, 13
possibility, 21–2
post-performance quartos, 71–2
poststructuralism, 3, 101, 143, 214–15
pragmatic behaviours, 62
pre-characters, 206, 210
presentational forms, 149, 179–81, 184, 190–1
presenter-roles, 180
private/public selves, 64–6, 69, 170–3
process, character as, 152
pronuntiato, 126
property-possession, 47–8, 98–100, 102–5, 107–9, 113, 204–6, 220, 223
props, 186–7
Proteus, 123–4
providentialist perspectives, 100, 102–3, 105, 107–8, 110–11, 113
Provincetown Playhouse (Chaurette), 92
Prynne, William, 153
psychohistorical relations, 54–5, 58
psychological approaches, 2–3, 24–6, 34–5, 42, 51–2, 54–5, 58, 162, 204–6, 218
public agent-concepts, 42, 51–5, 58–9
public/private selves, 64–6, 69, 170–3
purposes of playing, 63, 74–5

Q1 (Quarto 1) texts, 72–4
Q2 (Quarto 2) texts, 73–4
qualities and dispositions, 43
Québécois theatrical traditions, 92
quiddity, 62–3, 66
Quilligan, Maureen, 240–1
Quintillian, 126, 128

Rabinal Achi, 89
race issues, 9–10, 12, 24, 64
Rackin, Phyllis, 234, 244, 246
Rasmussen, Eric, 243
rationalism, 34
reader involvement, 5–7
readiness, 161–4

readings, 93, 161
realism, 41, 55, 57, 113, 163–4, 170
antirealism, 49–50
and appreciation, 58–60
response-dependence, 44, 48
real people, characters as, 21, 37–8, 49, 58–60, 214
reason, 26–7
reciprocity, 42
recognition, 29, 32
Regan, 103, 106–7, 111–12, 237–8
rehearsal processes, 148
religion, 12, 224–5, 229
  see also Christian culture; Judaic traditions
Renaissance, 87, 98, 160, 178
representation, 86, 91, 121, 124, 149, 154, 179, 181, 184
response-dependence realism, 44, 48
responsibility, personal, 29–30
Revelation, 102–3
rhetorical traditions, 68, 75, 123, 125–8, 164–5, 185, 242
Richard II, 6, 234
Richard III, 244
risking of characters, 140, 147–9, 151
Roach, Joseph, 123, 126–8, 130
Rodenburg, Patsy, 161–5
Romeo, 69, 73–4
Romeo and Juliet, 69, 72–4
Rosalind, 28–9, 158

Saga of the Wet Hens (Marchessault), 92
Salarino, 24–5
Salerio, 9, 24–5
Salisbury, 216–18
Sartre, Jean-Paul, 143
The Satin Slipper (Claudel), 93
satire, 203
Saül le furieux (de la Taille), 88
Saussure, Ferdinand de, 95
Sauvage, Roland Brisset du, 88
scenic *personnage*, 86
scenography, 93
Schlegel, August Wilhelm, 2
Schwartz, Kathryn, 235
Scofield, Paul, 199
seating, 149
Sebastian, 32

258 Index

secretly open artifice, 179–80, 188
self, 26–7, 29–30
  plural/single, 26–9
  private/public, 64–6, 69, 170–3
self-awareness, 215–17
self-consciousness, 63–6, 151, 153, 185
self-construction, 64, 67
self-criticism, 204–5, 208, 226
self-deception, 225
self-impersonation, 28–9, 31–2
self-presentation, 68, 75
self-preservation, 28–9, 31, 64
self-reflexivity, 141, 143, 155, 181, 218, 230
The Self-Torturer (Terence), 92
Selkirk, Myrna Wyatt, 15, 139
semiotics, 89–90, 174
separate rehearsal, 70–1
sets of wit, 75
sexuality, 234–5, 238, 242
sharers, 70–1, 73
Shylock, 9–12, 24–5, 38, 207–8
Sinfield, Alan, 214
single-mindedness, 199, 203–4, 210
single/plural self, 26–9
SLD (stroboluminescent displays), 42, 45–8, 54–6
Slights, Camille, 16–17
social distance, 182, 185, 188–90
social relationships, 30
social status, 63, 68, 220
soliloquies, 7
sonnets, 33, 36
Souhait, François du, 88
The Spanish Tragedy (Kyd), 128–9
spatio-temporal elements, 47
spectators' experience, 117–19, 123, 125, 128
  embodiment, 130–2
  privileged awareness, 189–90
  spectator roles, 145–6, 148, 155
  see also actor-audience communications; audience engagement; participation
speculation, 21
speech effects, character as, 62–4, 67, 199–201, 204
Spenser, Edmund, 235
Spinosa, Charles, 25

Spinoza, Baruch, 93
split structure, 206
sprezzatuta, 160
Spurgeon, Katie, 145–6, 156
stage interaction plots, 71–2
stage-practices, 63
staging, 149, 232
  early modern, 232–3, 246
  see also theatrical space
Stallybrass, Peter, 4, 8
Stanislavski, Konstantin, 128, 145, 165
States, Bert O., 62, 152–3
stereotypes, 64, 66, 68
Stern, Tiffany, 70
St John the Divine, 102–3
stock types, 87–9, 121
stoicism, 37
Strasberg, Lee, 165
structuralism, 160
Stubbes, Philip, 125
study-practices, 63
subjectivity, 100, 119, 128, 160, 173, 214, 230, 242
surrealism, 90–1
symbolism, 89, 99, 102, 111, 186

Taille, Jean de la, 88
Tamburlaine, 101
The Taming of the Shrew, 7, 89
Tartuffe (Molière), 90
Taylor, Gary, 239
Terence, 89, 92
text and character, 161–5, 169–70, 177–8
textual agency, 159–65
textual variations, 72–4, 110, 201, 239–40
theatrical emptiness, 142
theatricality, 151
theatrically interactive modes, 68
theatrical magic, 139, 155–6
theatrical metaphors, 83
theatrical space, 93–4, 158, 180
thematic criticism, 141
Theophrastan characters, 85, 88, 100, 120–2, 129
Thersites, 180–1
third space of theatricality, 93–4
Thomasson, Amie, 51, 55

Thomson, Leslie, 232
Throne of Blood (Kurosawa), 43–4, 47, 50, 52–4, 56–7
see also Washizu
Timon, 89, 197–211
　animality, 207–10
　contradictions, 200–2, 205–6
　as tragic hero, 197–9, 203–4
Topsell, Edward, 209–10
tragedy, 87, 92, 142–3, 203
tragic heroes, 197–9, 203–4
tragique, 83
transactions, 117
transformations, 117, 120–3, 128, 130
Tremblay, Michel, 92, 139
Troilus, 180
Troilus and Cressida, 179–81, 198
trugedy, 86
Tucker, Patrick, 70
Turner, Henry, 25
Turp, Gilbert, 93
Twelfth Night, 28, 30–3, 139, 167
Two Gentlemen of Verona, 34, 186
typecasting, 166, 172

Ulysses, 180, 198
unaccomodated man concept, 23
unconscious mind, 91, 111
unicorn motif, 209–10
unities, 94
universalism, 214, 229

Vahed, Roxana, 145–8, 150
Valeriano, Pierio, 126

Van Tassel, Wesley, 163–4
verbal manipulation, 63–6
　see also language; speech effects, character as
verbal use of 'character,' 33–6, 38
Villon, Francois François, 87
Vincentio, 102
Viola, 28, 30–3
virtualities, 92–4
virtue/vice, 36
vocal elements, 126
Voltaire, François-Marie Arouet, 90
vulnerability, 23–4, 65, 69

Waisvisz, Sarah, 139, 146, 148–52
warrior women, 232–6, 242–5
Washizu, 43–4, 46, 49–57
Webster, John, 123
Weimann, Robert, 6, 16, 74, 124–5
Weis, René, 239
Werner, Sarah, 17
Wiles, David, 122
The Winter's Tale, 139–40, 144–53, 188–91
Woertendyke, Max, 146–7
Worthen, William, 128, 152
Woyzeck (Büchner), 89
Wright, Thomas, 126–7
writing/ink metaphors, 33–5, 37, 98–101, 103, 109, 119–21, 125–6

Yachnin, Paul, 15, 108, 139, 159, 179
York, Michael, 164–5
Yu Jin Ko, 32

CPSIA information can be obtained at www.ICGtesting.com
Printed in the USA
LVOW07*1057240216

476514LV00004B/21/P